ACTIONS INTO LEADERSHIP

Robert Bulloch

Published by Robert Bulloch
© Robert Bulloch 2014
All rights reserved. First published 2014

ISBN-13: 978-0-9575863-0-7 (paperback)
ISBN-13: 978-0-9575863-1-4 (eBook-Kindle (AZW))
ISBN-13: 978-0-9575863-2-1 (ebook-ePub)
ISBN-13: 978-0-9575863-3-8 (ebook-PDF)
ISBN-13: 978-0-9575863-4-5 (ebook-mobi)
ISBN-13: 978-0-9575863-5-2 (hardback)

Abstract

There are many competing ideas of how to be a good leader, but the majority of them do not examine what is meant by leadership. It is taken for granted that a good leader 'gets results' and earns recognition for them, which has produced a great deal of literature revealing the 'habits' or 'traits' of good leaders, there to be studied and emulated. But each setting in which leadership takes place is different, and it no more makes sense to think of leadership in terms of specific and universal traits than it would to ask a painter to fix a car.

Instead, the concept of leadership must be understood as contextual, and therefore on display all around us. It is not simply to be found in the boardroom of industrial giants or on the pages of *Fortune* magazine – it is to be found everywhere, in every setting where an organised response perfectly satisfies an expressed wish. It is good leadership that ensures your morning coffee is just as you expect it to be, and that explains why contented employees show up to work on time, even when the boss is away.

The study – and therefore the development – of leadership skills must start from an understanding of organisational purpose, and from this study the function of leadership in context can be distilled and improved. This book provides a template of general principles for understanding the role of leadership within an organisation, allowing leaders to understand their own role without the need for psychology or acting classes.

With leadership placed in its proper perspective, and the importance of organisational purpose asserted, the book then guides the process of mapping out a leadership schematic specific to each organisation, making clear how each role in the organisation relates to the overall purpose. This schematic can then be used to clarify the role of individuals, focus development and training, and foster an environment in which initiative, innovation and creative thinking can be brought to bear on the bottom line, by spreading an understanding of the organisational purpose and allowing individuals properly to understand their relation to it and gain possession of the purpose.

The task of a leader is to increase the correlation between individual and group purpose. In order to do this, leaders need first to understand the organisation that they seek to lead, grasping its core purpose, and then nurture the living threads of leadership that bind it together. To do this, it is first necessary to dispense with the veneration of leaders, and replace it with a clear understanding of, and respect for, leadership.

Robert Bulloch
December 2014

Acknowledgements

I would like to thank Susan Zhang for the cover illustrations, tables and Venn diagrams. Stephen Sharman's patience, balance and feedback on the concepts as I formulated and tested them with him were invaluable. Finally, Ian Kingston is also thanked for his expertise and efforts in editing, formatting and general consultation in matters publishing. The end result is a vast improvement on the confused collection of thoughts Stephen was presented with and the strangled English that Ian was given at the start. Any success in this production is very much due to their ability to help define and make possible the effective communication of these ideas.

Author's profile

Robert Bulloch born in London, UK ,and raised in Canada and the UK, before joining the British Army in 1985. He was commissioned from Royal Military Academy Sandhurst to the 1st Battalion 2nd Gurkha Rifles. During his service with British Army as an officer, he served in conflict areas of Northern Ireland, and also in Bosnia with the UN protection force. Other countries and cultures experienced during his military service with the Gurkhas and various units were Brunei, Nepal, Hong Kong, New Zealand, Singapore, Kenya, Canada, Belize and the UK.

After 10½ years he resigned his commission and worked with Jardine Securicor (later G4S) in an operational role in Hong Kong, Taiwan, Singapore and Thailand, finally setting up the company's mainland China operations. After 7 years he resigned to set up his own consultancy in Shanghai, providing leadership-related services to predominantly multi-national organisations in China and Asia Pacific. Shanghai has been his base for the last 11 years while developing tools and programs to make understanding and applying leadership more effective and efficient.

In the course of these experiences many team sports were an influencing factor, with ice hockey being his first team sport and rugby union played at a representative level. Languages learned Nepalese and Mandarin.

Table of Contents

List of Illustrations, Tables and Examples

Preface

While researching the many hundreds of books and self-help guides on leadership a couple of important things struck me. Firstly, none of them can define what leadership is. Having been a trainer in the military, an operations director in a corporation and now a consultant based in China, I cannot find a consistent definition of leadership. Many will describe leadership and what it should look like, but this is rarely specific and almost always situation-specific. Secondly, the focus of much leadership study and reading by the individual is done to find a quick short-cut to being 'successful' as an individual. The cynic may state think that this is the wrong reason to be a leader and would prefer the group to benefit more from the relationship than the individual. If done well, all parties can benefit.

This desire to be a leader is understandable and positive in as much as it recognises that a leader is important and can add significant value. Beyond that it usually comes down to what do you mean by successful? Questions like why and how it adds value don't often get asked, let alone answered.

My experiences suggest that I have a better chance of knowing about leadership than most, purely because I have been in the position of a leader for longer than most. Despite the excellent training I received at Royal Military Academy Sandhurst, and my experience in the corporate world, for a long time I did not feel I could define leadership in any specific meaningful way other than to give comparative descriptions in similar terms to the books and my teachers before me.

The aim of this book is simple. It is to define leadership in such a way that individuals can apply the lesson to the groups they work with. Academics can use the definition to understand, analyse and recommend; however, the primary intention is that applicators can apply this to their groups. The definition is done so that applicators can apply and teachers and leaders can teach.

The study has drawn on common and well-understood theories and, most importantly, from practices honed by many years of application and refinement. Using well-known cases and existing systems that create a leadership environment makes it easier to analyse and be understood. Yes, I fall back on military experiences, but not on the often used process of situation analysis. Instead I focus more on the language of interaction between the levels and groups in the military.

Those who, once they have read this book, come to the conclusion that the concepts contained within are obvious and nothing new in practical terms will find that I agree with them. If this is the case they will continue to do what they do, yet they will now know how it works. For those who reflect and choose to experiment and test the theory themselves, good luck. The tools designed are new and are there to help demonstrate the concepts. The concepts should not be new, as all groups have a relationship in them and therefore readers should have experienced at least one or two of the types of relationship referred to in the book.

The tools will allow easier analysis, definition and planning of relationships. In the event that they wish to engineer a change in the relationship they now know how. The decision equation tool has multiple uses and links the individual to the larger scale of the group.

The book has been written to enable those readers who only want the short-cut method to do so. To short-cut the process of understanding leadership, just read the final chapters of each of the six parts. It is written as a journey from the question to the answer. It is a book about the Theory of Leadership in general, and it focuses specifically on defining what leadership is.

On the journey, many other questions about leadership and management are answered. The power of the decision equation, combined with how to use it can only be judged by those who read the book and choose to apply it. We who have used it know it to be very powerful, and it is simple to apply. This of course is a skill in itself. Applicators will attest to the fact that the application of understanding and ownership of a concept is very different to just knowing the theory and that is the subject of another book.

PART 1: Initiating the search

Chapter 1: The study of leadership

'The function of leadership is to produce more leaders, not more followers.'

Ralph Nader

The study of leadership is interesting at a personal level because it involves humans and the way groups interact to resolve challenges presented. It is something all have touched at some point in their lives. Some consider the study of leadership very time-consuming: too difficult and similar to looking for the right direction to swim in very muddy waters. If a leader finds the right path it is perhaps more by having chosen good examples to copy, chance or being in the right place at the right time. To many it is a pleasant surprise or a nasty shock.

There is a huge amount written specifically about the concept of leadership as well as on leaders and their activities as a commentary on their leadership. The topic of leadership has been raised to an almost mythical or magical status. It is, and has long been, one of the key objectives of those who plot a route to power and success. Successful leadership and attaining the privilege, recognition and power that goes with it, is based on how individuals define success and similarly how the word leadership is interpreted.

Xenophon's book [1] *Cyrus the Great*[1] is wonderful, recounting of the experiences of Cyrus of Persia and focuses on how the young prince, and later king, exercised his leadership. The book is considered to be one of the earliest studies of leadership in the 'leadership library'. Reviewers comment that in this book are laid out some of the core principles of leadership. If so, why do others write more on the subject? Perhaps they do not agree with Xenophon's analysis or that it is not broad enough. Perhaps later writers wish to reinterpret the lessons of Xenophon in a more modern context or they simply take the view that different lessons can be drawn from different situations.

Since those early times the study of leadership has progressed in context, range of situations and depth of detail. There are now thousands of books on leadership. The range is very wide: what leadership is, how to get it and then how to maintain the position and privilege once the throne of leadership has been reached.

The increasing volume of leadership studies, examples of leadership and the purchase and reading of these accounts is testament that leadership is a subject that continues to engage and that the earlier studies are not enough. More knowledge, a different leader to focus on or a more applicable interpretation are being sought. This is an uncontrolled trend which is non-specific in its search.

The continued search also reveals something about the nature of what is being written and how it is being interpreted. Some studies are becoming more focused and accurate in their measurement of commonly attributed aspects of leadership. There are more and more interpretations of examples and principles where one may assume they should be better at communicating the ways of leadership.

Looking more closely, one cannot discount the possibility that many may be merely repeating the same lessons in different formats, interpretations and situations. The answers that some readers are searching for are just not there. Of course, readers may just be reading to gain knowledge on the subject of the biography, but often there is a deeper motivation, which involves finding out if the reader could use the knowledge gained for themselves in some way. There are now so many self-help books on leadership or management that it suggests the current publications are not providing the answers.

A few key points can be gleaned from the current mass of publications on the study of leadership and the demand for greater understanding of leadership. Firstly, those who seek to understand, apply and use their understanding in order to enjoy the multiple benefits of leadership and those that write about and train others in the theory and application of leadership do not have a common agreed understanding of what leadership is. Secondly, the search exists because of a belief, gnawing suspicion or even hope (in some cases) that there is perhaps a unifying factor or key principle that can allow an individual to lead groups, be it the smallest sub-group or a very large complex overall group. The possibility of an easy, or at least easier, route to the top spurs readers.

The nature of this study of leadership is complicated by the capacity and speed of the human brain and its ability to deal with incredibly complex layers of information and group-related behaviours to be able to function and survive as well as they have. Readers of any book on a particular leader or situation will attest to the fact that the examples given in the book are different from their own. This immediately makes the application of leadership an exercise in abstract thinking: it is never as easy as it is written in the book. Books often relate situations that are vastly more complex and different from those that the reader has experienced, because of every situation's uniqueness in time, circumstance and participants. Readers are often overcome with a sense of awe and wonder at the solution that was achieved. More importantly, they have an inability to abstract the lessons learned into their own application and situations.

The complexity of factors and considerations creates what the cartoonist Scott Adams has labelled seemingly never-ending inter-related loops in his cartoon strip *Dilbert*. While it describes the perception well, it also points to a common deterrent to studying and applying leadership: it is considered very complex.

Figure 1.1 Scott Adams' *Dilbert* cartoon showing circular reasoning[2]

In Figure 1.1, Adams is linking two very general terms such as the 'right' people and 'success' when Dilbert proposes his plan. The general use of these and other terms, like 'leadership', highlights the difficulty of applying leadership theory. Vague terminology places any process on undefined rocky foundations. There are a number of questions raised by general terms, like leadership, such as the difficulty of determining what is specifically 'leadership' related and what is not. Not having a specific understanding of what the word 'leadership' means is the source of a common confusion. As usual, Adams is pinpoint accurate with his very revealing humour. General terms result in never ending general loops.

As the field of science (in particular neuroscience and psychology) unlocks the vast complexity of the human brain, it adds to the information for consideration. It will increase the possibilities available for interpretation and at the same time it may explicitly clarify earlier proposals in behavioural studies. The study of neuroscience will help us to understand the way individuals think and therefore how decisions are made in the group. Already, an understanding of the functions of parts of the brain is helping to unravel some of the mysteries.

How this will help the study of leadership will be related to how our behaviour patterns as individuals are caused and actioned. Like each neural network, thoughts and actions are unique to each individual. How the pathways are formed and the cause of these thoughts maps the process of thinking, and will provide an overlapping point with the study of leadership. These thought patterns or processes will be examined at that overlap, where they affect our behaviours as a culture and the decision process.

The experiences, ability, understanding and supporting factors that surround an individual or the group further confuse the study, as it is difficult to have exactly the same understanding and empathy for the circumstances, and therefore the motivations that others have found in that situation. Everyone sees things differently. Individuals with different motivations and understanding will communicate an idea differently to those in their group, who of course will be different from those in another group. Getting the groups to the point where a decision is made and actions are taken in the same direction is quite an achievement. The differences of each individual from another in terms of both external factors influencing them as well as their experiences shaping the way they make decisions ensure that every situation in each group is different. Yet groups still manage to work together to varying levels of success and humans continue to thrive. Somehow, there is a feeling that there exists a common thread between different groups. Is it leadership?

Leadership exists in groups everywhere and in every time period. It is impossible to count the number of different situations that have existed in order to do a study of them all and write a set of principles that applies to each situation. That said, this fact can be countered with the proposal that there must be a common factor that exists to get these groups to similar results. Leadership, in its general sense, could explain it, as could the situation making that result inevitable. Finding that common factor is a matter of asking enough questions of the situation and the group in order to differentiate what is a leadership issue and what is situational, and it applies to all individuals equally in the group the same way.

Finding the common thread between groups and understanding what allows leadership in both very large groups the very smallest of sub-groups has been compared to the grand unifying theory (GUT) of physics. In this, the scientists are attempting to prove that the laws of physics that apply to large bodies are one and the same, somehow linked to the laws used in quantum physics. Leadership theory readers are looking for that similar solution. What is the common link that allows one human to lead large complex groups and another human to do so in small groups, but with same devotion or commitment? Do small and large groups share a common thread in their leadership theories?

On reflection, it would be wonderful if the common unifying factor of leadership were just like a physics formula and its equations, in order to further its understanding and application. Often in physics it is the simplicity of the solution that highlights the beauty in its discovery. The more complex a theory gets, the more exceptions and randomness are thrown up. Physics and its theories are represented in nature; similarly, leadership is present in each group, large or small. Ideally, the formula in itself would allow those who analyse and study leadership in order to understand it to explain what leadership is, and at the same time it could allow those practitioners to be able to apply leadership by using a simple formula. A formula like this would also allow those who sit in the middle – the coaches, mentors, trainers and facilitators – to teach others how to apply the theory of leadership. A grand formula that would be!

At a simple level, to achieve this unification an author would need to understand and define what leadership is first before then moving on to explain how it could be applied. Authors often write about the application of leadership or its associated functions as a description of how to lead, rather than defining leadership itself. This helps the reader looking for a path. However, the author misses out on the challenge of defining leadership specifically and understanding the reason why it exists.

The continuing supply of books on the subject demonstrates that the demand for them is still there. The need is to understand what leadership is specifically, and why it exists – all this so that it can be applied and evaluated by the readers themselves in their situation, rather than being told how to do it in different situations. The understanding provides the road for the learning experience of application itself rather than the solution. If successful in defining leadership, the second step of application would be the motivation for achieving self-actualisation by using the proven definition of leadership rather than someone else's interpretation. The formula defining and explaining leadership would provide the bridging skill of linking the theory to the application for the reader. Again, a very grand formula that would be indeed!

This book starts by identifying the question to be asked about leadership, approaching the subject conventionally enough with what is known already or assumed to be correct, and asks the question again using this simple question as a guide: Is this specific to leadership or does this apply equally to others in the group or situation? The book seeks a definition of leadership that applies to all situations; it seeks a non-comparative definition of leadership. Identifying the right questions to ask is fundamental in the search to answer the general question: What is leadership?

As is often the case, an apparently simple explicit question frequently turns out not to be simple or explicit. It raises more questions. Therefore, this book answers a series of related questions to find a simple, precise and explicit answer to the now general question 'What is leadership?'. A set of questions are derived from the main question and listed here: How is leadership different from other similar terms? Why does leadership exist at all? How to define leadership as a noun? How to specify it when describing it as activity? And finally, how to define it as a function for useful application? The summary of these implied questions can then be formed into a simple, precise and explicit answer to the original general question, 'What is leadership?'. The answers reveal far more than the author expected.

Chapter 2: The approaches thus far in leadership theory

'The most dangerous leadership myth is that leaders are born – that there is a genetic factor to leadership.'

Warren Bennis

Leadership exists, of that there is no doubt. Xenophon is one of the earliest authors found on the subject, but he is by no means the last. He helps establish the assumed fact that leadership and the study of it has been with us since the beginning of human groups. He also gives us an understanding of what was interpreted as leadership at the time. There may have been a very diverse understanding of the word then, but Xenophon's is one of the few surviving books from that period. Currently there are volumes of recorded opinions and interpretations of what leadership is. There are now so many different sub-branches of the study of leadership it is difficult to grasp the full range of subdivisions, let alone be an expert in all of them.

The body of work that is labelled the 'Theory of Leadership' is not one set of established principles, but is a general understanding of concepts, with no one individual or group claiming sole authorship. It is a collection of the progression and diffusion of thoughts on the subject. This progression in itself implies that there is no clear, accepted single theory. In terms of its historical development as a study of concepts it takes shape in the early Great Man theory,[3] where inheritance, nature and superior qualities are the defining aspects of leadership.

The Great Man [2] theory was essentially the study of those qualities that differentiated the leaders from the masses. These specific qualities became the basis of identifying the traits of those commonly agreed by a culture to be a great leader. This school of thought evolved into the Trait theory [2] of leadership. From this stable platform the study of leadership theory has fanned out further to many different branches and sub-branches of leadership study.

There are now many sub-branches, with the type of leadership being described providing its name, such as environmental, situational, transformational, servant–leader relationships, gender-based or religious leadership. The name itself explains the type of activity performed or group to which it is assigned to achieve a leadership position. Many are comparatives of one style against another which leads to polarised understandings for simplicity and prompts confusion when behaviours of different styles are exhibited in different situations by the same individual. There are a large number of ways to describe how leadership is conducted and applied. Added to this there is no appointed authority on the matter. The subject is one of opinion and conjecture, owing to the non-specific understanding of the term 'leadership'.

The latest collection of application theories follow a few different lines of thought. One concept was published by John Adair in his book *Effective Leadership*, [3] first published in 1983 and continuously in print since. Adair[4] is a British academic who focuses on what he calls Action-Centred leadership, and has since authored many books on this theme. He is currently Chair of Leadership Studies at the United Nations systems staff college in Turin. His study focuses on the three functions of leaders: the task, maintaining the team and the needs of the individual.

Another current application theory is by Paul Hersey and Kenneth Blanchard, who are known for developing their concept of situational leadership. This deals with the effectiveness of a group, and therefore the leader will be dependent on the functioning maturity of the followers in the group. Scales and methods for determining these levels have been designed and used as tools to help the applicator in their approach to performing leadership. Both of these approaches have developed the common language of leadership and some practical applications for the practice of leadership.

In Paul Hersey, Ken Blanchard and Dewey Johnson's [4] '*Management of Organisational Behaviour – Leading Human Re-*

sources[5] there is a collection of definitions, all of which are follow
a similar theme. The definitions summarise that after reviewing
other writers, the authors agree that 'leadership is the process of
influencing the activities of an individual or a group toward reaching a goal achievement in a given situation' They then conclude by
saying based on this 'the leadership process is a function of the
leader, the follower, and other situational variables' They then create a symbolic equation to represent the definition, $L = f(l,f,s)$.[6]
This is a good agreement and collection of thoughts, but again very
general in its construction and difficult to apply. While it does not
define leadership itself, other than to say it is a function in general,
it does go on to state that leadership is done to influence the activities of an individual or a group toward reaching a goal achievement in a given situation. This is the closest and most precise
definition so far encountered.

Other contemporary academics involved in recent leadership
theory development have proposed the concept of transformational
leadership [5] starting with J.M. Burns[7] and developed further by
Noel Tichy and his 'leadership engine [6]'. Again, the contemporary leaders in the theory are developing the language and tools of
explaining leadership as well as confirming the need for leadership, but few derive a concise definition of what leadership is. Jim
Collins's [7] approach is a contemporary example of a continuation
of the process of distilling the qualities of leaders from examples in
a method reminiscent of Trait theory. Warren Bennis [8] provides
many comparatives of management and leadership in his studies,
but does not tie down what leadership is specifically.

The history and recent development of the study of leadership
theory is very crowded and well documented. In the last 100 years
it has become very wide ranging. Fortunately, R. M. Stogdill's
Handbook of Leadership [2], first published in 1974 brings together this collection of sources. His large handbook is a source book
summary and in it is Stogdill's interpretation of the findings of four
decades of published research (reportedly over 3,000 books and
articles) on the topic of leadership. His book was later revised and

expanded in 1981, with the help of Bernard Bass, to incorporate more recent theory.

Alas, Stogdill does not attempt to provide a summary resolution to defining or explaining leadership, but it does provide a very good place to confirm sources and what is, or is not, established in the study of leadership. The most important comment in Stogdill's book, for this author at least, is in his preface. Stogdill has written a statement which is copied below and it mirrors the conclusion arrived at by this author after many weeks and months of searching and before referring to Stogdill's epic on the subject of leadership study.

'The endless accumulation of empirical data has not produced an integrated understanding of leadership. There is a need for stocktaking [...] Leadership practice should be based on valid experimental findings. Future research should be designed to explore new problems rather than repeat what has been done in the past.'[8] [2]

The study of leadership has, in the main, taken three paths. One of the paths is to study leadership for the sake of studying it, as a scientist would a laboratory experiment. The study is done purely to derive or prove a theory. These academics have looked from a distance and have therefore a distal understanding and feel for the actions and results. They do however have the advantage of a lack of distractions from the demands of leadership that the second group suffers from.

The second path, that of the applicator, definitely has the distraction of the applicator's intimate involvement with the demands of leadership while taking the 'on the job' route to studying the subject. This path is the practical route to reproducing leadership, in order to effect better results in the organisation. Often successful, applicators have no real understanding of the established theories of leadership but have learned through experience. They have found the good, the bad and hopefully the 'best practices' that help achieve the objectives of the group.

The third path is that of the trainer, consultant or facilitator, who is either tasked with, or chooses to act as, a conceptual bridge between the two paths. The facilitators understand and interpret the group's accepted theory of leadership in order to develop in others an understanding of the theory and techniques so that others can better apply leadership for the benefits of the group and individuals. The third path is taken usually after one of the first two has been taken for a time. An agreed understanding of what constitutes leadership is established in the group and then the facilitator is tasked with finding ways of communicating this group understanding to others in the group. This can be a simple enough task if the facilitator agrees with what the group understanding of leadership is.

Many applicators, whilst engaged on the second route, have turned to the academics for help. Likewise, those applicators later added their thoughts to the academics' theories, based on experience, in order to help paint the theory with the colour of reality. There are those applicators who have gone on and become perceived as gurus on the issue of practical applications of leadership and are able to cross from one path of academic theory and back again to the path of the applicator. In the case of the applicators, given the quantity of literature on leadership, few of them have or could take the time to read the wide range of leadership concepts whilst applying and proving the theories.

The applicators are kept busy learning by experiment, experience and survival of the fittest, or perhaps the luckiest, in the harsh realities of leadership in groups. Some write of their experiences in a 'lessons learnt' format. These are practical application books and are often written in simple terms for easy uptake and repetition.

These self-application books more often address the question, if ever asked, of how to survive in situations that the author has encountered or the reader is most likely to encounter. The books do not address the specific issue of what leadership is, but are more concerned with the situation that the author has encountered. A reader seeking an answer to the question 'What is leadership and how can I do it?' will be further confused or misdirected if the situation that he sees and the one that the author writes about are not the same. More opinion and general haze are being created about what the term 'leadership' means and how it can be applied, and the reader's core question of 'What is leadership?' is not being answered.

Overall, across many books this creates many different understandings and further interpretations, usually based on a current or past theory of leadership expressed by an academic or senior applicator, and these interpretations are mixed and confused with general terms like financial 'success', or John Adair's book's subtitle 'How to Be a Successful Leader', or (generally speaking) 'winning'. With no specific definition of leadership it is difficult to know if the facilitator achieves the group's aim or not let alone leadership specifically. The group determines its traits and qualities needed and appoints them. The facilitator may still be required to find a simple easily applied pattern for leadership, one that can be taught, proved and developed in a more effective manner.

Xenophon's book certainly did not try to tell us what leadership is: he only described what Cyrus the Great's leadership was like. Xenophon, a well-respected Greek military leader some 100 years after Cyrus, praises the leader Cyrus. More importantly, the book is specific to Cyrus the Great and the situation he was in. It could be seen a precursor to behavioural and situational leadership studies of the 1930s and later. It is doubtful (but not known) that Xenophon was writing the book in response to a direct question of 'What is leadership?'; rather, he was relating an experience. It is written in story form to be used as recorded history, from which perhaps lessons could be learned on many subjects, one of which was leadership.

Cyrus the Great is written in story form, which is typical of the times. Many others have written in the same format since. The common process of storytelling was to build a character and therefore a picture of the individuals in the story. These spoken portraits describe the characteristics and traits of the leaders. Typically, these stories recounted the exploits of heroes, gods, kings and the greats of the times.

Rarely did stories relate to the commonplace or failures. If writers took on the subject of a failure it was written as a tragedy, and again the main players were the gods, kings and the greats. They were chosen as they had further to fall, and thus the greater the tragedy. Many leadership descriptions and ideas come from this genre or have inherited this form. It may be one of the reasons why leadership is commonly linked to the level of the gods, kings and greats, despite its presence in every group, even the most insignificant.

The practice of describing the qualities and specific traits of these individuals may be a precursor to an early version of the Great Man theory, which later was a foundation for the Traits theory. Many applicators, facilitators and institutes attempt to select and reproduce cultures that reflect these traits in organisations to somehow ensure more of the same success that Cyrus or others had enjoyed earlier. These stories serve to describe examples of leadership rather than define it.

Trait theory was distilled from the Great Man theory, and this trend of using descriptions of traits and characteristics of leaders continues in the selection, development and recruitment of individuals into the group. Whether this process was effective in meeting the demand for leaders or supplying academics with their theoretical proofs is not of major concern right now. What is important is that it had a fundamental effect on the study of leadership. This acceptance of Trait theory when studying and applying leadership in many ways galvanised the focus of leadership study on the leader itself. It established that the leader, as an individual, was at the centre and the only focus of the theory of leadership.

When the progress of leadership theory is presented like this it is not surprising that progress has continued along this blinkered path. Firstly, current theories on leadership seem to want only to describe what the leader is like, and secondly they are focused on the leader almost in isolation. Almost without exception, subsequent study has continued adding more and more literature focused on the same myopic view without conclusion or addition to what leadership actually is. The path has become diffused and further subdivided into more and more detail about the leader. The hope of finding an answer to the question 'What is leadership?' when going down this path gets more remote the further the examiner goes on.

When analysing the study of leadership it evokes the advice of the pioneering astronomer William Herschel in his letter to the Royal Society in 1785 [9]. At the time, advancing technology was increasing the opportunities to peer into and study space. More and more data and information was being compiled, written and published on many aspects of the heavens. In his paper Herschel advises the Royal Society in 1785 as follows:

> 'On the construction of the heavens, … merely 'adding observation to observation', without attempting to draw conclusion and explore 'conjectural views', would be equally self-defeating.'[9]

Much later, in the unconnected field of the study of leadership, R. M. Stogdill's advice sounds very similar:

> 'Future research should be designed to explore new problems rather than repeat what has been done in the past.'[10]

A new way of thinking is needed.

Chapter 3: A new approach; but first, what exactly is the challenge?

'Two roads diverged in a wood,
and I –
I took the one less travelled by,
And that has made all the difference.'

Robert Frost

Many of the early accounts of leaders describe what the leader is like in terms of the traits that are relevant to his assessors. In the search for a description of a leader there would commonly be a list of characteristics that the leader should possess in order to be effective. Typically, there is little detailed reference to the group that they are leading, so one does not know if they need this characteristic in greater or lesser amounts than the members of the group.

Secondly, there is no mention made of attempts to ascertain whether the leader needs these characteristics because the group does not have them or whether it is just as a way of differentiating the leader from the group, in as much as he has more or less of a quality than other group members, and is therefore by implication is the leader. Traits are being used to help establish the hierarchy of the individual in the group, not necessarily their applicability to leadership.

A third reason for the traits to be listed would, of course be because the situation demanded these characteristics. Traits in this instance are being used to match the individual to the situation of the group. The general situation is not specific to the leader but to all members of the group. There is a tiered application of Trait theory when using it to find the best leader of a group. Often the wrong traits are used, and without a clear understanding of what a leader's function is within the group it is not surprising mistakes are made. Without knowing the reason why these characteristics were important it becomes difficult to identify the importance or relevance of the trait. Why groups have leaders becomes a fundamental question in the search.

The lists of traits and characteristics used is by no means a fixed master list. Additionally the meaning of each characteristic or trait is open to interpretation. The characteristics are easily confused and mixed with functional abilities or qualities that may be in abundance or lacking in the team. Courage, fortitude, boldness and wisdom are all words that demand interpretation and a shared understanding. The traits present themselves differently in different people, cultures and situations. Would a band of thieves need honesty as a quality in their leader? Perhaps they would internally, given their own code of rules within the group, but certainly not with respect to others around them. Here the trait works internally but not externally. Linking traits to the group or the external environment creates some of the confusion and it becomes difficult to see why a specific value is needed in its leaders.

Different lists of characteristics can be created for different situations, groups and environments. The military identify specific types to recruit, as do large multinational commercial companies. These traits apply to all the group members and some to the leader's positions. As the theory of leadership has progressed, study has focused more on factors that influence these traits, such as the situation, the environment and the group, rather than focusing specifically on what leadership is within the group. In most situations these factors affect all group members, not just the leader: they are not specific to leadership.

With the ever-advancing levels of communication and global trade, as well as increasing populations and competition, change is ever present and speeding up. The increase in the speed of change places new demands on groups and it will change some aspects of the ability to perform leadership. Without knowing what leadership is, relying on a list of traits that are linked to the situation or environment, rather than leadership, will only be effective if the situation or environment remains the same or similar. Adding factors such as the situation and environment to the study of what leadership is certainly adds complexity to the study, because it dilutes the focus of the study. A focus on the situation and environment because they are easier to see and analyse distracts from study of what the leadership function is, and the reason why it is needed in the first place.

Competition, more efficient communication and logistics leads to an increasing frequency of change needed, and will increase the demands on groups to perform more efficiently and effectively to meet these demands. Leadership is needed for this to happen. Whether it is in the fight against disease or responding to the need to supply a customer before another does, there is a need to improve the efficiency and effectiveness of leadership in those groups. If the study of leadership digresses into the study of the factors surrounding the group rather than the specific definition of leadership, its functions and why the leader is needed by the group, then the lessons and tools learned in the past will eventually only produce more of the same results as before. Current theory and application will not be enough to meet demand.

Thomas Kuhn [10] identifies in his 1969 book *The Structure of Scientific Revolutions*[11] that in order to identify a new paradigm of thought, one must leave the normal patterns of scientific development and thought. These departures from the normal patterns are where the scientific revolution starts. Establishing and defining the specific question is the start point. What is leadership? The need to find an answer is the root cause for the volumes of literature written, no matter which path you have chosen to follow: academic, application or facilitator. A return to the fundamentals of how leadership is studied in practice is needed in order to look at it from another angle.

What is known about leadership? Leadership occurs all around us but it is not fully understood: it is a paradox. It can be recognised when it happens and while some claim a 'gut feeling' on the subject, others rely on comparative judgements made where one person is a better leader than another (often themselves) in a given situation. Few, if any, are able to define in specific terms what leadership is so that it can be applied in all situations and groups. There is a distinct lack of skill in identifying what 'action' or function the leader displayed that compelled the others to follow the leader other than to use the word 'leadership' as a general descriptor.

It may be possible in some cases to identify a financial bonus or specific words and phrases that spurred the followers into action but there still remains the challenge of knowing whether this fits into the general leadership term. It feels like it does, but how do these motivators weave into the complex web that links leaders and their followers? Because there is no definition of leadership, influencers like these seem very difficult to place in the leadership process. They do not have a formal link to the concept of leadership in terms of a definition. This therefore means that it may or may not be leadership.

If leadership is to be fully understood, taught more effectively and repeated, a detailed definition is needed – one with specific terms that links these influencers together into a common understanding and framework of functions and reasons why that allows analysis of any group situation in order to create and maintain a leadership plan that follows a process that can be taught and repeated. This appears to be a considerable challenge, and (as in leadership itself) the challenge must be clear and specific in order to draw the correct conclusions and answers. The specific challenge is identified as follows;

> To define what is leadership is, in order to be able to list its functions in order to allow for more effective and efficient application and development of leadership.

Chapter 4: Why is there such confusion?

'Leadership is one of the most observed and least understood
phenomena on earth'

J.M. Burns

The confusion also arises because of the way in which leadership
is studied. Leadership is the result. It is a solution that is to be acquired. The study of leadership is actually more about finding the
path that can get to that solution. Previous methods, as seen, are
the acceptance of a divine order of things and of the situation as it
unfolds, as there is no alternative concept. The Great Man theory,
rather like the Great Chain of Being,[12] is the result of this approach
[11] and is akin to gathering everything known about leadership
and admitting that it is too difficult to sort out the detail or to know
whether one is right even if it could be done. This approach has
been superseded by the Traits theory in an attempt to respond to
the needs of groups for more effective leaders.

Taking into account all of the possible options and putting them
under one microscope in an attempt to study all the options to find
a focus point of commonality can be overwhelming. The scale of
the search for the path to leadership brings to mind the statement
made by Michael Ventris, a young British architect, when asked by
a BBC correspondent how he deciphered the ancient language
called Linear B in 1952.[13] He said,

'It is rather like doing a crossword puzzle on which the positions of the black squares haven't been printed for you'

In the case of leadership puzzle there is only the word 'Leadership' in the middle of the blank white crossword grid. The only
clue is the word at the centre of the grid. Working backward to find
how this solution was arrived at is a truly daunting challenge to
most people – a very specific challenge that has the journey itself
as the prize, because the solution is already known. Being able to
fill in the other words and phrases around it so that the whole puzzle is completely filled and then creating the corresponding clues

to match the originator's clues would be an extraordinary demonstration of coincidence. Random retro guessing is not an effective approach.

Trait theory is a different approach, however, due to the many different interpretations of what the word 'leadership' and the host of traits listed actually mean, with a shared understanding that makes it difficult as well. As has been seen, the traits are not always linked to leadership specifically and are distracted by the situation and influences that all those in the group face. This situation brings to mind the old adage 'If you don't know where you are going any road will get you there.' The need to specify the meaning of leadership is a step towards the first goal of finding a way to make more effective leaders more efficiently.

Returning to what is known, a different approach can be started. There is a common concept or a perceived feeling of what leadership is. Some readily recognise it in others. The terms and expressions are in regular use and it is a clue where to start the search for the elusive definition. Leadership is something that can be differentiated from other types of relationships because of the actions of the group, or more specifically the actions that the followers and leaders perform that make up the group. The body language, the posture, the expressions and communications, or lack of them, along with many other signs, serve as indicators that give the perception of a leader, distinct from the followers in a type of positional hierarchy.

By looking at other social animals, such as lions and the great apes, it may help to recognise and confirm what humans mean by this phrase 'a leader–follower hierarchy'. Humans have extended the terms commonly used in human groups to describe leader–follower hierarchies to other social animals. Groups of social animals are given many different names, such as flocks, packs and prides. In these groups, humans have distinguished that some groups also have followers and leaders that can be differentiated.

Labels such as the alpha male and female in the pride, the king of the jungle and the leader of the wolf pack are given to these groups. Whether they are actually the leaders of the pack is not the issue here. The important point is the human application of the terminology based on the human perception of the animals' actions and behaviours in the group. These social animals display actions and behaviour patterns that humans recognise and label as typically displayed in 'a leader–follower relationship'.

The recognising and labelling of leader–follower relationships in social animals has implications. Even when explaining merely the limited leader–follower positional or hierarchical situation there is often an assumption attached to this label: that the leader must have leadership skills. From the word *leader* is derived the verb *to lead*, and this understanding or assumption by implication extends to the relationship. A leader–follower relationship implies that leadership (*the noun*), as a thing, exists in the group. From an etymological point of view it is correct, but there are those who would question this assumption or implication. This displays a semantic difference in the terminology. It demonstrates a general understanding of the word and its derivations. One could say that in general the leader is demonstrating leadership, but that is not what is meant by some when addressing a 'true leader' when using examples of those that lead through inspiration of others.

There is a divergence of understanding when it comes to specifics, and this is where a great deal of the confusion is rooted. The large number of different interpretations of what leadership is, as well as a lack of a precise definition leadership causes this confusion. Other social animals display actions and behaviours that humans understand in general terms as being typical in a leader–follower hierarchy, and this is important. Humans have a common understanding of the term 'leader' and the implied general meaning of leadership has a common root.

This general understanding holds true in many other languages, not just English. Not surprisingly, many of the Indo-European languages have this general understanding but it is also true in some of the Sino Tibetan languages that the author has encountered, such as Mandarin, Nepalese and Thai. Also true in these languages is the common perception that this is a general understanding and that it does not apply when looking at specific situations and describing specific relationships. Some situations are used as examples of great leadership but are then rejected by others as not 'true' or 'authentic' leadership, only examples of coercion. The confusion arises when the general description of the positional relationship in a group is extended to every individual situation or relationship. This is easy to clear up by being specific in the use of terminology.

Being specific, though, requires a shared understanding, and the confusion starts again. When looking closer at the term 'leadership' as a description of the situation it is given a label or 'type of relationship' rather than the standard leader–follower hierarchical relationship in order to clarify that situation. The type of relationship description refers to how and what actions and behaviours are different in that leader and relationship. The differences are pronounced and help in the analysis of leadership, as they provide the details that help us to zero in on the disputed meaning of leadership.

These different actions and behaviours of the leader will help describe the type of relationship and have led to a huge amount of study on the different types of leader relationship there are. Again, these are studies that distract us from the fundamental question needed to answer before finding out what leadership is. Why does a leader–follower hierarchy (or for that matter any other type of relationship) exist, irrespective of its label? When this is known then an examination of what leads to the differing actions and behaviours of the leader can be explained and labelled more explicitly and a shared understanding can be gained.

Chapter 5: Breaking down the clues

'A journey of a thousand miles begins beneath one's feet'
Lao-tzu

One clue is in the word 'leadership'. The word itself has an action aspect that is specific to the leader and differentiates the leader from the followers. Also, there is a common interpretation that leadership actions are different from the actions in a management relationship or a dictatorship. All three describe a positional leader–follower relationship. What those actions are and their differences have significance in this study and is an important question to answer *en route* to resolving the specific challenges of 'What is Leadership?', and how it is to be defined.

Leaders exist in groups. Indeed, at the basic level a leader is a position in a group. The word 'leader' is a noun and it explicitly describes a position in a group. While the word is simple to understand on the surface, it is most important to note the implications of the word. The position of leader belongs to a group. The word leader implies a follower and therefore a group. The group, the followers and the leader belong to each other. The group, leader and followers are co-constituents. While the word itself may not explicitly state this (or one may not consciously think it), the implication and subliminal understanding is there. It is the way our language is structured and consequently interpreted.

The implicit meaning of the word is learned through experience and instruction in the group. Words are the way in which the group confirms specific meaning and derive an overall understanding amongst the individuals of the group. Direct instruction in the meaning of a word is complemented by experiential learning to ensure that any double meanings and its use in different circumstances are understood. The group's understanding of the word creates part of the culture of the group.

The linguistic importance attached to words and the order in which they are used is taken for granted by most. Greetings in dif-

ferent groups take many different forms in words, phrases and actions, but they are all greetings. Even the order in which the words
are assembled into phrases provides meaning and implication. It
creates a priority of understanding and action. Addressing the name
of the person at the front of a sentence or instruction gets their attention and emphasises the need for that individual to listen more
carefully. Similarly, it allows others to reduce their alertness to the
briefing and continue with another task in hand.

An understanding of the group and its intentions comes from
both the explicitly stated and implicit meaning of the words, but
also from the order in which they are used by the group. This is
something that is learned through observed actions, direct instruction and the subsequent important linking of the actions, instructions and experience.

The understanding that comes from a combined use of language
and actions is different in each individual. Experienced individuals
may need only an action or a few words in a short phrase to understand what is meant. It is this understanding in the group that will
help define a group culture. This group or cultural understanding
of a leader–follower hierarchy concept could be along family lines
all the way up to national, religious or racial groups, or (as demonstrated) even across species. Language and actions will define the
understanding in a group. It will also lead the thoughts and perhaps
unintentionally blinker the thinking of a group

Continuing on the path to a definition of 'What is leadership?',
by establishing a common understanding, a start point can be
found. A leader is a position in a group and implicit in the word
'leader' is that there will be one or more followers and therefore a
group. A leader without a follower in common understanding does
not exist. The correct term for the members of the group that are
not the leader is the 'followers'. It is worth mentioning here that a
definition of a group can be as simple as 'two or more individuals'.
The group, the leader and the followers, are co-constituents of the
group. They are three distinct entities or parties in their own right.

The term 'leader–follower hierarchy' describes a relationship in a group. It implies a priority and a value chain. It also does not mention the group. In the past, the study of leadership has revolved around the leader as the focus. The followers, if mentioned at all, are merely bystanders or, as implied in the label, of secondary concern in the relationship. The group exists of course, but it is not even implied or mentioned when studying this type of relationship. When the concept of servant leadership was developed by Robert K. Greenleaf,[14][13] as revealed in the 1970 publication of his essays entitled 'The Servant as Leader'[15] it promoted the follower to the main stage, but only as a bit part in the main production. They are explicitly given the part as the subject of the leader's attention and focus, but with no lines, whereas previously they had been merely an unseen presence in attendance in the theatre of leadership theory.

Hersey and Blanchard continued in the same vein of promoting the follower to the main stage. This time they had an influencing role in defining how the followers affected the leader's role and performance. Hersey and Blanchard create a method of defining and grading the followers' characteristics or traits and how their functioning maturity will affect the leader. This term 'functional maturity' is a significant addition to the lexicon of leadership study and Hersey and Blanchard use it to describe an aspect of the follower and their ability to contribute to the group in terms of their function in the group. In order for leaders to deliver a more effective performance they must choose followers that are at the appropriate functional maturity according to the roles they play in the performance.

This is a promotion to the main stage from the wings of the theatre and the group has also gained a significant role on stage. This is a considerable promotion from the roles they occupied in the Great Man theories, but they are still only present to highlight the position of and actions of the leader as different from the followers.

In the servant-leader relationships proposed and described by Greenleaf the followers are the primary focus of the leader and he identifies what the leader must do in order to get the followers to act. Hersey and Blanchard refine this approach to assist the leader in their ability to find the right followers for the right part in the group and balance the performance to get the best results. Both theories represent significant advances, but are still supplicant to the language and thinking patterns of the leader–follower hierarchy.

This represents a move away from previous thinking by placing the emphasis of the leader's focus more on things external to themselves and on the followers, but it still leaves the third party, the group itself, in the wings. The studies themselves are still studies of the leader as an individual, only they focus on the traits of the leader and the followers. Although servant and situational leadership concepts have developed as another sub-branch of leadership theory because it is different, and more effective, it is still only an advancement of the Trait theory. Both are still primarily a study of the leader himself. The study of leadership must go further than this and involve all three parties explicitly and equally in reference to the relationship between them.

The followers and the group are of fundamental importance in the study of leadership because they are the reason why the leader exists. To exclude the group as a major party in the relationship is to blinker the study. It is a partial reflection of what actually happens in reality; similarly with the followers. It is understood that leadership theory focuses on the leader explicitly, but it cannot be done effectively without all three parties being linked together as co-constituents within the overall framework of the group. This will allow a balanced overall view of what leadership is, the functions of a leader and why leadership is needed in a group.

The ability of the followers to understand and work as a group depends on the followers' ability to understand and work within the group, and with the leader. In practical terms, a group leader is often chosen according to the group they are expected to lead. There are very good practical reasons for this. The survival of the group does not just depend on the leader, but also on how the followers perceive the challenge or threat to the group. The followers must understand the leader's communications and that will help determine whether the challenge is given priority by the followers and how effective the group will be in meeting that challenge. Taking it a step further, where competition between groups exist the group's role is easier to see and communicate. When there is a challenge that threatens the existence of the group, the group members' (both the leaders and the followers) perception of the group and why it exists will be very important. The challenge being faced will influence the group's response.

The level of cooperation between the group members and their perception of the group in relation to the challenge will vary. This is a group-specific issue taken in light of the competition and challenge that the group faces and not the individuals' perceptions of their place or reason for being in the group. Who is to decide on the value of one individual in the group when faced with a challenge? It may be the leader or the group as a whole. This cooperation between the three parties will determine the nature of the relationship and therefore can be used to define the relationship, rather than the success of the group in competition with other groups.

The response to that group-level challenge depends very much on the followers and what they perceive the group to be. If their perception is different from the positional leader's then the group may reject the positional leader in favour of another. Alternatively, the group may reject the challenge as one that is not relevant to them and individuals will abandon the first group in favour of another group. Eventually the group may cease to exist due to a lack of members that empathise with the group's stated cause. Political parties are good examples of this. Within fixed populations the group's appeal to the population is based on the cause of the group they represent and it is the reason that the followers give their membership and support.

The term 'leader–follower' may have influenced the study considerably or perhaps the studies reflect what is perceived to be the dominant type of group relationship. There are groups that reflect a follower–leader hierarchy, such as dominant unions within companies and cooperatives. For the name to be truly reflective of the relationship, all groups should include an element of the group as an entity itself that influences the followers and leaders. The label perhaps should be group–leader–follower relationship in order to prevent the implication of a greater importance to any one party. Language influences the thinking of a group. There is a need to disenthrall the theory from the focus on the leader in isolation to get a more clearly understood and effective application of leadership in the group.

Few organisations in practice appoint a leader of a group without considering how all three parties – the leader, followers and group – will meet the challenge. Factors such as understanding of the followers' functions, their language and culture, and the environment are considered. An interpretation of the group challenge is presented by those appointing the leader. The considerations are present; however, the actions involved in appointing leaders often do not reflect the considerations. More often, it is an exercise in recruiting for a title or job description carried out by someone removed from the challenge facing the group. The followers' perception of the challenge facing the group is rarely given an airing in the process.

The process of appointment differs in each group. However, the practice usually reflects the group alone and their needs rather than the challenge facing the group or the followers. The practice of appointment of leaders often reflects only one party's view of the group and it is not the whole picture. With no specific definition of a leader as a function or a reason why, selectors can only use an example of what has worked before. The interaction of the group, the leader and the followers together in light of the challenge will form a relationship and make the group effective, not just the leader in isolation.

The focus of leadership studies should be on how the leader, the followers and the group relate to each other rather than on one party against the situation. More specifically, focusing on how the three-party relationship manifests itself in practical terms will help identify the components of the relationship. This will then help to define the details of the relationship and allow a definition of the type of relationship that it is when compared to other relationship that use different techniques of relating. The actions and behaviours between them will define the relationship.

Any definition of leadership must focus on the relationship between the leader, the followers and the group. The definition should specify the relationship in terms of why, what and how the parties interact with each other in order to be a definition that can be understood and applied to make leadership more effective in terms of the application and resolution of the challenge the group is presented with.

The challenge facing the study and understanding of leadership in some areas, such as business, is made more difficult due to the increase in the speed and reach of communications and therefore competition. The increased scale of competition has highlighted needs not previously considered. These needs are manifested in the need to change and adapt more quickly and in a wider range of activities and industries. No longer is it just emergency, war and matters of life, death, injury and provision of the basics of life that demand this speed and comprehension to improve leadership. This competition drives the need for greater effectiveness and efficiency of leadership across industries, economies and nations.

The study of leadership at an academic level is following the trend predicted by Stogdill,[16] moving along ever increasing and inwardly tightening spirals of detail that are not addressing the issues of what leadership is. Rather, they describe the situations that surround it. Improved or faster change management, better communications allowing centralised decision making and authorities at a global scale have focused decision making where it is best, but have not made leadership more effective or widespread. If anything, it has reduced it to a more centralised few.

Even with the increase in competition, leadership continues to exist in groups all around us. It is being passed from generation to generation as the speed of change increases. 'On the job learning' is probably the dominant method of transmission. It is done in response to the needs of the situation and given the requirements it will probably remain the dominant process.

It is in the 'group' where leadership is present and the human brain's capacity to perceive 'the group', whether virtual or real, as an entity in itself is a common theme in all leadership scenarios. The 'group' also has an advantage in that it can be perceived as an individual is perceived; it has its own character and personality. It is a motivator in its own right and can develop over time to represent something quite permanent in itself. This property as a third party and as a separate motivator in of itself in an individual's decision process reflects reality in the relationships of groups. It therefore should be reflected in the study of the theory of leadership.

Increased competition requires more effective leadership at all levels of groups. Leadership is happening in groups every day. It is to the practical application that the investigation turns to examine what part they play in the relationship. It is something that has been happening and will continue to happen with or without the advances and speed of technological change, so it is something that has existed as long as groups have.

Leaders clearly perform a function in the group and add some value to the followers and the group. Where competition exists, if the leader did not add value a new leader (if the option were present) would be found. The group similarly adds value to the leader otherwise the desire to be a leader would not exist. This is borne out by the fact that not everyone wants to be a leader in all situations they experience. There are those that are quite content to be followers in positional terms as well as in actions. It would be wrong to consider the follower to be an opposite to the leader. The followers, the leader and the group are co-constituents in the relationship.

Seeing the group as an entity in itself reflects practice and is something that is not reflected in the academic study of the theory of leadership. The relationship between the group, the followers and the leader has a common uniting factor and all serve as motivators to each other to be linked to each other. In each individual party the motivator may well be different, and it is the unique combination of these, and how and why they interact, that creates a relationship and unites the group. The group as an individual entity is implied in the word 'leadership' as is the follower, and each is a vital component in the study of the theory of leadership.

Chapter 6: And the binding agent is?

'The only real training for leadership is leadership.'

Sir Anthony Jay

What is it that the three parties add to each other to hold them together? What is it that the leader, the group and the followers add to the relationship? In the case of a follower, there is the thought and muscle contributed to the group to ensure that the group's plans are met. These actions of the followers, and sometimes the leader, are the obvious addition to the group, but there is more. Depending on the interaction between the three parties, the results can vary substantially.

The relationship between the leader, group and followers is identified to an extent in the communications that they share. Whether it is the body language or (more commonly) the spoken language, it is the actions and reactions displayed that define the relationship. The communication of ideas is the connecting point of the three parties in as much as it is the physical element of the passage of ideas and intentions from one party to another. It is the starting point of the connection and it is the method used to establish and maintain a relationship over time. These ties can lead to bonds that go beyond logic to emotions and prompt decisions into action that in some cases defy the rule, principles and predictions of economists and behavioural scientists.

The three parties need something from each other and they combine to meet their collective needs. How they do this will determine the nature of the relationship, and its effectiveness in resolving the needs of each party. There is a need demanded by the group from the group members and vice versa from to its group members. The group members are both the leader and the followers who have different needs and likewise different expectations from the other two parties in the tripartite agreement. How the three parties meet those needs will define their relationship in specific terms as to what type of relationship it is. It is not enough to label it in terms of a positional hierarchy group. It will determine whether it is a relationship that is called leadership, management or coercion. Individuals will join groups to meet some of their needs. At a basic level the need for food, protection from the environment (such as harsh extreme weather, dirt and disease, crime, abuse and theft) and personal security are just some of these needs. Not all the individuals' needs are always met by one group, and individuals will belong to multiple groups that may be separate or nested within each other, like Matryoshka dolls. Larger groups that contain subgroups will cater to different needs at different levels. If basic needs are met by other groups then they may join a group for reasons that appeal to other aspects of their individual needs, such as the need for recognition through money, status, opportunity or awards. There are many types of needs and they are specific to each individual. Needs are driven by individuals and they motivate the individual to make decisions into action. Groups are a collection of individuals all claiming membership in order to meet their needs, however complex or simple they are. Motivation is an individual thing, not a group thing. Belonging to a group is an individual impulse that motivates the individual to join and remain as a group member.

Groups are made up of individuals who are there either by choice of the individual or because of circumstance, such as your place of birth (deciding your passport, nationality, culture or environment) or a lack of options, perceived or real, to chose to do otherwise. It maybe that the individuals are in that group because they have been forced there by the laws of that country, such as a military draft, or they are in the group under duress. Groups have subgroups and the members are members because they choose to be, even to the extent that the situation would be worse as an isolated individual, however reluctant that individual is to join the group. There are all manner of individuals in groups and this leads to different types of relationships being formed.

Whether the group is one of volunteers or not, the leader must focus on two sets of needs. One set of needs is what the followers expect to get from the group to meet their individual needs. The second set of needs is what the group expects to get from the followers. There is no order specified and that depends on the group and its circumstances.

The leader is also an individual group member and will have an individual's needs from the group. The leader is similar to the followers in this respect and like any individual in the group, his needs will be different from others. The leader may realise that his different skill set affords him different value to the group when compared to many of the followers. The differing sets of needs create a balancing game. When labour is in short supply compared to vacancies the individual has a bargaining position between competing groups. This situation happens often enough in isolated locations. Labour shortages can lead to major social change, such as in Europe after the Black Death: the shortage of labourers for harvesting and other basic needs of common life led to great changes in the social structure of countries in terms of the relationship between leaders and followers.

When followers are in abundance, groups have the better bargaining position due to the competition amongst labour. This is a simple supply and demand situation. This is similar to labour with specific skill sets such as engineering qualifications, multiple language skills or experience in specific areas. The ebb and flow of demand and supply may be perceived or real, but it will determine the market value for these skills and therefore the relationship between the individuals and the group. Leadership is often seen as one of those specific skills.

It is often assumed both leaders and followers as individuals know what they want. In reality, many do not know without some careful thought. Experience is a great teacher and individuals spend a period of time learning what they don't want rather than what meets their needs. Then as they find what they want their needs start to change. Genghis Khan eventually found the challenge of expansion and warfare his area of expertise and maximum challenge, and hence enjoyment. He left the management and stability of peace to others in his wake. To find out exactly what those individual needs are, is important to individuals in their pursuit of their goals as well as to the groups and the establishment of stable relationships.

Needs, called motivators by psychologists, cover a wide spectrum from the basic physical requirements of food water and shelter to intellectual challenges that are new and engaging. The individual's needs of all types, physical or mental (such as for recognition of the person's value in a group), are subject to constant change as some are met or abandoned. A good tailor measures his returning customer every time they meet to ensure they are fitting for a great solution at that moment in time and the foreseeable future, not for the shape the customer was at the last fitting. Each of the three parties in a relationship should be constantly reassessing the needs of the other as they change, in addition to allowing for the external competition, factors and fashions.

The needs of the group are placed on both leaders and followers as conditions to gaining membership and group benefits. For the leader and followers it is important that the group's needs are understood in order for the group and its members to be able to create and maintain that balance effectively between individual and group needs. Initially the demands that the group makes of both the leader and follower become a uniting and common feature for the two parties in the group. These common demands often serve as a starting point for the creation of a relationship between the follower and leader. Once the leader and follower are joined the links can continue to be forged with each other and the group entity.

Individuals, whether leaders or followers, are assumed to have a reasonable understanding of their basic needs, although this is not always the case. Knowing the group's needs is the other half of the balance that each individual considers and decides on when considering group membership. The individual has a choice, and the decision to join or not is one of three options: positive action and join; inaction and find out more before deciding; or negative action and not joining (or even open opposition to joining if they have the choice).

To have an understanding of the group's needs is of importance to the individuals in the group. Once the individuals become aware of the group they want to know more about the group in order to know whether they wish to belong. The human need to belong to groups is strong and means there are thousands groups already in existence and waiting to be formed. It is a need that both leaders and followers have. In the case of the leader the urge to belong is of prime importance to the group as it is often the leader that is expected to represent the group both internally and externally. In the group-leader–follower relationship the balance between the group needs and individual needs will define the relationship between the group's co-constituents. The 'leader' is taking on a third party position in this relationship. It creates the two sub sets within the group, the sub set of leader and the separate sub set of the follower.

The balance of the needs of these three parties provides the framework for the components of leadership theory. To study only one sub set as mentioned earlier is myopic. How the co-constituents relate to their separate needs is sometimes referred to a group dynamics and in the past leadership confined to the sub sets usually just the leaders sub set and the individual that occupies that position. The study of leadership more accurately pertains to the relationship of needs between the three co-constituents and how they relate to each other as a whole. It is the needs of the three parties as individuals that is the binding agent in the relationship.

Chapter 7: The gap between study and application

'In theory, theory and practice are the same. In practice they are not.'

Albert Einstein

The parties need a balance in order to work as a group and produce a solution to the challenge presented to the group. In order to make the study of leadership more effective and efficient, focus must be placed on the relationship between the co-constituents and their interaction. The study of this relationship is separate from the application of leadership. There are those who understand it but cannot apply it, and others who, just through good experience and instruction and habit, perform it well without understanding why it works. Clarifying and increasing the understanding of group relationships will allow more people to apply and achieve more effective and efficient relationships earlier in life and more often. This is the ultimate goal of resolving the challenging question of 'What is leadership?'.

At a fundamental level there is a misunderstanding not only of what leadership is, but also of how and when the word should be applied. Firstly the title or position of manager does not automatically bestow the qualities upon the individual who occupies that seat. Most young team leaders find this out very quickly in practice, and in order to be more effective and add value they retrace, adapt and start again. It is a basic survival technique: change according to the needs or fail. They start to listen, engage and develop their leadership abilities within that group. This final phrase 'within that group' is an important addition to the last sentence. The experienced applicator understands, perhaps through harsh experience, that leadership of one group does not mean leadership in all groups automatically. One gains experience and develops new techniques and awareness for the differences of new groups of individuals and the new challenges that groups encounter.

The concept that it is possible to learn the theory of the process of effective leadership and that one can expect 100% effective solutions on first application all the time is laughable to the experienced applicator. Effectiveness depends on many factors, not just the co-constituents in the relationship. The relationship is not a one-stop-shop solution; it is a process that is constantly evolving. Just looking at the process in practice will demonstrate this. When a challenge is presented by a customer the group must work out the plan, confirm it, execute it and arrive at a solution. The customer will assess the solution, and if largely effective, and in the absence of a competitor's more effective solution, the customer will ask the team to repeat their efforts. Any adjustments and minor improvements will be included in the next effort to make it more effective. The concept of getting it right first time, every time, is good in theory, but often not realistic in practice, and does not take into account the customer, who often adds to the requirements with hindsight of the solution. This is a simple representation of the challenge resolution process that is repeated many times in many situations. It is a familiar process and it follows a predictable chain of events, whether it is in a commercial organisation or a smaller group such as a family. A challenge is presented and identified, a plan is made, a decision taken, actions are performed and a solution is the result. Using the key stages as identifiers the process is called the Decision $\rightarrow$ Action $\rightarrow$ Solution chain, or DAS chain for quick reference.[17]

The DAS chain is a general description of the actual process that happens in groups. Currently the first time this process is studied in any depth is at universities and higher education facilities in the form of Business Administration (BA) degrees to prepare individuals for the commercial job markets. Unfortunately these institutions limit themselves to dealing with only one part of the chain: the decision process. Many BAs and higher level MBAs or EMBAs advertise that they help improve the leadership of the participants.

By addressing only a limited aspect of a part of the process they cannot develop leadership, and this is because of the limited understanding of what leadership is. Typically the programs run by the universities use case studies. These are sample cases that are designed and explained in great detail. The case studies are often specific to a situation and the details are used to set up the guidelines and parameters of the situation. More detail is often done to focus the thinking towards learning specific lessons.

Much of the explanation, when using a case study, is taken up in outlining the terms of success, such as monetary figures, marketplace solutions, or finding concepts in the application of a process and projects. The case study will outline for the participant the solution in the form of targets, KPIs and the goals that they hope to achieve. The participant must try to find a path to the expected solution of these terms defined. Individuals or small groups of managers, leaders or 'titles' take time to assess and later present solutions. All is done in isolation from the group and followers. All is set up and appears to be prepared well, even though it lacks key elements needed for leadership to be experienced even in these theoretical scenarios.

Seldom is the relationship between the leader and followers addressed. Lessons are drawn from these situations and proofs derived into a theory matched against an existing theory in the use of assets and markets etc. Discussions are very important in revealing new ideas and approaches as well as highlighting and revising lessons that have been forgotten. Without a firm understanding of what makes up the relationship between the co-constituents in the relationship the case study will often digress into an asset allocation exercise rather than a study on how to create and apply a relationship between the co-constituents in response to a challenge that the group is faced with.

These case studies, while important in building a set of studies of business asset allocation, do not address the relationships that are at the foundation of the study of leadership. Of course, most universities state that the programme is a Master of Business Administration and not leadership specifically; however, the advertising or the market has wrongly perceived the programme to somehow bestow the participant with leadership abilities.

Working on case studies of this type and in these settings focuses on only one aspect of the decision process: the assets and their allocation. The followers are considered as one of the assets or as a resource to be used. This is just one aspect or link in the chain. Just as looking at only one party in the relationship is myopic and limiting, so is believing that only one party in the decision stage of the process is going to develop leadership ability. It will develop the planning of assets and options to be taken based on the knowledge learned and discussion experienced, and this is important.

The exercise may also practise the presenting and communicating of a plan to shareholders if this is part of the exercise. The communication function is important, and practice in these areas is good, but planning and communicating to a limited group of asset allocators is only a sub-link in the DAS chain. Development of leaders must happen across all links in the chain and in tandem with the three parties in the chain, in order to develop relationships and to maintain them.

Each group in reality is made up of different individuals and the challenges presented to each group are different. Each case study has limited value in terms of the application of a relationship in a group. The participant walks away from the case study with the knowledge that this is something to do with business theory, but it is only an exercise in asset allocation. It does not take into account the actual followers or actual customers.

Even after the programme is completed, the participants exhibit a continued demand for case studies that reflect the former students' actual situations to be discussed and for a third party view to be expressed in order to clarify and give confidence to the individuals once they are in situations that demand decisions. For many this is the first time that they experience a real challenge, and it now has implications that will reflect on them and their position.

While at university it is difficult for students to imagine the challenges to be faced in terms of real followers and group representatives making demands of them. By creating very specific models in the absence of a formula that can be applied in any group it creates a dependence on the scenario which has done much of the thinking for them. The targets, KPIs and goals are set out in accordance with shareholders' (asset managers') requirements. There are no tools for the students to be able to self-assess their effectiveness other than what they are told to do. The real thinking is removed from them.

The case study has reduced them to being able to respond only to a task required of them. While it is unusual for a newly appointed manager to have the future of the group in their hands, the ability to analyse, assess and process what is a challenge to the group is a key part of the decision process. It is often the assessment of this unknown factor that will determine the rest of the plan and the effectiveness of the group they below to. The ability to think at this level with effective models that help lay out the format of a relationship is a key requirement in forming a relationship. Participants who are unable to abstract from the theory into the situation that they face are of limited use, whether in an asset allocation exercise or in forming relationships. Differences in the ability to abstract from theory into reality highlight the difficulty of this type of 'unreal' application learning.

Groups exist all over and at every age level. It is possible to teach, exercise and experience the creation and maintenance of a relationship in diverse groups of individuals at all age levels. Currently it is practised haphazardly, with little common focus or adequate tools other than on-the-job experience, application from previous practice and repeating known recipes. By defining what leadership is, the way that thinking is required of leaders can be more easily understood and systematically applied in any group at any age level. The learning experience can be improved for the benefit of the group as well as for the individual, in as much as they gain more from each experience rather than receiving the same experience many times before learning which aspect needs to be changed to be more effective.

The process of developing leaders is ongoing and does not stop at the decision stage. It moves all the way through the whole chain. It must be based on real situations and on real experience across many different groups. Large organisations often move individuals on a regular basis to different functions, locations and cultures to experience working in different groups. Recruitment agencies will use simple indicators from an individual's CV to assess their ability to change across function, culture, geography and language groups. Companies take this approach to develop the individual holistically in their company, across many disciplines and groups.

Some individuals actively seek new challenges and environments which will present them with the need to learn new experiences and adapt new approaches, broadening their horizons. In leadership terms each new group experiences has an R&D phase when the leadership learning curve is at its steepest and opening new horizons for the individual as a leader.

The search for the precise definition of leadership is done in order to enable applicators to be able to create their own relationship models and apply them. The definition must reflect the environment of practical application as it happens in groups, all around, all the time. The uniqueness of each situation requires the definition and tools of application to be simple enough to understand, formulate and apply into actual situations all around them. The concepts pertain to the actual relationship with their actual followers, not business models which remove themselves from the relationship and its co-constituents.

To study the process, the steps in the DAS chain are used. To become effective as leaders individuals must learn and apply the concepts themselves to experience each aspect of the DAS chain and relationship interactions in groups. These experiences will build knowledge of the nature and application of relationships and what defines them. The theory of leadership as mentioned is focused on the interaction and relationship between the three parties. The path to being effective in the leadership role is through its applied practice and experience.

Universities, not surprisingly, are not the place to study the theory of leadership. They could be, as they have the capacity to understand, teach and create the environment for diverse groups and their interaction. In this regard so do schools, sports teams and all manner of groups, right down to the simple family group where much of life's relationship learning is based. They are a starting point and could provide a basic foundation provided they address the planning of the relationship between the three parties involved in the DAS chain.

Universities are practising the planning and analysis of assets allocation based on market reports, financial predictions and shareholder demands. This is what an MBA or EMBA course explicitly states it does, and many produce very good administrators of assets. As a business leader who has expectations to develop their executive teams in leadership there are more productive ways to achieve this. Whether a commercial or non-commercial group, there are better ways to develop executives in creating and maintaining relationships in real situations in a focused manner with all co-constituents present. Leadership at any level is a function in itself and individuals start learning the process of leadership as soon as they become part of a group.

The process of group learning starts once a child becomes aware that it is an individual amongst other individuals. At this stage the child is said to be self-aware in that the child has the ability to recognise itself as an individual separate from the environment and other individuals. All future learning is done within this context and the group aspect remains with the individual throughout its life. Peer pressure, in any respect, it is ever-present in an individual's considerations.

The groups that the individual belongs to will have set the environment, language, expectation and culture that the group members will understand or be taught to use when communicating ideas and concepts. The study of leadership and its application is based on what exists in the group and is manifest in the interactions of the group. It is not limited to large organisations only: it exists in all groups, large and small.

For the theory of leadership to be accurate it must reflect what happens in reality. An accurate definition is needed in order to make the theory useful to applicators. From an accurate definition better understanding and tools can be extracted to improve the effectiveness of groups through better leadership. If this is not the purpose of a full understanding of leadership then the theory will remain just that: a theory with little use but to academics. The ever-changing nature of individuals over time and the evolving needs of competing groups demonstrate an increasing need for more effective leaders of groups. The enhanced need for leadership to be more effective drives the study of leadership theory. The theory of leadership must reflect reality and create the ability to improve the process of application of developing leaders to grow with or exceed the demands placed on them, so as to avoid being relegated to the depository of academic study.

Chapter 8: Leadership – more than just positional hierarchies

'In the past a leader was a boss. Today's leaders must be partners with their people ... they no longer can lead solely based on
positional power.'

Ken Blanchard

The study of leadership has evolved slowly and in practical
terms is more about how to find a path to more effective leadership. The word 'leader' refers to a position in a group. The word
also implies a group, and it could also imply that a leader does not
exist without a group. Similarly, the term 'follower' is a position
and does not exist outside of a group. A deposed king is a title that
is held, but as he is deposed he has no group. He is therefore not a
leader in a group but merely the holder of a title that is commonly
accepted as being part of a group. The title remains, but the grouping does not. These are terms that are not difficult to understand.
The leader may have a title, but only the group gives the word
'leader' or the title substance.

Followers are the second party in a group and the term is commonly understood to apply to those who are not leaders. They are
not, as is sometimes perceived, in opposition to leaders, but co-
constituents in the group. A follower is also a position that is sometimes also given a title or label within a group. Followers are equal
players in terms of position in the group. The interaction between
the group, leaders and followers will determine the type of relationship the group has. This style or type of relationship will
change over time and is dependent on many factors. However, it is
the follower who is often the party that carries out the actions of
the group and is therefore often a vital and equal party in the
group.

Humans think in groups and memberships of groups. More than
one individual creates a grouping of a sort. The human brain draws

up comparisons and highlights the differences and similarities between those in the group. Another individual is studied to assess aspects of the individual, such as whether they are recognised or not, their gender, size, age, whether they are known to be aggressive or passive, and whether or not they are a threat. Once an assessment is done, the target individual is placed in a grouping hierarchy at different levels; recognised or not, safe or not, threat levels (physical or mental) etc.

The groups take on a virtual form or a three-dimensional image/concept/character once a mental image is made and a label is attached to it. The group label, such as 'pirates', will immediately cause a positive or negative image/concept in the mind of the individual and can also invoke physical reactions (involuntary or otherwise). Groups are a very real part of human thinking and experience, and therefore motivations.

In the study of leadership it is necessary to focus on the interaction in the group between all three rather than just looking at one party. The history of the theory of leadership has been a slow random progression that belated reflects society, but is fast catching up with reality. Trait theory has developed many more descriptions of the leader and the types of relationship they create or maintain. The label 'leader–follower hierarchy' in itself creates in the mind a priority listing, with the leader superior or first and the follower inferior and second. The group is not even mentioned.

The third party, the group, is a term that is not so easy to see, but due to the brain's incredible complexity, individuals have the ability to give meaning and apply qualities, values, brand images and intellectual rights to a group. It can be an organisation that has legal status or it can be virtual and exist only in the mind. In many groups the leaders and followers sign a contract with the group, not the leader.

Corporate entities have been with us since Roman times and perhaps before. The Magna Carta, signed in 1215 between the English king and his barons, is another instance where the group as a separate entity was clearly defined and separated: the state (the group), the king and the freemen (non-serfs – a specific title of respect incorporating the word 'free'[18] to recognise their status as being separate from a lord or bondage). The leader was separated from the state (England) as an entity its own right and its freemen [15]. Much later, in France, Jean Jacques Rousseau reinforced this when he claimed that it was the people, not the king that embodied sovereignty in his Social Contract articles [16]. These laws and ideas express the conceptual understanding that the group is separate from the leader and followers, who are also separate to the group and leader.

The concept of the group has been with us much longer. It is a motivator or influencer of individuals, something that an individual could join or avoid because of the values, actions or causes that are associated with it. The group is an entity in itself. In practice it is individuals who create, represent and define the values of a group as separate from their own.

Given time and opportunity to spread, the practices, values and concepts can develop into traditions, history or even legends, and are the cause of the currently accepted way of doing things. Speech patterns, accepted meanings, laws, understandings and practices that the group adopts become features of the group and may define the culture of the group. Groups change, develop and adapt over time due to the challenges they face. They remain, break up or are broken, due to the circumstances they find themselves in. These features of a group help identify the group and give it physical and virtual representation.

Figure 8.1 gives a visual representation of a leadership relationship.

The Group

Figure 8.1 Venn diagram 1: the three parties in a relationship

This Venn diagram demonstrates the three parties: the group as a whole, the leader, and the followers as three separate parties.

1. The group
2. The leader (or leaders)
3. The followers

As individuals, the process of taking decisions into action takes place everyday. In terms of the study of leadership the group element is added. Taking decisions into action within groups is a familiar act. Within our own experience, this starts in families, then at school. The skills learned in the family group are tested and expanded upon. Interaction in new and different groups all the time and every day increases the level of experience in interacting and taking decisions into action. Absorbing raw data and facts, sorting it into packets of similar information, processing and analysing this information so that it can be compared and then selected for use for decision making and reaction, is a process that happens as individuals grow.

The process of moving along the Decision → Action → Solution chain is one that many are familiar with; however, little formal instruction exists. The process is not linked specifically with the theory of leadership or by application tools as there is no clear definition of leadership to clarify where it fits in the process. Universities are expected to be a likely place for learning leadership, yet again the link between academic levels and practice has shown a gap in the theoretical understanding and therefore the application. The gap needs to be filled to reflect reality and provide a more effective bridge between the theory and reality, where leadership exists in all groups but is not fundamentally understood.

The interaction between the co-constituents in the relationship is where leadership will be found. The study of the physical passage of ideas, concepts and intentions between the co-constituents is how relationships are created, and maintained, in addition to meeting the needs of the three parties involved. This phenomenon happens in all groups, whether we are conscious of the process or not.

The starting point of the DAS chains that occur in every group and relationship is where the search for the answer to the question 'What is leadership?' is initiated. The step known as the decision process is the focus, as individuals make decisions as individuals not as groups. Each individual has unique motivators for joining the group and while peer pressure will influence their decision it is only one of the influences. Decision making as individuals and the subsequent influences of other factors, like the group and other group members, must be included in the study of leadership and the relationships of the group. They are all inextricably linked to each other.

How humans learn and how the decision-making process works in terms of the chemistry, neurological pathways, networks and hardware behind the process is best understood in its parts by neurologists, psychologists, chemists and biologists. As an overview of individuals in groups the process can be seen all around in the actions and language used to give the group members' common understanding of the ideas of culture.

Geert Hofstede's 1993 book identifies the actions of groups that define its culture. His book is well named: *Cultures and Organisations: Software of the Mind* [17]. The identifiers of a culture can be found in the actions as a result of the thinking of the group. The software of a culture or group represents the programming language used to create the language and the interaction processes. As leadership exists in all cultures, the study of leadership can be considered equally as the study of the software and programming language of the group.

Geert Hofstede's work is the study of specified cultures and what identifies them and the differences between these cultures/groups in order to more effectively understand and bridge between cultures/groups. Hofstede is the first to warn that the group identifiers do not necessarily apply to individuals within the group, as they are general group identifiers.[19] This is where the study of cultures differs from the study of leadership. In leadership and the decision process in groups it is the study of the relationships within the group created by each individual's decision process in the group. Individuals are focused on. The DAS chain is an individual process and is the result of an individual's unique perspective. The group as a separate entity can also have its own DAS chain that represents the decision made by the group, which again is unique to the group and its co-constituents. The relationship in the group will determine how the group DAS chain is arrived at.

Initiating the search for an effective definition of leadership has given the outline of the process to be examined and the questions to answer. For the answer to the question of 'What is leadership?' the definition must involve all co-constituents in the relationship and explain the functions of the leader as well as why leadership is needed in the group. This is done in order to provide the theory of leadership with a more precise reflection of the nature of relationships in groups. A more effective definition will also provide more effective tools for the comparison and development of more effective relationships across all groups.

PART 2: Facilitating the rescue

Chapter 9: Deciphering the language of interaction

'The art of communications is the language of leadership'
James C. Humes

In order to carry out a full search for the answer it is necessary to find out the language that is being used. The relationship has a way of addressing ideas, concepts and intentions. It is necessary to work out this interaction-specific language in order to continue on the path to defining leadership. This language of interaction relates to the patterns of packages of data and information in decision making. How these packages are grouped and the order in which they are assembled will create patterns in our speech and give clues as to how different meaning, interpretations and behaviour are decided upon. It is similar to any language, in that rearranging the words can change a statement into a question.

Where individuals have worked out their proposed plan of action they must yet complete a process that gets the Decision stage into gear before moving to the Action stage. The leaders must take the plans and proposals for the DAS chain to the followers and group in order to get a decision to go ahead, or at least confirmation, that they know what is expected of them. It is an important stage and is often one of the more involved stages in a relationship for a leader. The transition from one proposed set of ideas into a decision by each party in the group can be difficult but necessary. Only then can they move ahead into action and towards a solution.

As with any chain, each link is important, and when one link breaks the whole chain is ineffective. There is, however, an alternative that will strengthen the DAS chain. Instead of there being only one chain representing the group and showing the DAS process, there could be multiple chains, one for each of the parties in the relationship, that are twisted and woven together rather like a suspension bridge's steel cables. This combination can effectively multiply the strength of the overall DAS process. Having the same process followed and agreed at every stage by each individual is effectively like combining chains and strengthening the relationship.

Most leaders have a choice of how they present the message to the group and followers. The military, of course, do not have a much leeway in the way that they present (particularly the content). They have a system for this: it is called the orders process or system. It is through this system of interaction that the physical manifestation of the relationship can be revealed.

The military are known for having systems for everything. They have many systems, but the specific system that they use (unlike in other groups, commercial or otherwise) is one that sets out how decisions, intentions and concepts are communicated in the group. This orders system is part of battle procedure prior to any expected conflict, large or small. The orders system gives a very structured procedure and accurate record of how the ideas and concepts are passed from the higher-up group to the subgroup members.

There has been, over many years, an attempt to replicate the situation analysis and decision-making systems used by leaders in the military. Business schools, universities and consultants in many countries have to some degree used these processes to limited success in creating their formulas to help apply leadership in organisations. Within the military this system of analysis is used to assist the decision process of the leaders as individuals.

Like in business schools and universities, it does have value, but it is limited as it is isolated from the three-party interaction of the DAS chain. It is not this system that is the focus of this study. This analysis process is the start of the leadership process in both the military and the universities. This helps the leader when drafting a plan. It is the next step of taking it to the group to get a decision or confirmation from the group and the beginning of the next Action stage which is the focus here.

As in any group or organisation there are good leaders and bad.

The military is no different in this, but the orders process provides a consistent record of the interaction. The orders process has a strict structure of how to extract and issue orders from commanders to followers. While the military system is strict it cannot be monitored at every instance and it will experience all types of relationships: leadership, persuasive and coercive.

The orders process of transitioning plans into Decision and then Action has been applied and improved consistently over centuries. It effectiveness is based on achieving the group's needs and at the same time meeting agreed individuals' needs within that group in order get the group's, leader's and followers' decision to go into the Action stage of the DAS chain. The orders process reveals the real nature of the relationships and can be analysed. The results reveal why the military is effective at developing leaders, yet at the same time attracts the perception that there is an inflexible dictatorial system at play. The system creates potential for leadership, but at the same time can equally lead to coercive environments. At the same time it reveals its interaction language.

Similarly, groups outside the military have the capacity to develop their own types of relationships and they also have their own interaction language. It is not exactly like the specifically defined terms typical of a profession like the military, but it achieves the same thing: getting decisions made and into action, whether in a large multinational company or a small family of three. Many of the interactions in groups are designed to process a DAS chain and therefore consist of similar packages of information. The patterns of how the packages are assembled are an indication of the how the interaction is created and can be used for identification and comparison.

In broad terms the similarity of interaction language is not that surprising, as a volunteer military is a reflection of the people is it recruited from and therefore the population as a whole. The population-wide nature of a military group requires a system that caters for all levels of education and types of background, and no doubt different experiences of relationships in that population. Like many large organisations it has systems designed to cater to the widest level of its members. It therefore must create a robust and comprehensive system to achieve its group goals and be effective in its purpose.

The comprehensive nature of this system allows it to be abstracted and applied to any situation and environment. It is a 'catch all' system designed to cover all eventualities in war. The system is designed to be applied to applications elsewhere, not just the military, providing the systems can be adequately translated for commonplace usage and understanding of its core meaning. If the specific terminology of the military profession is interpreted into normal colloquial speech, what was a formal set of orders sounds very much like that of a commercial organisation, such as a manufacturer's or hotel group's leader's project or daily briefing.

In the study of leadership proof is important to verify a proposal and measure its effectiveness. There is a need for the confirmation, verification and measurement process that is very important in proving the existence of leadership and its effectiveness. The military systems, due to the immediate nature of their work, are proven on an immediate and frequent basis, and are open to audit. In an operational military, proof is often immediate, and there are severe consequences in the event of the communications process breaking down or a situation change. Soldiers in severe fast-changing situations would not decide to go into action if their needs were not being met.

This is in stark contrast to some commercial groups, where a decision made does not have repercussions until perhaps months or even years later, if discovered at all. Secondly the only stake that followers have in the process is their salary when and if the consequences are discovered. They have the option of leaving the group long before and avoiding any consequences. The engagement of the followers in the relationship is even less than that of a shareholder who, stands to lose capital investment.

To a soldier, the option of getting fired and going home is an excellent idea on the eve of a life-threatening military operation;

almost like a 'Get out of jail free' card in the game of Monopoly. The shareholder in a military operation is the population that the military represents and the soldiers (as members of the population) are also shareholders who stand to lose much more than the capital invested. The immediacy of the situations that a soldier faces is reflected in the old soldiers' phrase 'I would rather be tried by 12 men good and true, than carried out in a box'. The situation is more physical and immediate, as is verification of the relationship.

The actions of a banking group or other similar commercial or even non-profit organisations can only be verified after a long period of time. By that late stage people have moved and any accurate record of the ideas and intentions and how they were communicated between the parties has been lost. The group and its members have often changed and the relationships are fundamentally altered. Even then the consequences of a perceived failure are the loss of a monetary bonus (normally separate to salary) or perhaps even loss of a job for a temporary period. The verification is individual and delayed and is distal – it is definitely not immediate, or a threat to life or physical endangerment. The effect on the group is diluted and minimal as an agent of change and improvement.

For the reasons above, the military orders system of interaction will be studied for its interactive language patterns. It provide a system that focuses on the interaction methods between parties and therefore the relationship. It is a system that is designed for all situations and environments. Finally, it is a system that has been tried, tested and refined over decades, if not centuries, with immediate verification and measurement. This provides a starting point and a model which can be verified and compared to other studies in related fields of human interaction and groups. Current groups and contemporary studies are used to compare and refine the model in order to provide an understanding of what makes up the interaction language and its application as proof. Identifying the interaction language will facilitate the search towards the ultimate goal of defining what leadership is.

Chapter 10: What do the parties need in simple terms?

'You don't need a title to be a leader'

Multiple sources

The question of 'What is it the group wants?' is important in helping us discover what the leader can add to the group. The British and other military groups identified some of this a long time ago and have implemented a system to ensure that the group provides those needs of the group to its members. The group needs to be effective in meeting many challenges. In order to do this effectively it needs to speed up the preparations for battle at all levels. The military has developed what it calls battle procedure. In order to get groups to react faster than the enemy and thereby gain an advantage, the military has constantly refined this battle procedure. Leaders are required to commit to memory the definition, and most importantly the aim, or reason why, battle procedure is carried out, in order to reinforce the purpose of the group and the leader in that group.

Battle procedure starts with the appreciation and analysis of the situation by the leaders. This process has been mentioned as often being copied or used by universities to help develop individuals' planning processes. It is the final step in that Decision process, where a leader presents the ideas and concepts to the group that will decide the nature of the relationship that he or she develops with the group and followers. Before looking at the presentation of the concept to the group and followers it is important to go through why the system is created in the first place. This is found in the aim of battle procedure[18]:

'The aim of battle procedure is to ensure that the soldier is launched into battle without a waste of time and with minimum fuss, knowing exactly what he has to do, and how he has to do it and knowing what support he has to do it with.'[20]

As with any profession there are special terms and interpretations of those terms, and this language can be an identifier to distinguish it as a profession. From the aim of battle procedure the structure of the message that is given by the leaders to the followers is drawn. The structure becomes a set of 'orders' in the military, while in other groups they are called instructions. Each group delivers them as and when required. In the military the structure is followed rigidly and orders are issued as a set of formal orders using all the headings, without deviations. Along with the content the orders are delivered with a tone that conveys this formality. The table below shows the information packages contained in the aim of battle procedure that starts the process of conveying the intentions and ideas of the group along with a brief note to explain its significance or meaning in colloquial terms.

Table 10.1 An interpretation of the aims of battle procedure in the British Army

'The aim of battle procedure is to ensure that the soldier is launched into battle without a waste of time and with minimum fuss, knowing exactly what he has to do, and how he has to do it and knowing what support he has to do it with.'

Information package (extracted from the Aim of Battle Procedure)	Meaning in general colloquial terms
a. …the soldier	who is the focus of the whole process and where they fit in the picture
b. …is launched into battle	a reminder of the reason why the group is formed, the purpose
c. … without a waste of time	an emphasis of the need for urgency: it is a priority
d. …with minimum fuss	again creating a sense of priority and focus
e. … knowing what he has to do	what the challenge is in detail and the expected outcome

| f. | ...knowing how he has to do it | what actions are proposed in outline and expectation |
| g. | ...knowing what support he has to do it with. | what help they have and their place in the overall group |

In order to ensure that all of these information packages are passed on to the followers and group the military has created a system of giving orders that everyone is taught to use and apply. Each of the information packages is included in headings that are standard and they structure the interaction of the three parties. The orders format ensures that all of this information is gathered accurately and communicated. Learning the format is important and part of the assessment for promotion at lower levels. The system of orders created directly reflects the aim of battle procedure. It creates a level of priority and allows for the leader to fill in the details that are specific to the situation and group they are part of.

Table 10.2 The orders format alongside the aim of battle procedure requirements

Orders heading	Information package (extracted from the aim of battle procedure)
1 Situation Enemy forces and intentions Friendly forces and intentions	a. ...which soldiers (1 & 2 higher units and higher level intentions) b. ...is launched into battle (concept of the plan at higher level including higher level mission and why?) e. ...knowing what he has to do (at 1 & 2 higher level) f. ...knowing how he has to do it (at 1 & 2 higher level) g. ...knowing what support he has to do it with (at a 1 & 2 higher level)
2 Mission (who, what, where, when, and most im- portantly why?) The group in	a. ...which soldier (who) b. ...is launched into battle (what) e. ... knowing what he has to do (why?) (where and when are specific to the operation)

Orders heading	Information package (extracted from the aim of battle procedure)	
question.		
3 Execution – actions and details of the subgroups	a.	…which soldier (the group being addressed)
	e.	…knowing what he has to do (at the group's level)
	f.	…knowing how he has to do it (at the group's level)
	g.	…knowing what support he has to do it with (at the group's level)
4 Service support Coordinating Instructions & logistics	c.	…without a waste of time (timings) and
	d.	…with minimum fuss (concurrent activity)
	g.	…knowing what support he has to do it with. (combat supplies, materiel, food, administrative support)
5 Command and signal	g.	…knowing what support he has to do it with (who is the command structure and communication methods)

This orders format system may appear to be taking away possibility for creativity of the individuals and not trusting individuals to think for themselves. At a superficial level it does; however, the content of the orders at their own level and below are filled in by the group leader. The plan, the concept of execution, tone, pitch, speed, body language and words used in the delivery will create the leader's style and convey his individuality. The format ensures that all the necessary information gets to the followers to allow them to make a decision on the actions they are expected to take.

Perhaps surprisingly – and contrary to popular perception – the orders format is designed to allow the leader to create the opportunity for initiative and his own type of relationship within the group. At the same time, it may be that the leader does not know how to do this or does not have followers with enough experience to do it. The orders format is derived to ensure that the soldiers do receive the information set out in the aim of battle procedure. There have been recent refinements made in the words and headings used, which highlights another key reason why the format is used. It caters for the lesson that is repeatedly learned in war and life in general: plans need to allow for situation change. The lesson so often learned is summed up in the soldier's oft-repeated phrase 'No plan survives H hour'. This refers specifically to the fast-changing situation on a battlefield. It is also used in peacetime, as the need for change from the initial plan is not restricted to battle scenarios. H hour is the time designated for the start of an operation. Using this term allows planners to get on with the planning of the operation and come back to considerations of the start time when it is known, which is often only closer to the event as the situation unfolds and plans come together. Nothing is one hundred percent predictable and situations change. To cater for this the orders format and the leaders that write them use word patterns that allow for changing situations and yet still provide adequate direction in the event of any change.

Recent changes to the orders format relate to the third heading of the orders format: the mission statement. Previously it was called 'the aim' and it was more of a task statement combined with the limitations such as time or location. Now it is called 'the mission statement' and is a more complete statement that serves to repeat the specific challenge and the reason why the group is chosen to resolve that challenge. The mission statement, in its new form, details the group it is being addressed to and the task that it is required to do, and can include the timing, location or other mission-critical information. It also adds the specific challenge and reason why the task is being done: in other words the purpose of the group is detailed.

The purpose is already covered once in the first heading: 'Situation'. Under this heading the orders format divides into two topics. The first subheading topic is 'Enemy forces', which in effect outlines what the specific challenge being presented to the group is. The second subheading is 'Friendly forces', which gives the reason why the group is formed to resolve that task. In very general terms the military purpose at times of war may well be to protect the constitution and way of life of the country from the threat specified in the 'Enemy forces' paragraph.

In an set of orders the 'Friendly forces' paragraph specifies which groups and subgroups are to be used and in what way to resolve the specific threat posed. This represents the specific challenge facing the group and the specific reason why that group is formed to resolve that specific challenge. Together they form the purpose of the group. The mission statement reinforces this by repeating it and linking it to the task expected of the group. The order of the packages of information in the mission statement reinforces the order of priority.

This purpose is placed at the beginning of an orders set in order to explain and ensure that the group understands the overall situation and its specific purpose in the overall scheme of things – to protect the constitution and way of life of the country from the threat specified in the 'Enemy forces' paragraph. This is repeated in the mission at the group level in order for the group to know the direction it should take in the event that the situation changes and there is no time to regroup, rethink and react appropriately with a new set of orders. The system is designed to allow individual leaders at lower levels to be able to act independently and take corrective action initiatives in the direction of the overall purpose of the group in the event of a change in the situation, if they are at all able to do so. The change in the wording is small and subtle, but can be very dramatic in its effect, especially in a situation subject to frequent change. The system has been refined to cater for costly lessons learned in operations. In order to prevent inaction, the orders format allows for initiatives to be taken in the direction of the larger group's needs in the event of change.

Table 10.3 An interpretation of the orders headings into colloquial speech

Orders headings	Colloquial interpretation
1 Situation Enemy forces and intentions Friendly forces and intentions	1. **Specific challenge** – this specifies what the challenge is 2. **Reason why?** – this explicitly states why the group is formed to resolve the specific chal-

Orders headings	Colloquial interpretation
	lenge.
	3. Support – this details the other groups that will be helping their group
2 Mission (who, what, where, when, and most importantly why?) – As applied to the group in question. It is a single statement that covers the information for that group.	**4. Proposed actions**
3 Execution – As applied to the subgroups of the main group in paragraph 2.	This is covered by paragraph 4 above
4 Service support Coordinating instructions & logistics	**5. Benefits balance** – food, water and shelter details that meet the individual's needs Timings etc. are covered in paragraphs 3 and 4 above
5 Command and signal	This is covered in paragraphs 3 and 4 above

Table 10.3 shows a colloquial interpretation of the orders headings and content and reduces the repetition. The complexity of military operations can be similar to that of other large organisations, and leaders in non-military organisations have the liberty to reinforce the message by repetition. Similar to the military, they can make the message that they give their subgroups more complex or simpler. The military system has evolved to ensure that all necessary information is given in a format that the individuals can predict and gain the group's priorities from. It is designed to be used by anybody with minimal training to be able to assist in getting followers to make decisions into action and provide the opportunity to know what direction to act in when the situation changes. It is a tried and tested system for getting groups into action to resolve a challenge.

This process of battle procedure is repeated throughout the British army at battalion level and below. Many other armies around the world issue their ideas and intentions using orders in the same way, with very few changes if at all. This orders process has been used since WWI in the Commonwealth armies and in the US armies since before WWII and is largely still used today by these forces and many others. The delivery method from unit to unit may be digital and much quicker to cater for the speed of warfare and to improve the chances of getting an edge in terms of time and decision making ability, but the process of creating and maintaining the relationship is still the same.

There is little change, if any, made to cater for the size of the groups being led, or the situations they are faced with. The process in general and the headings are not situation aware, but the commander is and he adjusts the missions accordingly. For a given situation, assets, tactics and timings would be adjusted as required. The process is designed that way. Most importantly, the process is designed to cater for the needs of the group. The basic needs in all situations are the same. Using the aim of battle procedure and the formal order headings there emerges a pattern which can be drawn up to represent what it is that the group needs from its co-constituents.

In the commercial world the customer represents a need in the form of a specific challenge. Back in the early 1900s in the USA (coincidentally a comparative period for the battle procedure process study), John Lincoln and his younger brother felt that the demand for spot welding two metal sheets together rather than riveting them was enough to develop a welding machine. They expanded their product line of electric motors to include welding machines. He and his younger brother James Lincoln went on to lay the foundations of the welding industry. In the early 1900s rivets were the common solution for joining two metal sheets together. Riveting was a technique widely used at the time in the construction and shipbuilding industry and both industries used huge volumes of rivets.[21]

The specific challenge of how to join two sheets of metal together was relatively easy for James Lincoln to resolve. Also, by measuring the rivet market at the time the Lincolns could measure the demand for a solution to the challenge and for welding to replace the rivet. The market for a cheaper and better join and therefore a more effective and efficient solution was easy to identify. He and his brother expanded Lincoln Electric to meet that demand.

The business case of Lincoln Electric Company is used for comparison as it is the most popular and most downloaded business case study of all time. It was compiled for and published by Harvard University and is used to here to provide an alternative case for comparison. Lincoln Electric identified a specific challenge of joining two metal sheets effectively and efficiently. They had a very good reason why they should be resolving that specified challenge: because they could. The Lincoln brothers knew how to and could do it better and more cheaply than anyone else. They could be of more value to the customer than the rivet manufacturers. The Lincoln Electric case is particularly well known as it provides one of the best examples of how to meet all the group's co-constituents needs most effectively.

The second component of the 'Situation' paragraph is 'Friendly forces' in the orders format, or in colloquial terms it is the reason why is the group formed. In other words, why should this group choose to resolve that specific challenge? Readers can conduct a further confirmation that individuals like to know the reason why a challenge is taken up by simply presenting a challenge to someone and listening to the responses. Depending on the nature of the task presented some individuals will just do what is asked of them, while others will ask questions to confirm the reason why. Questions like 'Why should I do it?', and statements such as 'it not my turn' or '….it's not my job' will be heard. This is especially true in the case of a challenge that does not have any connection to them specifically. With no obvious link to them the responses may come back as 'Why do you want me to do that?', or 'Why do you need chairs over there?', and 'Why can't somebody else do it?' and 'It's not in my job description'.

The responses may amount to a point blank refusal, such as when a child, told to go to bed, replies 'No, I don't want to', further backed up with 'I am not tired'. The child is addressing the assumed link between the instruction to go to bed and the reason why people go to bed. It is assumed, even by a child, that the proposed action will be linked to the reason why they have been told to go to bed in the first place. Some of the questions address the reason of why, specifically, they are doing the job. Other questions address the issue of why the job is being done in the first place. In all these cases the respondent is addressing the reason why: what is the specific challenge that results in my having to do this task? Where the specific challenge and action are linked is comparable to the army leader presenting the enemy situation and the friendly forces situation so that the soldier can understand why they are being tasked to do what they are expected to perform.

The Reason Why? is linked to the specific challenge presented. The challenge gives rise to the reason why the group chooses, or is chosen, to do the job. Indeed, without the specific challenge there maybe no reason for the group to exist in the first place! The Specific Challenge + Reason Why? are the first two components of what the group's co-constituents want to know about the group they are part of.

The Support component details the larger group's parts and where the individual fits in that larger group. This component addresses the conceptual aspects of the group's formation, hierarchy and command structure as well as the physical aspects of the group and its place in the larger group. It details who the individual is working with and his place in the larger group plan in relation to others in the larger group. This is linked directly to '…knowing what support he has' of the battle procedure and what resources he has to carry out the proposed actions with in the bigger scheme of things.

The mission statement is the fourth heading in the orders format and relates directly to '…knowing what he has to do' and '…how

he has to do it' in the battle procedure. The US Army adds the remarks 'Who, what, where, when and most importantly, why' as a
helpful reminder of how to structure the mission statement. It is a
reinforcement of all the elements in the aim of battle procedure. It
is structured as a single sentence and includes specific challenge-
critical timings and other factors to ensure that the message is received.

In both military and non-military groups there is a need from
the followers to know what the group needs them to do. The actions process is part of the message and is called the Proposed Actions component. When the Proposed Actions component is added
to the Specific Challenge, Reason Why? and Support components,
the four components complete what the group wants the followers
to know, and is similar to the mission statement.

The first four components clearly identify what the group is requesting of the group members, but it may not be clear how the
members are benefiting from the relationship. At this stage a fifth
component, called the Benefits Balance, may or may not be added.
This component has two effects on the individual. With only four
components the members are still not sure how they will benefit
from being part of the group. So far, this fifth component is not
fully represented and in the military is only partially covered in the
orders format. This is similar to most non-military groups, where
contractual agreements have largely done away with the need to
repeat or renegotiate the benefits afforded them in their employment contract at the start of each DAS chain. Where additional
benefits are expected they may be added or, as in a military operation, they will address some of the daily needs of the individuals,
such as food and water, if not part of the normal arrangements.

We can look at the relationship in terms of a negotiation between three parties: the group and its members, both leaders and
followers. It would seem that most of the demands are one-way:
from the group to the members as individuals. This is typical in an
established group. In a situation between two previously unrelated
parties there would be an element of negotiation on these points of

benefits. Typically there would be conditions, measurements and terms, and also perhaps penalties laid down.

Included in the Benefits Balance are many long- and short-term benefits or penalties, which can be divided into two sections. Intellectual benefits may include peer recognition (proving oneself to be of value to the group); being part of something that is bigger and more important to one's belief system; or a test of one's ability. There are as many conceptual benefits to being a group member as there are physical benefits, such as protection, security, convenience, and the rewards that allow individuals to follow other interests outside of the group, if and when the opportunity arises.

These benefits are individually based and not always known to the individual at the time of joining the group. The benefits and penalties of group membership are very dependent on the group and are difficult to explain for each situation. It is a component in the relationship and decision process that both the group, and the individual need to understand, balance and prepare for at their level. The individual assesses each one on its merits in a theoretical balance and decides on a positive action to join or negative action to not join – or perhaps just stalls on the decision of membership and finds out more or limits the period of his membership.

In terms of the question of 'What is leadership?' and the challenge of identifying the component parts of a relationship, the balance of benefits and penalties is labelled the Benefits Balance. This component is added to the first four components and the five together make up the component or information packages in the individual's process of decision making, and helps define his subsequent actions in terms of group membership.

By identifying the components or information packages in the interaction language of a relationship in the military, as listed in Table 10.3, it is possible to understand the relationship better. The components relate to the needs of individuals to help them make decisions in a relationship, whether they are the group, the leader or the followers. It is necessary to take all needs into consideration to form a relationship between the three parties. To maintain a relationship over a longer period of time it is necessary to maintain that mix and balance over the duration of the relationship.

In the theory of leadership, to teach the multitude of situations possible in a relationship is both inefficient, due to the length of time it takes, and ineffective, as it relies on the memory of the individual to sort through all the situations learned and select and apply a solution to the situation being faced at the time. This ineffectiveness is proved in situations when time is of the essence, correct information is unavailable and the options are limited.

To include all situations in a definition of leadership or an analysis of the relationship would create confusion and take us down the multiple paths that Stogdill referred to earlier. The definition does not need to go into the details of each specific situation and group design. The components are grouped into general terms for ease of remembering and use. In summary below is a list of the five components that make up the information packages that the group can provide to its members to make a decision and to make them more effective in their task of resolving the specific challenge. At the same time it provides the leaders and followers with the information they need to know in order to decide on membership of the group.

The Specific Challenge
The Reason Why?
The Support and resources the group needs and has available
The Proposed Actions
The Benefits Balance

Further details and how the co-constituents interact using these components are given later in Part 3 of this book. Identifying the five components helps summarise the information packages needed by individuals into manageable chunks. Which components are used and how they are used in the interactions between the three parties will determine what type of relationship will be formed. The initiating, facilitating, defining and communicating of these components will also determine how effective the leader will be in transitioning the leader's plans into a decision and into action towards a solution by the group.

Hersey and Blanchard, in their concept of situational leadership, outlined that the group's performance will be based on the followers' maturity in their function. This embraces Chris Argyris's [20] immaturity/maturity continuum[22] as well as his single and double loop learning concepts.[23] This means their ability to perform their function combined with their ability to learn, unlearn and change quickly when required. It describes the functional maturity of the followers. This is correct in the case of the followers, and their functional maturity is important and will effect the outcome of the group and the leader's capacity to perform.

Functional maturity also applies to all the parties, including the group and leaders, not just the followers. Can it change and adapt quickly? Small groups often change more quickly than large groups. The leaders themselves also need to be aware of the needs of both the group and the followers in order to act as a bridge, while at the same time being conscious that they themselves are a member of the group. Applying the functional maturity concept only to the followers will miss the other parties in the group.

The group must provide, maintain and promote an understanding of the interaction language components of relationships. The group itself must be functionally mature in these matters in order to create the environment where the systems are designed to pass information, concepts and intentions effectively. The military examples used show a functional maturity of the group in the use of systems, training and procedures in the command and control of groups.

In the case of the military individuals come to the group with a basic but built-in knowledge of how to work in groups. Knowing and developing the functional maturity of this knowledge in the co-constituents of the group will make the group more effective as a team. Table 10.4 reflects the five component information packages needed by groups to create an environment with the potential to make them effective.

Table 10.4 Military orders format given colloquial interpretation

Order format headings	Colloquial interpretation
1 Situation Enemy forces and intentions	1. Specific Challenge – this specifies what the challenge is
Friendly forces and intentions	2. Reason Why? – this explicitly states why the group is formed to resolve the specific challenge.
	3. Support – this details the other groups that will be helping their group
2 Mission (who, what, where, when, and most importantly why?) (group level)	4. Proposed Actions
3 Execution (details for sub-groups)	This is covered by paragraph 4 above
4 Service support Coordinating instructions and logistics	5. Benefits Balance – food, water and shelter details that meet the individual's needs Timings etc. are covered in paragraphs 3 and 4 above
5 Command and signals	This is covered in paragraphs 3 & 4 above

Chapter 11: The building blocks, but what about structure?

'if you give a man a fish he is hungry again in an hour; if you teach him to catch a fish you do him a good turn.'

Ann Isabelle Ritchie

The military system not only provides a record of the interaction between leaders and followers, but the record identifies the components of what knowledge is needed. As shown in the preceding chapters, the components are packages of information that have been assembled from single words joined in a structured way to make sense. Pronouns fit to nouns, and verbs describe the actions of the nouns or objects, and this is taken for granted as grammar. The way in which it is assembled has evolved and been structured in a format that allows the words to make sense and be analysed in a meaningful way according to our group or cultural learning.

This is done in order to allow analysis and conclusions to be drawn from the raw data. The components have been assembled into a structure. The way they are assembled is important. Bricks can be laid differently and will produce different buildings with different functions according to their design. Similarly, interactions and relationships will be different according to how the interaction language is assembled. The words or bits of data are assembled into packages of information or phrases, according to the rules of grammar. Similarly, again, these packages are assembled in sentences and then into paragraphs and on into larger and larger groups of information.

The example used earlier is the records of interaction between the group, the leader and the followers in the military called the orders format. This process of collecting and structuring converts the raw bits of data into information. The structure allows it to be analysed and turned into knowledge. The interaction language structure presents the information in a way that makes it easier to be analysed and understood. The structure can be changed and augmented over time in order to make it more effective and more efficient for analysis and converting into knowledge.

This evolutionary process of assembling patterns and augmenting, mixing and developing structures in a set of rules called the grammar of a language. The structure of a language gives linguists the ability to generally determine the language's functional maturity. The language's ability to convey meaning and intentionality can be evaluated in terms of effectiveness and efficiency, and thus its functional maturity be determined. This expression can be used to apply to a group as an individual entity in its ability to provide the information necessary for the effective passage of ideas, concepts and intentions. Its use is not limited just to the followers in a group: it can be adjusted according to what information packages are assembled with it in a sentence.

The structure adopted in the orders format also gives a sense of priority – not so much in terms of which task is to be performed first, but more in terms of which components are priorities in the analysis of the information once assembled. Similar to most languages, the orders format does not just contain content: the way the content is assembled also has meaning, both implied and explicit. Things such as group identity, social stratification and humour, can be found in languages, and therefore in the orders format. Language is much more complex than is commonly understood, and because of this the orders format does not just transmit content: it also communicates intention and feelings.

Languages are drawn together by semiotics, which are the interpretations of the combined meanings of signs (body language, tone and speed of expression are some of them), meanings, codes and the semantics that connect those meanings. This is the language of interaction, where the complete meaning, intention and full feeling of a concept is transmitted. With reference to a language, the full extent of what is meant by a word is often taken for granted. Does it include the semiotics or is it just referring to the written represented language in a word by word analysis? The expression the 'language of terror' elicits more than academic understanding of the word's contents. It incites terror, fear and hatred usually, because of the semiotics that go with the language content when expressed. When the expression 'interaction language' is used, it intentionally means to include the additional semiotics when expressing the content. It is the personal face-to-face semiotics that often makes the interaction language effective.

In the case of the orders format used, experience has led to revision and progression in the terms used in order to make the system, and therefore its leaders, more effective at transmitting the concepts and intentions. The military also focuses a lot of its training on the semiotics of the interaction language to make it more effective. The system is becoming functionally more mature in the transmission of ideas and intentions.

The consistent application of the military orders format has provided a method of analysing the interaction of the co-constituents very specifically rather than just taking a surface look at the happening in a group. Although it is not possible without actually being present when the orders are given to see the full extent of the delivery and the semiotics attached to the words, it is possible to use the format to give a detailed look into the interaction of the group, leader and followers.

The sequence of the order format gives, by design, a level of priority. The level of priority reflects the way that the military have found most effective in getting the message across. It is user-friendly in colloquial terms. The Specific Challenge and Reason Why? are applicable to all in the group. These start the orders sequence. The Mission Statement is also applicable to all in that group and it reinforces all the vital information packages in the orders sequence in one sentence. Interestingly, it changes the order of the packages from the orders sequence to again reinforce the learning process.

The Execution paragraph continues with the different information package order, which is more specific to the subgroups and the roles they play in the overall picture. This allows the individual to realise their value in the hierarchy of the group more effectively than going from the individual to the group level. The orders process then returns to details that apply to all in the group.

In terms of being able to analyse the information it starts with the Specific Challenge facing the group and reminds them how this applies to their group. When detailed focus on individual subgroups is needed the packages of information (components) change sequence. The component detailing the specific group's title (Support) is placed at the front to gain the attention and focus of that group, and then the task (Proposed Actions) is presented. This process is not exclusive to the military: it merely reflects what is done in society and everyday speech practices.

The process has been refined over many years based on the same process that adults face when speaking with children. The child is not very old when it starts to ask questions about the tasks it is being instructed to do. When a child replies 'But I am not tired' to the instruction 'Go to bed' the child is addressing the reason why it is being told to perform that action. This continues as the child matures and questions his tasks with simple questions like 'Why is it his turn?' further backed up with 'It should be my turn after her'.

The process used in the orders format reflects the process by which an individual goes about collecting data into information packages for analysis in order to make a decision. The next step is familiar to most parents: the child goes into action in favour of the task or continues to delay the action with more questions related to the Specific Challenge and Reason Why? The other option is to move to outright resistance and negative action to counter the specific Challenge and Reason Why? as the child perceives it: a temper tantrum.

The orders format provides a ready-made system of components that already takes these very complex processes into consideration. Using the orders format system to help decipher the first clues in the puzzle towards the answer of 'What is leadership?' is one path. This path starts at the base of the human interaction process and works upwards through layers of increasingly complex compounds towards a solution that may turn out to be leadership. This is a very different path than working from the crossword puzzle solution and searching back down to find a path. The packages of information or elemental components are the foundation stones on which interactive relationships are built. The stones or components grow up into a range of peaks or relationships, and one of the peaks is the relationship called leadership.

The orders format provides an entry point on the path and it is very relevant to the application of the theory of leadership, as a military population reflects the general society that it comes from. The orders format is part of a system that is based on common thinking processes and the military has refined that process to enhance its effectiveness and the efficiency of communicating its ideas and intentions. This is similar to any professional language. A profession creates its own language within a common language. The two languages have a common root.

It is by stepping down one level from the terms used by the military group that the colloquial level of all groups is reached. This is just a matter of interpreting the terms from military speech and the orders format into colloquial terms. Relating it to the thinking process behind the information package formation is what gives the terms a common interaction language base, or root, that can be used when in groups. Translating the components is simple enough, as these are just terms and phrases. The real importance is the process of assembly that the military interaction language or the orders format has demonstrated. The orders format shows that the information packets or components can be assembled for different effect in the decision process. It is the way the components are assembled that allows a relationship in a group to form, function, maintain or destroy itself.

The next step is to focus on how the components are assembled to form the latticework between the co-constituents on the way to a relationship. These patterns apply to individuals in all groups and will facilitate the analysis of the interaction of the parties. Looking at the structure of the interaction language of a relationship and how the components are assembled may help to identify some of the differences in the resulting relationships. These patterns can be analysed to confirm if the differences are useful predictors and definite indicators of relationship types.

The military orders format suggests that there are different results created when different formats are used; hence the firm application of the orders format throughout the system. From there the different methods of assembling the components can be linked to relationship types. The components pattern can act as a defining element to the differences between relationship types. Linking patterns and the common understanding of types and actual groups will be where the study of the theory will meet the application.

Definitive differences can then be linked to commonly understood descriptions of types of relationships. These different types will have differing patterns and the relationships will be named more accurately. With a path that is based on specific component patterns in the interaction language the relationship can be studied and revealed. Among the differing relationships will be one that commonly associates with leadership as described by many different sources.

The different patterns will make relationship type easier to distinguish. The patterns will become the path to the solution. From the pattern will also emerge methods of application to create a route towards a solution. These are paths towards more effectiveness and efficiency, rather like genetic engineers grow GM crops. Similar to GM crops, relationships can only be confirmed after application because of the myriad of influences, both external and internal. The target relationship is no different in that leadership can only be confirmed, verified and measured by the application in groups; however, the current process can be fundamentally altered.

Identifying the interaction structure in group relationships will allow the identification of those relationships that are not leadership relationships and further help define the differences between many groups. The structural differences will define the relationships. The structure of the decision process in individuals is the key to the interaction of the group. The next step is analysing the structure of this interaction to progress further along to finding a path towards leadership.

Table 11.1 shows the comparative labels of the components or information packages in the decision process between the co-constituents in military groups. This extends to most individuals in general when the terms are interpreted to colloquial terms, as the military is a cross-section of its population. The process, whether in the military or civilian groups, is designed to get decisions from individuals. The components provide the packages of information needed. The orders format provides a sequence for the components in the orders format headings. This sequence provides a basic structure which is logical in the respect that it starts with the specific challenge, which is the basis of reference for all the other components in the sequence.

Table 11.1 Comparison of military group terms and individual colloquial terms in the decision process

Military group – Orders headings	Individual colloquial interpretation
1 Situation	1. Specific Challenge
	2. Reason Why?
	3. Support
2 Mission	4. Proposed Actions
3 Execution	
4 Service support	5. Benefits Balance
5 Command and signals	Administrative details of hierarchy and communication channels which change constantly.

When taken together they can be added up in the order to assume that these are the components that allow decisions to be made. How they are assembled and re-ordered in the sequence will define the relationship. It is the components and the basic sequence that facilitates the search for the answer to 'What is Leadership?'.

PART 3: Defining the message pattern explicitly

Chapter 12: The decision components defined

'Would you tell me, please, which way I ought to go from here?'
'That depends a good deal on where you want to get to,' said the Cat.
'I don't much care where –' said Alice.
'Then it doesn't matter which way you go,' said the Cat.
'– so long as I get *somewhere*,' Alice added as an explanation.
'Oh, you're sure to do that,' said the Cat, 'if you only walk long enough.'

Lewis Carroll

The five components identified are pieces of information that help individuals make a decision into an action or expression of action. In order to present the five components more easily and express them on paper, the components are arranged in a symbolic logic formula. Putting the components into a symbolic logic formula, similar to a simple mathematical equation, has the function of making it easier to communicate to the many groups across the world. The format used is the same used for simple addition of numbers in mathematics, for example $2 + 2 = 4$. The format is one of the most widely recognised languages in the world: mathematics. Symbolic logic is used here to help demonstrate aspects of relationships in groups.

The symbolic logic formula or equation allows the simplification of an otherwise complex message in the common language of the group. It renders words, phrases and sentences into components of the decision process. In short, it simplifies. Once the components are identified, the equation can be formed and analysed in order to confirm and ensure that the correct meaning is conveyed to those listening. Each component is defined according to its explicit and implicit meaning. This approach in defining very specifically each component will highlight the importance that the words and phrases in the components have for group members. With some individuals the implied meaning is more pertinent than the explicit meaning of the word with respect to affecting their decision-making process.

The symbolic logic equation format also allows the components and their perceived meaning to be compared to other terms and accepted theories in the field of human behaviour and motivation. This check against other theories in the study of human behaviour helps confirm definitions and perceptions of meaning. By checking and comparing against other fields of expertise it also helps to act as a guide to further definition and confirmation of direction in the search for the definition of leadership. The process of combining the components is done in order to get a decision. Therefore the symbolic logic formula used is called the 'decision equation' for short.

The decision equation – with full component names:

Specific Challenge + Reason Why? + Support + Proposed Actions + Benefits Balance => decision

The equation components are abbreviated into capital letters that are representative of the component. They are in capital letters as they can be subdivided into smaller parts. The symbol 'd' for decision is written in lower case as it is specific to this challenge, and its unique combination of components and their contents and cannot be subdivided without changing the components.

The decision equation in symbolic logic format:

Example 12.1 The standard decision equation

SC + RY? + SP + PA + BB => d

The directional equals sign (=>), when translated from symbolic logic, means more than just 'equals' in common prose; there is a material implication. It represents the phrase 'in order to…, followed by a verb such as *get, achieve, allow* or *commit,* or some other verb used to create the correct prose to join the phrases. It helps in the decision equation to explain the relationship of one component to another and it allocates prioritisation of the sequence of components and material happenings. The direction arrow indicates which direction the prioritisation and application goes. For example, the basic decision equation shows that the components are all added up 'in order to get' a decision.[24]

Other mathematical symbols are used, and they function as in normal formulas. This is the decision equation based on the military orders format sequence of priority. It is logical, as all the subsequent components are based on the specific challenge presented to the group. This decision equation is the base equation, although others will be presented with different patterns and sequences of components in later chapters.

Specific Challenge (SC): This is an explicitly stated situation that is presented by an individual or group that invites resolution. It is different from a statement or a common challenge in two respects. A statement does not expect any response, whereas a challenge invites a response; the issuer of the challenge expects a response. Secondly, the challenge is made very specific: not just that it is a challenge, but also that the nature of the challenge is detailed and very specific.

What separates a statement from a challenge will depend on a number of factors, including body language, tone and a host of other things that are included in the delivery, and not just the content, of the words. Additionally, how individuals perceive the statement will also determine whether it is a statement or a challenge. This is easy to demonstrate. When the boxer Muhammad Ali made the statement 'I am the greatest', to him it was a statement of fact. At the same time it implied and was interpreted as a challenge by some, while others accepted that it was a statement of fact. Some choose to qualify it, and think 'in a fight, yes you maybe the greatest but I am a better chess player than you'. Each individual has their own line that separates what is a challenge or a statement and what is worth challenging. Some may just treat it as fact, and therefore a statement, and therefore there is no need to reply. In a specific challenge there is an explicit request for a reply or resolution of the challenge.

In the case of a Specific Challenge, it is the explicitly stated challenge to resolve a specifically identified situation that is presented. The Specific Challenge may also include time limits or other resource limitations to help make the Challenge Specific. In issuing a Specific Challenge the request for a response should be clear. Defining a Specific Challenge can be done by anyone: for example, a customer or person outside the group, or a group member who identifies a threat to the group – or even an opportunity. In the case of the military orders format the leader often personally explains the Specific Challenge. It is communicated by re-defining it so that the group understands it fully and accepts ownership of it as their challenge.

The Specific Challenge is not the same as the task. The word *task* describes an action. There is confusion between the terms, and it is often assumed that the requirement of the customer is the Specific Challenge that they have given the group in the form of a Request for Tender (RFT) document. This RFT is often written as a task, with little reference to the reason why the product is needed.

John Adair's action-centred leadership identifies the Specific Challenge as the task in his well known Three Circles Venn diagram, which links the task with the leader and the team in terms of a leader's function.[25] Adair's use of the term *task* here is not specific enough and does not separate the actions from the requirement. The needs are very different from the actions taken to meet them. The leader often does have to identify the Specific Challenge, but it is not exclusively his responsibility. In large commercial organisations it is often the sales team that identifies the task from the customer. Adair's book succeeds in identifying the need to specify the task, although it would be better to call it the Specific Challenge rather than the task. It is important to do this as the Specific

Challenge will greatly influence the other components in the decision equation, and it is fundamentally different from the actions taken to resolve it.

The Specific Challenge is a term which can apply to the short or long term. It can be limited by time, quantity of products or financial resources available. The limitations will be a critical factor in determining whether the Specific Challenge is real and applicable to the group. This will be assessed as part of the Decision section of the DAS chain process. In contrast to this, the specific challenge may be a long-term ongoing responsibility of the group which remains as long as the challenge exists.

Reason Why (RY?): This is the explicitly stated reason why the challenge is to be resolved by the group. Why does this group choose to accept the specific challenge and resolve the challenge presented? The reason why a specific challenge is accepted is part of the decision process and will be different for each individual in the group. When assigning tasks the leader should bear in mind the functional maturity or suitability of the individuals being assigned these tasks in order to assign the most suitable individuals in order to achieve the task effectively.

In some cases the leader may even explain the specific reason why an individual is chosen for his task once the group's Reason Why? is understood, as it may be different or specific to that individual: for example, to give that individual the experience needed. Again the Reason Why? needs to be stated explicitly by the leader in order to be clear to those involved in the resolution of the specific challenge. This explanation of the Reason Why? may also go into the details of how the larger group expects to resolve this challenge and thereby give an indication to the subgroup of their place and value in the overall plan and how they may be expected to perform their role.

When a group accepts to resolve a specific challenge there is by implication an acceptance of ownership on behalf of the group. This is a reason why identifying the group as an entity is an important concept: it reflects the commitment to the group and its cause or Reason Why? This ownership is reinforced with signatures in the legal world of contracts and risk evaluation, with oaths, pledges and even terms such as moral contracts in other scenarios. This acceptance of the specific challenge by the group further adds to the commitment to the group by individuals. It also highlights the difference between the individuals in the group and the group itself. What is a concept in the mind becomes an entity in legal terms when licenses and contracts are involved.

Support (SP): These are the groups, people, materials, resources etc. needed to perform the resolution of the specific challenge, in line with the reason why the group has accepted the specific challenge. It will also be in line with the proposed actions if they are known at this stage of the decision-making process. Typically support is based on who the target of the actions is, which could be an individual or a subgroup in the group. It includes the equipment and resources needed or allocated to complete the Proposed Actions to resolve the Specific Challenge. Examples of this of this are specialist equipment, vehicles, budgets, portions of time allocated to the group, outside groups of people and other assets needed or allocated.

The words or titles used to describe the support component indicate the groupings, function, rankings or position within the group as required. Titles that indicate a hierarchy, such as manager, supervisor, ambassador or nicknames, will add personal value to the content of the description and impact. Group labels also indicate function, such as executive team or key accounts team, lead auditor, sniper team or operations department. These group labels will indicate to groups and individuals their importance in the plan and special status in the group. Group titles and names will also have reputation, history, importance attached to them such as 'the Screaming Eagles', the Office for National Statistics or the United Nations. These titles will give them importance and position in the group and therefore their value in comparison to others in the group. These titles are peer recognition systems, which gives them a specific position of value and status within the group and to those outside the group.

Proposed Action (PA): This is the action being proposed for the group, subgroup or individual to complete in order to resolve the specific challenge presented to the group. This can be as simple as 'make a list', as complex as 'build a nuclear power station', or even as vague as 'to liberate the people'. The actions allocated to an individual or group will indicate to them their value and importance to the overall group. The functions assigned to them will convey importance and value in comparison to other functions in the group. Again, like titles, functions can be attributed to individuals and subgroups.

The Proposed Action is different from the Specific Challenge presented to the group. The difference is easy to see in the case of a drill manufacturer. They design, source and assemble drills in order to resolve the specific challenge that a customer has to hang a picture on the wall. They need a hole in the wall in order to put a screw in so that a hook can be secured to the wall in order to hang a picture on. The specific challenge can be resolved a number of ways. The drill manufacturer performs the task of building the drill in order to resolve any number of specified challenges, one of which maybe make a hole for a screw to hang a picture. How the picture owner decorator chooses to resolve the challenge is up to them. If the drill suits the customer's needs and compares favourably with other options, it will be used.

John Adair identifies 'defining the task'[26] as one of the key functions of the leader. This is an area of confusion due to the language used. As mentioned in the Specific Challenge paragraph, identifying the challenge and detailing it specifically and explicitly is very important. The Proposed Actions is different from the Specific Challenge. Practice shows that it is not always a function of the leader. Often the group leader is not the functional expert in the actions needed and they can be done by individuals other than the leader of the group.

Benefits Balance (BB): This is the combination of explicitly stated positive benefits and negative penalties that arise from the actions taken to resolve the Specific Challenge. Some benefits are specific to the customer, or even the customer's customer, that created the challenge in the first place. It is possible to list benefits in sequence, such as customer's customer, then customer-related, group, and finally individual benefits. This follows the sequence of the decision equation starting with the customer and Specific Challenge-related benefits, then the Reason Why? and group benefits, followed by subgroup and individual benefits in order to instil an order of group-first priority. There can be positive benefits or negative penalties, many or few, real or imagined, present or potential and not yet proven. An individual will analyse and balance these benefits and penalties to provide them with the ability to have a reasonable level of knowledge of the outcome and help them make a decision.

Risk analysis specialists, economists, financial analysts, business or unit managers and similar titles typically cover this field, usually at group level, but they can also work at an individual level. The individual's position in the group, their background, personal situation, the reason why they chose to be a member of the group and many other factors can place a greater weighting on the individual's benefits to join the group.

Often the balance and decision comes down to a focus on the asset measurements. At a group level the Benefits Balance could include shareholders' profits, staff bonuses or a loss. At an individual level it could be salary, bonus, extra costs or loss of job. It can also include intellectual or conceptual benefits, or sometimes soft skill factors, like 'exciting challenges', 'gives opportunity for my ideas', 'gives people purpose' or even 'develops my experience and confidence in the decision-making processes with that group of people'. It is important to know what the individuals in the group value and to use this knowledge to help meet their needs.

This knowledge comes with focused inquiry and experience.

The Benefits Balance allows individuals to asses their value in relation to others in the group and other groups. The salary or rewards they receive can be compared to others in the group or outside their group. The opportunities for travel, new experiences and advancement can all be listed alongside the penalties they may endure as a result of membership or certain actions taken in the group. This immediately gives them a feeling of worth and value in the group and outside. These individual value terms are powerful motivators of the individual in relation to the group.

The terms of the decision equation are the components that are used in forming relationships in groups. The sequence and assembly will define the types of relationships in the groups and how decisions get actioned. The components are defined and encompass the information needed. Each specific DAS chain will need to have its components defined by the group and processed. This process of assembly is where the individual needs of the relationship co-constituents is negotiated and actioned.

Chapter 13: The decision equation compared to other systems

'Things that coincide with one another equal one another'
Euclid

Before going on to use the five components of the decision equation and demonstrate the equation in relationships it is worth looking at the components in comparison to other studies in order to confirm them as key components in human behaviour. In a separate field of study, the psychologist Abraham Maslow published a paper called 'A theory of human motivation' in 1943 and a second paper in 1954 called 'Motivation and personality [21]'. His study is widely acknowledged and his theory has other parallel studies in the field of human developmental studies. Maslow identified the terms *physiological, safety, love and belonging, esteem* and *self-actualization* as the five levels that human motivation develops through. Maslow pointed out that motivation is specific to the individual and that his model applied to the individual, not the group. Maslow's hierarchy was assembled into a pyramid by others to help demonstrate his concepts and the levels. The pyramid was designed and drawn by someone other than Maslow as a way of graphically representing his terms and to impart the sense of ascending development toward the top of the pyramid. It is shown here (Figure 13.1) and demonstrates the level of priority that certain things have for an individual's motivation. Maslow emphasised that motivation is specific to the individual, not the group. This is similar to the decision equation.

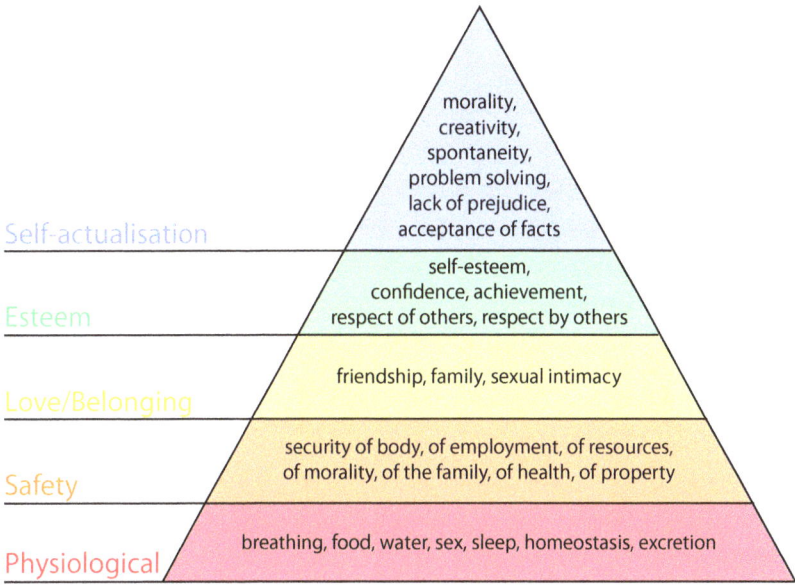

Figure 13.1 Abraham Maslow's hierarchy of needs

The terms Maslow uses are specifically defined and relate to situations faced by individuals, not collective groups as a whole. The terms are also interdependent of each. Each level is a stage that an individual progresses through on their way to another. They are not to be taken in isolation. The most basic of human needs (physiological) must be achieved before the individual will motivate themselves to consider the second level, safety. His theory proposed that an individual human will progress through these various levels of motivation during development. Using the terms and descriptions on the pyramid for reference there is a correct assumption that the pinnacle is the highest level and it marks the highest level to which humans aspire to reach. The pyramid presents the different levels in an ascending order of needs progression.

Individuals will only achieve motivation at the higher levels when the previous level's needs have been met. If the first four levels' needs have been met then they will be meta-motivated and focused on this final stage, which Maslow labelled a B-need (a being need), as opposed to a D-need (a deficiency need), which describes the previous four stages and is related to physical needs. Maslow further divided the five levels into two different subgroup sections, the first being the higher order of motivations (self-actualisation and self-esteem) and the second section being what he called 'lower order', containing the remaining three levels. While many have viewed the hierarchy as a rigid path for progression and have therefore criticised it, Maslow stated that it was a general path and not a specific one. He was quick to point out that humans were at any one time dominated by one or another of the terms, rather than always having to progress through each consideration before moving up a level to consider a more mentally focused task than the previous one. The human mind is flexible and very complex and is capable of concurrently processing the focus of its motivations towards one and suppressing other needs when required. The needs are ongoing and multiple, and Maslow's purpose was to identify a general path of progression once the lower orders were met.

The important ideas in terms of leadership theory are the terms and levels that Maslow identified. Maslow's five terms have been expanded on by others in the field and they further re-define these terms, which has also seen greater detailing of where or how an individual could be identified in terms of a motivation pyramid or chart of related terms at any particular given moment. A number of additional factors that motivate individuals have been identified. More detailed lists have expanded from Maslow's five terms: for example, the 16 intrinsic needs study by Dr Stephen Reiss.

Frederick Herzberg published his 'two factor theory' or 'dual structure theory' in 1959 [22], where he developed a more simplistic approach for the workplace environment in order to be easier to apply. He followed it up with his 1987 article for the *Harvard Business Review* called 'One more time – How do you motivate employees?'(23). The papers introduced the terms 'intrinsic' and 'extrinsic' motivators to the 10 factors that motivate employees. Herzberg considered the intrinsic motivators as factors that are pleasurable and are of interest in themselves rather than working towards an external reward. These he listed as achievement, recognition, the work itself, responsibility, promotion and growth, ones which give job satisfaction. He called this first group simply 'Motivators' or satisfiers.

Motivators were different from the extrinsic factors, which he described as externally based influencers such as a job done to achieve an outcome or a reward given for achieving externally determined objectives. He labelled these factors as 'Hygienic factors'. Examples of these include things like pay and benefits, company policy and administration, relationships with co-workers, job security, salary, contract and fringe benefits. They were called hygienic factors because, like hygiene, if present it they are not noticed as a motivator but when not present they are dis-satisfier or demotivators. Similarly, in the work environment things like salary, fringe benefits and job security are good, but once they are present, adding more of them does not necessarily add to job satisfaction in the same way that recognition, responsibility and the other intrinsic motivators do.

These detailed studies are a result of and further refinements of Maslow's work. While some reject the order of priority in Maslow's work or its value in terms of its predictive abilities for all individuals and some cultures, it is widely accepted as the foundation work in the field of motivation. There is a large amount of work done in this field and it continues to be reviewed and refined under ever larger and more powerful magnifying glasses. This book uses it as a field of research that is well accepted and established, and it provides an ideal study with which to compare the components of the decision equation.

For the comparison of components in the decision equation, Maslow's simple five terms will be used, with the subgroup sections using Herzberg's popular 'intrinsic' and 'extrinsic' labels being used later to highlight distinctions in the components. Maslow's five terms and general understanding of priority are useful for placing the components of the decision equation alongside to obtain a better understanding, further identification and comparison in the study of relationships. Maslow's and Herzberg's work and terms are all useful in helping clarify the terms, concepts and intentions of the levels and components – their similarities as well as their differences. These differences have allowed subgroup labels such as B or D needs, higher/lower, intrinsic/extrinsic, or motivators/hygienic factors respectively. All this serves to clarify and understand the labels better and what they imply in terms of motivating an individual.

The decision equation is representative of the relationship and the process between the co-constituents in the process of getting decisions in the tripartite relationship. It is representative of the balance of needs between the three groups. Table 13.1 positions the components of the decision equation alongside Maslow's terms to compare levels and terms demonstrates a level of similar interpretations. Each component can be referenced to a level in Maslow's hierarchy of needs pyramid. The descriptions of the levels can be compared across to the names the components listed to see the similarity of the motivator and the decision equation component. The interpretations can be seen as directly compatible or compatible with an adjacent level. Not all are exact; they are, however, all very similar, with an amount of overlap. The overlap of the description with the component is in brackets. All the overlaps are with an adjacent level.

Table 13.1 Maslow's terms of motivation and the corresponding decision equation components

Maslow's term	Description	Decision equation
Self-actualisation	Morality, creativity, spontaneity, problem solving, lack of prejudice, acceptance of facts	Specific Challenge (+RY?)
Esteem	Self-esteem, confidence, achievement, respect of others, respected by others	Reason Why? (+SP)
Love and belong-	Friendship, family, sexual inti-	Support (+RY? PA)

Maslow's term	Description	Decision equation
ing	macy	
Safety	Security of: body, employment, resources, morality, the family, health and property	Proposed Actions (+SP, BB)
Physiological	Breathing, food, water, sex, sleep, homoeostasis, excretion	Benefits Balance (+PA)

The table allows the components to be further understood by equating Maslow's terms and descriptions with the decision equation's component terms. When applying the decision equation components to an actual situation it is possible that the components can be better understood when using Maslow's descriptions, as they use more familiar terms related to the human motivations rather than packages of information although one causes the other.

The table provides a better understanding of the link between motivation and the information packages/components provided in the orders format and decision processes of individuals. Both are important in the study of motivation, and it is the motivation of individuals that is paralleled in the study of the theory of leadership. Understanding what motivates individuals to take decisions into action is the focus of all these studies. The decision equation is a tool that helps interpret these terms and put them in a process of application that helps one individual apply it to another individual or group relationship.

While the comparison is close in descriptive terms, the level progression in Maslow's pyramid is also very close to the sequence in the decision equation components. Again the components are not a direct comparison but a close match. There is an amount of interpretation and overlap needed, but the comparison can be seen in both the individual components and also the order of priority. The overlap is with adjacent components. This will give a better understanding of the component and its rating in terms of motivational value for the group's members.

The decision equation is distilled from the military orders process. It is using a practical application format as a guide, which when compared to motivational theory provides a bridge between the two applications. Each group will use its own descriptions to apply to the components. For example, further interpretation in terms of the basic needs, such as the safety and physiological levels, labelled in the decision equation as BB, could be salary, bonuses and pensions. Each benefit will depend on the environment and system that the group belongs to. While the term *salary* is explicit and can easily be grouped in the Benefits Balance component, its nature can also imply other levels of motivation, which the individual will make their own interpretation of. A salary itself implies a level of recognition and respect, as it allows individuals to choose for themselves what they value, depending on their priorities and motivators. Also, a salary, when compared to that of another individual in the group, will imply a value of the person in the group and therefore a place or hierarchy in the group.

This demonstrates that it is not easy to equate all these factors exactly and rigidly attribute them to one level or another, as individuals' interpretations of the factor or component will sometimes differ. The decision equation in its most simple interpretation acts as a bridge between general terms, motivational theory terms and the military orders format. From a wider perspective, the decision equation provides a key to the language of interaction between parties and the group they belong to. The five components are labels that can be used in any situation that contains the factors that motivate an individual to make decisions. At the same time it also provides a structure for sequencing these components to make a pattern, with their factors inside, in the decision process.

The decision equation provides a grouping template for a multitude of factors that are faced by each individual in the process of making a decision. Which factors are grouped into which components is defined, and the structured pattern chosen by the individuals in the group will provide a record of the interaction of the individuals in the group. Using these common component terms allows a common terminology to be applied to Maslow's terms for any situation in any group.

The bridge between Maslow's terms and the military orders format is shown in Table 13.2. The general terms of the decision equation are in the centre column. The military terms place some of Maslow's terms together under one heading: *Situation* applies to *Self-actualisation*, *Esteem* and *Love and belonging*.

Table 13.2 Maslow's terms of motivation and corresponding headings in the British Army orders format, with the decision equation bridge in the centre

Maslow's term	Decision equation terms	Military orders terms
Self-actualisation	Specific Challenge	Situation
Esteem	Reason Why?	
Love and belong-ing	Support	
Safety	Proposed Actions	Mission and execution
Physiological	Benefits Balance	Service support
		Command and signal

Military orders formats have a heading at the end called 'Command and signal' (communications details such as frequencies, passwords and codes). This comes last because it is subject to daily changes and does not apply to all in the group. It is predominantly specific to the leaders of the various groups and subgroups. The military, like other organisations, does not repeat details that do not change, such as salary, pensions and benefits, as these are set out in contracts and terms and conditions that remain in place throughout the individuals' careers. Some terms in military orders are repeated to gain reinforcement. For example, the mission statement in a set of military orders will repeat some elements of Support and the Specific Challenge and the Reason Why? The mission statement is issued in a different pattern and provides a distinct pattern to the decision process and the relationship in military groups.

Organisations in general will strive to complete the full spectrum of the terms used by Maslow when recruiting or employing their groups. Once in daily operation, most organisations, including the British Army, try to put all of the lower needs out of the concerns of the group members so that they can focus on the issues at hand. The assumption is that once in the group the individual has agreed to these terms and it does not bear repeating; otherwise it may become a subject of negotiation at each briefing. It presumes and demands a higher motivation to focus on the Specific Challenge and the Reason Why? the group is formed in the first place. In the event of these changing it is up to the group representatives to involve the group members in the change in the components and factors to re-establish the new DAS chain.

By establishing and confirming long-term conditions for the lower order motivations the group can focus on the higher order motivators to effect decisions into action and solutions. This requires training and preparation to achieve this. The rewards for the group are greater levels of creativity, morality, spontaneity, problem solving amongst the group members. This level of motivation does not happen automatically and needs prior preparation, planning and practice. The decision equation provides a template that equates to known theories and accepted practices of motivation.

Chapter 14: The equation in a non-military group

'Do unto others as you would have them do unto you; this is not just a Sunday school ideal, but a proper labour management policy'

James F. Lincoln

Non-military organisations similarly strive for the ability to produce groups focused on higher level motivations. James Lincoln, one of two brothers who founded Lincoln Electric, was from the outset very focused on ensuring that his group fully understood the model he was pursuing. He outlined the Specific Challenge and the Reason Why? they were doing what he wanted the team to do.

He took inspiration from a number of sources and he made his message very clear to his workers, customers and shareholders. James Lincoln's goal was to provide more and more product, at better and better quality, at lower and lower prices, for more and more people. He prioritised the order of focus. He listed the customer as being the key stakeholder, then the employees, and finally the shareholders. He believed and proved that if the customer and employees were treated according to his interpretation of the golden rule, the shareholders would also benefit. James Lincoln's golden rule was taken from a phrase in the bible. The phrase went like this in his version of the book: 'so in everything do to others what you would have them do to you'. In more colloquial speech it equates to 'do unto others as they would have you do unto them'. In USA around 1900 it was perceived to be a good moral standard to apply to life, and James Lincoln choose to use it as a guide for business as well as a good way to convey his concept with an already familiar and accepted phrase.

The specific challenge was the application of the golden rule to the challenge he perceived in the marketplace, namely that of producing more product, of better quality, at lower prices, for more and more people. This was, and still is, a considerable challenge. The reason why the Lincoln Electric company was choosing to resolve the challenge presented by the customer of fixing two metal plates together was that they had the techniques and experience, and they agreed with the moral principle of the challenge. Getting this under way as a business was not easy or done in a standard way. Lincoln's negotiations with labour were certainly counter to common practice at the time, which viewed labour as the enemy of the management. Again his application of the golden rule in respect to the employees was simple: the employees needed food and shelter, as did the management, but the workers' needs could only be met after meeting the needs of the customer. While this approach is logical, it needed to be put into a more holistic and detailed approach in order to convince all concerned that it could work. The development of his six applications of the golden rule in respect to customers, employees and shareholders was very clear from the start and later became a central part of his books relating his experiences in business.

James Lincoln's six applications of the golden rule – do to others what you would have them do to you – are taken from Joseph Maciariello's book [19] *Lasting Value – Lessons from a Century of Agility at Lincoln Electric*:[27]

1. Recognize that workers' greatest economic need is for income and security in that income, and that both labour and management have the same interests. But the workers' need for security in income can only be met by satisfying the needs of customers on a continuous basis. Therefore, the customer is the key stakeholder whose needs are to be satisfied, and this should be done by applying the golden rule in the relations of the company to its customers. He believed this should be the goal of industry.
2. Achieve the needs of the customer on a continuous basis by staying in touch with and in front of the needs of the customer. This happens when both management and the workforce apply continuous efforts to increasing quality, customer service, and productivity, which in turn provide the customer with new and

improved products, higher quality products, and reduced prices. Thus, Lincoln advocated a 'cost-based approach' to pricing.

3. Provide the workers with the most modern tools of production (materials, methods, and machines) and with continuous training and skill development, and encourage them to participate in solutions to all kinds of work-related problems. Besides raising the productivity of the workers and the quality of their work, these efforts also develop their talents and raise their dignity, creativity, and self-respect.

4. Achieve continuous cost reduction and pass its benefits on to the customers in the form of lower prices. When combined with continuous increases in quality and the development of new and improved products, the golden rule is fulfilled as far as the customer is concerned.

5. Reward increased productivity, quality, and innovation via a merit system that puts no upper limit on what a worker can earn. On the other hand, workers should bear the penalty for lack of productivity, poor quality, absenteeism, and the absence of teamwork in fulfilling company goals. The incentive system should provide strong formal rewards according to variables that matter a great deal to the customer and increase the economic and social status of the worker. In the process, the worker becomes an entrepreneur.

6. Recognize that the shareholders deserve a fair return on their investment. James Lincoln differentiated between a shareholder who helps to finance a new operation and one who simply trades shares for gain. Lincoln believed that to the extent a company is already launched and profitable, a passive shareholder does not contribute much to its success and is not deeply committed to its customers or its workers. A shareholder who finances a new venture, however, adds great value and deserves a return commensurate with the risk of the new venture.

These are James Lincoln's six applications and it is very clear about the needs and priorities allotted to those needs and payments made. It is a broad approach and covers all parties: the customers, the workers and the shareholders, even to the extent of differentiating the risk-taking shareholders from passive investors looking for a safe return. The six applications are covering all aspects of what the followers need in terms of Maslow's hierarchy of needs and being able to make a decision in terms of a set of military orders. Further detail was added to this in the 1950s when the workers were given guaranteed continuous employment measures for USA-based Lincoln Electric employees. Those employees who had been with Lincoln Electric for more than three years were guaranteed 30 hours a week employment. This was in order to ensure that it would provide the environment for the employees to want to find efficiencies and increases in product quality without the threat that these efficiencies would cost them their jobs.

Like the different levels of Maslow's hierarchy, the components of the decision equation, the headings in the army orders or James Lincoln's application of the golden rule, they are all interlinked in their component parts and interdependent within their formats and situations in getting the complete message across. The challenge of the customer (Application 1) and problem solving, creative self-actualisation of Maslow's level 5 is reinforced throughout the message and is in brackets in Table 14.1. The whole message is communicated to the follower and, like a negotiation, it is there to gain compliance and agreement to the proposed actions. The decision equation has five components that provide the follower with the information to assess and make a decision on whether or not to go into action. Again, interpretation will create areas of overlap and it is important that these areas of interpretation are clarified by good communications and experience.

Table 14.1 A comparison of Maslow's hierarchy terms, the decision equation components and James Lincoln's six applications

Maslow's hierarchy levels	Decision equation components	James Lincoln's six applications
Self-actualisation	Specific Challenge	App 1 and 2
Esteem	Reason Why?	App 2 (App 1 challenge)
Love and belonging	Support	App 3
Safety	Proposed Actions	App 4 (App 1)
Physiological	Benefits Balance	App 5 and 6 (App 1)

The Harvard Business School's Lincoln Electric-based case study is used widely in the business world, and is currently one of the most downloaded case studies. It is based on a model that places a very clear outline on how the parties involved are to interact. Although this is a general conceptual overview, it is a record of how the founder and the followers were expected to interact. The fact that Lincoln Electric's USA branch has gone on to be a successful company based on returns and consistency is unusual, as it has a clear record of the concepts ideas and intentions of interaction that were explicitly expressed at the start and maintained throughout. The Lincoln Electric case study is often referred to as a model case for use in studying labour relations and motivation.

The components of James Lincoln's six applications approximately correspond to terms that are identified with levels of motivation. These terms correspond to headings and applications in the organisations identified. Maslow's theory and terms have been widely accepted by many organisations as indicators of where to focus efforts when designing systems to attract, motivate and maintain individuals. The needs and motivations in any group should be approach in a holistic manner as part of the whole DAS chain process.

The completed message of the decision equation is the desired situation. However, rather than looking at each component separately in isolation and then trying to jam them altogether at once into the final decision equation as a complete whole, there are intermediate stages. The message can be built in stages and grouped into subgroup sections in order to approach it in a piecemeal fashion. This is similar to the way that Maslow grouped his five levels into B or D needs or higher order or lower order, and Herzberg's intrinsic and extrinsic labels, and motivators and hygienic factors. Some of the components in the decision equation can be grouped as physical components and some as intellectual. In a similar way to a mathematical equation, individual parts can be put together first in bracketed subgroups and then the subgroups added to make the whole. Some parts of the equation can be worked out separately from each other, such as the potentially very technical and manufacturing orientated SP + PA components separate from the SC + RY? components. The components stand on their own, but at the same time form part of the overall message and can be used flexibly and sparingly before being presented as an overall decision equation in the leader's formal presentation.

This is often what happens in practice. A conversation between a leader and some of the followers will go back and forth before the leader makes a decision as an individual. It is also seen in other situations, such as a negotiation when recruiting staff. Components such as BB are put down in front of the potential group member as a proposal and they are added to until both sides either agree to group membership or not. By deciding to look for another individual in the case of the group recruiting agent or the individual looking elsewhere for a position in a different group, one party or both feels they have not met their perceived match. Some individuals may make decisions based on only one component, while others need all five. The decision is made as an individual; what the group does may be (and often is) one of the factors in that individual's decision process. Looking at the components in subgroup sections is the next stage before moving to the equation as a whole.

Chapter 15: Group purpose

'The meeting of two personalities is like the contact of two chemical substances: if there is any reaction, both are transformed.'

C.G. Jung

The decision equation is a tool and it is used to represent the decision process in a relationship. The decision equation concept is applicable to the individual and therefore this quality allows it to be used in very small organisations as well as large ones, as seen in earlier chapters. The components and the subgroups sections, to be shown later, help define terms which many have heard of but have not before seen defined specifically. By learning the next stage up from the individual components – the subgroup sections – an individual will be able to construct a second layer up from the foundation stones of the components from which to communicate and form the relationship of the group. An individual, like an architect of communications, will be able to construct their own decision equations and help design the relationship in the group.

The five components in the decision equation can be grouped into two larger sections that have different properties. The subgroup section groupings are similar to how Maslow and Herzberg split their five levels or factors respectively (Maslow's higher and lower orders and Herzberg's intrinsic and extrinsic factors or his motivators and hygienic factors). The first section of the decision equation is composed of two components: Specific Challenge coupled with the Reason Why? When added together they form the purpose of the group.

The purpose is an important subgroup section in the decision equation. In defining purpose this way the group is identifying not only the Reason Why? a group is formed but what the root cause for the group to form is – the Specific Challenge. Understanding the Specific Challenge and therefore the Reason Why? the group is formed to resolve it is important, as it sets in motion the need for the remaining components of the equation. The Reason Why? does not exist without the Specific Challenge and they are forever linked together. The Specific Challenge is implied by the very presence of the group. The decision process starts with a Specific Challenge and leads to the formation of the group. When the Specific Challenge is resolved the need for the group also disappears.

It is important to be explicit about these two components, as it will reinforce and give reference to the Specific Challenge the group is attempting to resolve. These two components can be described as concepts, ideas, goals and principles and can therefore be described as the intellectual or higher order components of the decision equation. The purpose will give an indication of the direction in which subsequent components should be used in resolving the Specific Challenge. For example, in a military scenario, a threat composed mainly of armoured units would logically be countered by having units comprised of anti-armour weapon systems deployed against it to destroy, block or channel it.

Specifying the challenge in the case of joining two sheets of metal would be met by Lincoln Electric in a different way than their competitors in the early days, by offering to join with rivets the sheets of metal. The Specific Challenge presented is resolved in a different way from the rest of the market at the time. The customer did not have a shortage of rivets: they had no way of joining the two sheets of metal. The ability to define the Specific Challenge and then resolve it in a better way has been an ability through which fortunes have been won and lost. Lincoln Electric managed to persuade the customer that their solution was stronger, cleaner, cheaper and essentially better value.

The difference between the actions requested and the Specific Challenge is important, as it can produce very different solutions. If the customer just told the suppliers to produce 15,000 rivets then they would have been given proposals for 15,000 rivets by both competitors. It was a brave and innovative move by James Lincoln to persuade the customer of the value of their product. Most importantly, he addressed the Specific Challenge, not the actions requested.

The Specific Challenge needs to be explicitly stated to assist in the decision making of which solution is best to resolve the challenge. In the case of Lincoln Electric their technical knowledge and advantage in this area of expertise created a very good reason why they formed a company: to provide better value to the customer. They proved themselves to be better engineers and solution providers than the competition. In the case of James Lincoln, his long-term Reason Why? may well have been to prove that it was possible to use the golden rule as a moral compass in business. In the decision equation the purpose is represented like this:

Example 15.1 The purpose components in the decision equation

Specific Challenge + Reason Why? => purpose
SC + RY? => p

The term *purpose* is defined in the dictionary as 'an object to be attained; a thing attained, the intention to act, resolution, determination' for the noun. The verb format is defined as 'to have as one's purpose; design, intend'. It is in common usage and is a term that relates to the thing to be attained or resolved. The dictionary is not clear on what exactly is to be resolved, and as pointed out earlier it is only implied.

'What is the purpose or objective of your actions?' Similar words, such as intention, targets or missions, are terms more familiar to the military, but are now used increasingly by non-military groups. These groups are many and varied. The term *purpose* is simple and makes up the intellectual part of the individual's decision equation. The Specific Challenge and Reason Why?, or Purpose, is, as Herzberg identified, a very powerful motivator.

When asked if to volunteer and donate blood to help hospitals maintain a large enough blood bank to carry out blood transfusions for future patients, the individual is being presented with an option to decide. The purpose has been explained in outline and could be a good enough reason for him to decide to act and donate. In the situation where the patient knows the recipients it may be easier to agree.

In another similar but different scenario, where the individual is asked to sell their blood to the hospital or a third party, they may question the reason why they should sell their blood. In this new scenario the motive for asking may not be to help save lives as much as it is to make a profit for a dealer between the donor and the patient. In the second scenario the individual donor is suspicious and the donor cannot be sure the purpose is genuine. The profit incentive or dealer's Benefits Balance and the purpose are being questioned.

Many countries will offer other non-monetary rewards for donating blood. Italy offers a day off work and Singapore has a very extensive national recognition system for the donation of blood. Other countries have made it illegal to purchase blood or body parts. The purpose (that it saves lives) and the thought that it could be the donor who needs blood one day is a good Reason Why? to donate. The actions are seen as the right thing to do, and peer recognition is a powerful motivator.

In some cases, without the purpose, a specific identified challenge and a reason why, some individuals see only the demotivating factor such as profit (BB), and do not trust the agents. The term *de-motivator* relates to Herzberg's second subgroup section, the hygienic factors. The mistrust created by the potential for third-party profit, lack of quality control and not being purely purpose driven provides a disincentive and prevents donations.

The second subgroup section consists of the remaining three components of the decision equation. These are the physical components. This subgroup of the decision equation is called the Group section. Each component explicitly describes either the physical material assets or actions of the decision equation. Each component, when related to the individual, gives each individual an indication of the value of that individual in the group and of that group's value in comparison to other groups. The three components are all similar in that they give the individual his value in terms of the others in the group, and the group with other groups and individuals.

The group is an entity in itself and a specific name or title in that group brings with it certain characteristics and perceptions from the individual's understanding. One group's perception of the title will be very different from another group's culture. For example, the individual whose nickname is 'the Owl' in one language will may be perceived as a wise all-seeing bird of prey, whereas in another language and culture he may be viewed as very stupid because an owl stays up all night and sleeps in the day. Each group will have its own understanding and meaning of the title. Within certain cultures the title of manager conveys a value position of importance, and while the individual may not have the same abilities when compared to a manager in another group, the value perception is still there. The desire to have the title of *manager* is very real in many cultures because of the value perception that it has.

The Proposed Action component details the role and importance that individuals have in the overall group if it differentiates the individuals and group from the other groups. Their function indicates the value to the team as a whole. Those with specialised and rare skills are considered more valuable than others in their own way. The Benefits Balance will give them greater monetary rewards comparative to others in the group. These physical components explicitly express the material assets and actions of the group. These components by implication speak to each individual within the group directly and relate to them their importance and the value placed in them by the group.

These three components in the group section link the individual to the group. The link to a group as an entity and its purpose provides a focus on a motivator such as the extrinsic motivator term *esteem*, as well as the extrinsic hygiene-related terms of *belonging*, *safety* and *physiological* motivators. To some in the group their titles, honours and the kudos from their peers, who recognise the group they are attached to, are powerful motivators to become members or remain in the group as an entity. The membership of the group results in pride and esteem in what they do within and outside the group. The Group components are represented in the decision equations like this:

Example 15.2 The Group components in the decision equation

Support + Proposed Action + Benefits Balance = Group
SP + PA + BB = G

Separately the words describing these two sections of the decision equation have their own specific meanings. Both the Group and the purpose sections describe two different types of motivators or levels of motivation of all the individuals in the group. Both the leader and the followers are linked to the group's intellectual and physical motivating factors, as they fulfil their individual's need in terms of both intellectual and physical needs.

The group is formed to resolve the purpose rather like the SC is linked to the RY? in the purpose. The group exists because of the purpose. One gives rise to the other; the group exists to resolve the purpose. There is interdependence between the components and sections of the decision equation. The SC leads to the RY? when the group is formed and the SP, PA and BB are designed with the SC as a guiding factor to be resolved. At the section level as well, the components identify the specific links, both physical and intellectual, to the group as an entity. The purpose represents why the group is formed, and the Group section explains how and what the group plans to do to resolve the SC. The five components are known collectively as the Group purpose:

SC, RY?, SP, PA, BB are known as the Gp[28]

As the Group purpose is formed, it is presented to the members who are then required to make a decision whether to accept it as their Group purpose and to take action or not. The decision equation represents the Gp and the decision as a completed process. Before the decision is made there is the function of initiating, facilitating the definition of the Group purpose. There remains the function of communicating the Gp to the group members, and its members as individuals making the decision to confirm that is their

Group purpose.

The Group purpose is a collective name for the five components before the decision is made. It is a phrase that adds simplicity and meaning to the collective of the five components. When the decision is made the decision equation is written using the symbol Gp, meaning Group purpose. Using these sections the decision equation can be reduced to a simpler form:

Example 15.3 The short form of the decision equation

Gp => d

The distinction of the group purpose as opposed to individual purpose is important in studying the relationship. As pointed out in the earlier chapters, the group is fundamental to any case of leadership. If a group member refers to or takes action in the direction of another purpose they risk losing their position in the group. The common term is that they are deemed to be suffering from a conflict of interests.

The leader is there to represent the group as an entity. Often a person is the leader because that individual can understand, define and communicate the Gp both to the followers and to others outside the group if required. The position of leader is often dependent on the ability to represent and confirm the Gp. If they are not able to do this they may not remain the natural leader much longer. When the group is confronted with an SC that is difficult to resolve and the leader reveals they do not agree or are not prepared to act in the direction of the Gp, the followers may well ask the same question and choose not to act towards the Gp either.

In the event that the leader is seen to act in a way that is contrary to the perceived Gp there is a potential for a misunderstanding of the Gp and a conflict of interests. Also added to this perceived conflict is that members in the group may have given up some of their individual pursuits to align with the Gp. It may be considered as unfair that the followers subsume their individual purposes for the group purpose when the leader does not.

The level to which this is acceptable varies according to the Gp proposed and the individuals in the group. The differential between what is fair and not fair is a factor that affects the relationship. On a national scale income inequality is often quoted by economists and politicians as an example of one of these differentials. It is a measure of the difference between nations and individuals in groups and is a highly contentious issue because of perceived conflicts of interests between individuals and the groups they belong to.

In many groups the Gp is what the leader defines it as. The leader is seen as representative of the Gp. Often the followers will only receive their Gp from one person, and this reinforces the leader's position as the sole definer and communicator of the Gp. If the Gp is in line with the individual member's beliefs or interests it will be easier to motivate them to sacrifice everything or do anything to resolve the Gp.

The key function of the leader is to get this motivation towards the Gp into the group. The leader knows that their position as leader could very well depend on their ability to motivate the followers to be effective in pursuit of the purpose for which the group was created and organised. It may also be that the group has been forced together and it is in their interests for survival and protection. The group members may be in a group that is forced together and they cannot opt out. As individuals they are better off being in a group and will suppress their individual motivators to a greater degree than usual.

There are many types of groups and different types of interactions that form relationship patterns between the co-constituents. It is understood that the leader of the group is assumed to be in a position to represent the Gp. Ideally the position is awarded or allocated to the individual or committee that can best define and communicate the Gp. Where the Gp is initiated from, facilitated, defined and communicated in the group will decide what type of relationship the group has.

Chapter 16: Group purpose, benefits and results

'There are no bad soldiers, only bad officers'
Commonly attributed to Napoleon Bonaparte

The group purpose is specific to the group and not the individual. Benefits can apply to both the group and an individual. This difference can have large implications when motivating members of the group and preventing conflicts of interest, even if they are only imagined conflicts. Benefits in Maslow's and Herzberg's levels are understood to be lower order or extrinsic motivators and describe a reward of some sort or payment such as a salary, profit or bonus. Benefits or penalties are often at the forefront of an individual's mind when presented with a challenge. It is 'Radio WIIFM', as explained by Bob Johnson, a popular American trainer. It is the world's most popular radio station, as everybody at one time or another is tuned into it. WIIFM stands for 'What's In It For Me?'.

The distinction between Group purpose and individual benefits is small but significant, as demonstrated. To motivate individuals there needs to be an appeal to either their intrinsic or extrinsic motivators. 'What's in it for me?' has the word 'me' in it at the end, which indicates first that it is driven by the individual not the group. Individuals make their decisions as individuals; however, their decisions could be based on group-linked motivators or be totally focused on their own motivators. All five components can be linked to the Gp. The BB are a mix of customer or SC based benefits, and group, team or individually based benefits.

The Gp gives a sense of the challenge and the direction, and perhaps instils desire or ambition in the group members. This ambition to achieve and attain the target can be understood as an intrinsic motivator. It is the challenge and recognition of being able to resolve the group's Specific Challenge and to be recognised as having appeal in itself. The recognition can be reflected in the Group section's components by titles, honours, better conditions, greater responsibility and other benefits.

The possibility of more responsibility and/or recognition of the ability to resolve the challenge within the group and recognition external for the group is important. Job satisfaction and the ability to improve and grow into something better is often quoted as being a key motivator. Clayton Alderfer later published his 'ERG Theory'(24) which identified this need for growth as a further development on Maslow's hierarchy of needs. In addition to incorporating Maslow's needs under the headings 'Existence' and 'Relatedness', he further added 'Growth' to encompass Maslow's needs for esteem and self-actualisation. The word 'growth' more easily explains this motivator in terms that are understood immediately.

Within the Gp there will be competing individual purposes or motivators, such as the individual's growth. It is sometimes an expected function of the leader to align these individual needs for growth within the group to achieving the group purpose as a priority. Growth can similarly apply to the group within a larger group. Many groups are driven by shareholders to grow and continue growing each year in order to continue increasing returns. The individual's need for growth is aligned if possible within the group's drive for growth.

The leader is often the person who has the role of defining or giving exact meaning to the purpose of the group so that the group can understand it and act upon it. This may appear to be a simple task of explaining in clear terms the purpose behind the actions, but it must be done in a way that is specific to that group. In practice, the group purpose will often come from a higher group level. How does the leader deal with this common situation?

An important skill of the leader in this situation is to be able to translate, from the larger group purpose to his group, their own specific group purpose. The purpose section must contain the key information from the overall group purpose, yet it must also relate to the subgroup it is being communicated to. Just to repeat the larger group's purpose as if it is the subgroup's purpose does not always serve adequately in giving enough information to allow the group to understand, accept and decide to act in its favour.

Occasionally, subgroup leaders will exclude information about the larger group purpose on the assumption that the subgroup members will not be able or willing to understand or be interested in the overall reason why. This may not appear to be important on the surface of it, but it cuts away that ability to know what the desired result of the larger group is. This larger group purpose is sometimes called the 'Big Picture'. Knowledge of the larger group's desired solution is what enables individuals in the subgroup to see their value in the big picture.

There is a difference between the purpose and the group and individual benefits gained as a result of the actions of the group. The latter two, as benefits, are dependent on the purpose of the group being resolved. The group is formed to resolve the SC, and without it there is no RY? to create a group in the first place. Group and individual benefits that come from being in the group should come as a result of achieving the purpose.

Many organisations choose to pay steady salaries rather than for piece work. It is common practice in most groups and is the first step in de-linking the straight line path along the equation from the SC and customer to the BB rewards they are paid. They have contracts and salaries, and this method, for most, is a preferred way of hiring and motivating employees to resolve their individual needs of physiological and security needs, but it is not the only way.

Sales staff are often paid a monthly salary, but then are also paid an additional sum which is linked directly by a commission system to sales agreements they make with customers. There are some sales commission systems that are driven only by individual benefits and not linked to group benefits. A typical example can be found in industries where the individual commission is paid on signing of the contract or payment of the contract, with no link to the resolution of the specific challenge being given to the customer.

Senior managers of companies are also linked to company success this way, with options on company shares and many other methods of benefits. It is a balance that is struck and a link that needs to be retained, otherwise the individual pays greater attention to the act of signing a contract than the group's goal of resolving the SC. They become de-linked from the SC of the group. This can have dire consequences for the group. Scott Adams' cartoon again hammers the point home.

Figure 16.1 Scott Adams' Dilbert cartoon of a situation with a de-linked CEO[29]

In Lincoln Electric, at some locations in their global empire, spanning 20 countries and 160 distributors, such as the factories at the company's home base in Cleveland, individuals work on a 'piece work' basis. This work model directly links the workers' behaviour with the customers' and the SC presented by them. How this works in groups is to a large part dependent on whether the group members agree or not when given the option. In the case of Lincoln Electric workers, they work when there is work presented. The company guarantees them 30 hours a week, but if there is work lined up for 50 hours a week or more, the group members are obliged to work 50 hours a week – no holidays, no sick leave, no overtime. Also, because of this 30 hour a week guarantee the company's sales force are focused on finding the work to ensure there is enough for them to do.

The employees on piece work are well rewarded for it. In the Lincoln Electric Cleveland branch they annually earn more (sometimes double) than the average factory employee in similar fields of work. At annual bonus time at the factory, the local car dealers are lining up outside the factory gates. James Lincoln was very clear in his six applications of the golden rule that the three parties he defined had an order of priority: customer, employee and then shareholder. The customer came first and only after the customer's challenge had been resolved satisfactorily would the employees benefit. Piece work is a model that makes this system of priorities very obvious.

In the Lincoln Electric model, the shareholder would be paid last after the employees. Even then James Lincoln distinguished between types of shareholders as well. Although they are treated equally in many ways, his attitude was that those who risked on new developing business would be rewarded before those shareholders who just bought stock to get a return without involvement and interest. It is not surprising that he openly encouraged his employee to buy shares in the company. He believed it was only right that they should be given the opportunity to invest in something they could influence the outcome of. Additional to this, as shareholding employees they could see where the money went more clearly, rather than just 'away from them' as is often the perception on some factory floors.

In James Lincoln's case and the piece workers model there is a situation in which the leader defines the Gp and makes it very clear from the outset, with his organisation structured around it to reflect in action the Gp. Overseas branches of Lincoln Electric do not all use the piece work model, and there are more convention models employed in other locations. This model is restricted in some countries by legal requirements in the employment of labour. Some markets do not support the quality or tailored approach they take. Choosing to work in this way and de-link the direct connection from the customer's SC through the four components to the BB is a choice made by the leadership in the organisation in each situation.

Ideally, benefits should be seen as a result of achieving, or actively participating in resolving, the SC. This is not always an easy task for a number of reasons, such as the size and length of time of the project. Selling a type of aircraft or a nuclear power station, for example, is no short-term simple task. The leader of each group is required to examine their specific group and its Gp. Linking the overall group and their subgroup purpose can maintain this link with the SC of the customer and the customer's customer. The RY?, SP and PA all flow from it to the BB they receive if the SC is resolved and they complete the actions according to the plan.

Each model is different and will lead to different actions being focused on by the individuals in the group. To the followers, the way the organisation is led by its group leaders at each level will effect how the Gp is defined and put into action. This relates to the benefits that an individual gets from being part of the group compared to what he would be getting if he were not in the group. From the followers' perspective these benefits of belonging to the group divide into individual motivators (intrinsic – job satisfaction) and hygienic factors (extrinsic – job security, contract, salary).

The leader must act in favour of the Gp. The old adage 'we judge others on their actions' is very apt. The leader will quickly see who is not fully behind the Gp. Similarly, the followers will quickly spot actions that a leader takes that are not in favour of the Gp. If the leader is shown to be acting outside of the Gp then it has the potential to jeopardise his position as a leader of the group.

The UK MPs' expenses scandal in 2010–2011 is a good example of how leaders acted contrary to Gp. Individual members of parliament allegedly misinterpreted the law with respect to their expenses and claimed much more than was allowed, or deemed not in line with what was expected. The scandal exposed these MPs' actions. Accusations were made and some of the MPs were proved to be guilty of unfair and unlawful behaviour and convicted. Others, although not convicted, were forced or obliged to resign their posts, either by the electorate or their political party. The effect on the leadership of the country at the time was to the detriment of all parties concerned and the relationship of trust in the position of

MPs as leaders has been shaken.

Gp is the uniting feature of the group. In some cases the Gp of one group is in all groups' interests: for example, as a species, reducing disease or preventing the spread of a virus. In these groups, where the members are motivated by intrinsic and extrinsic self-interest, the Gp has an obvious focus. When the Gp is not clear and followers are being asked to decide to take action based on limited or misunderstood information the relationship and getting decisions into action becomes more difficult.

Often the individual joins a group purely to get the benefits of being in the group. They are not motivated by, or perhaps not even privy to, the group purpose of their team and organisation as a whole. They are de-linked from the decision process and concerned only with the physical Group section components at an individual level.

In another scenario the group's leaders can turn away from the SC of resolving the customer's challenge to pleasing the employees, or focusing on the results for the shareholder. This redirection can inflate costs or reduce quality to the point where customers no longer buy from the group, and then the reason why the group was created is called into question. This change in focus can be seen by leaders at all levels in groups. The terms of benefits may be allowed to take priority, and while this may horrify shareholders it will also change the ambitions of those leaders and followers in the group.

Individuals will often use the example of the leader as a justification for their actions. There is the unwritten rule of fairness and equality of application of the rules and or guidelines. If the leaders misdirect the efforts and assets of the group to their own benefits, the followers will, in some cases, use this as an excuse to do the same. Napoleon is reputed to have said 'there are no bad soldiers, only bad officers'. While this is a general statement without a specific case to refer to, it has been quoted by many leaders (using slightly different words) in order to impress upon leaders the commonly held expectation of leadership. What the followers will accept of their leader is very much based on the expectations of fairness in similar groups around them. This is knowledge that they have been given as they have grown up.

Leaders at all levels can become more focused on their own position or title in the group rather than the purpose the group was created for. Leaders are, after all, individuals within the group, and join the group in order to benefit from the group. Organisations that have a clear, well-distributed and active focus on the Gp, have an environment which is easier for followers to function than in groups where the purpose is not clear, or the leader's actions do not seem in line with the Gp.

Without the Gp there is less of an intrinsic link to the group, and it is much easier for an individual to leave the group. With no link to the Gp, membership motivators for the followers are limited to the extrinsic motivators; love and belonging, safety, and physiological. Benefits are limited to the physical rewards they can get from the group.

A salary can be converted into many different things to fulfil the extrinsic needs of an individual. Not surprisingly, the followers seek only a salary rather than any intrinsically based motivations that the group can provide. Over time the followers become less prepared to work with or for other members of the group for the benefit of the group members. Followers are encouraged to defend their position and job description rather than look at the group as a whole.

When leaders define Gp as the shareholders' results, they are focusing on the wrong end of the equation. They are correct in stating that it is a desired result or objective to be achieved, but only after the SC is resolved. Without linking it to the SC it becomes more difficult for group members to link their actions to the results. Key Performance Indicators are very useful tools in focusing employees' efforts, but if they cannot be linked to the Gp at any level then the result may well be a product or service not fit for task. Such a product or service does not always get rewarded by the customer and then the benefits that the group is looking for cannot be achieved.

Secondly, when the leader links the results for the shareholder to the followers' actions, the followers may also do so. The group members probably did not join the group in order to put money into a shareholder's pocket. When leaders speak of profit or shareholder returns, the group members do not see it the same way.

In business it is accepted that shareholders receive rewards in the form of payments for their investment provided there is a profit. Meeting a customer's challenge has a purpose, and if done well, rewards are the result – which includes the shareholders' rewards. In the event that the group members do not perceive their results and benefits as comparing to those of the shareholders then this becomes a de-motivator.

When the link to shareholders is emphasised as the reason why the followers are employed, the motivation for the followers changes. The followers' perception is changed and they see the results just going towards another swimming pool for an investor. It is not surprising if the followers' dominant motivators change from the ones that helped them join the group in the first place. When given this situation the followers start to question their decisions into group membership in a different light.

Within the decision equation the lower case 'd' for decision reflects that the decision is specific to the situation and components when the decision was made. It is unique to each member and situation and therefore cannot be subdivided. A new situation will lead to the components being redefined and a new decision being made. The followers may still take action, but the decision is based on a different combination of components and motivators.

If there are alternatives presented, such as a better Gp in another group, the individual may well take the alternative option, where they perceive the Gp will be a different and better combination for them. Napoleon's phrase is complemented by the adage that 'staff don't leave companies, they leave their bosses'.

In a country, region or local election, voting rights link the individual to the benefits of having an influence in defining who the leaders are and what should happen in the country. They are being involved in the process of choosing who is to be their leader. The policies that the leader is proposing will affect the individual. Voting is the expression of the individual's decision. He has the choice to vote for the good of the group or for himself. Do the candidates address the specific challenges that the voter faces? The candidate can use the group benefits to appeal or the individual benefits. The candidates will define the challenges and then propose actions and claim everyone will benefit.

The different motivators of voters were highlighted to the author when a friend's wife was asked if she was going back to her home town to vote in the national elections. Her reply was revealing: 'the price they pay you to vote for them [approx. US$15 equivalent] does not even cover the cost of the gas to drive there, so no, I am not going to bother'. This is a clear case of the group purpose being left out of the process and the direct link from the action to the benefit had been forged.

Another instance of how far distanced the concept of voting and engaging in the group had gone from the link to the Gp, social contract and the proposed actions of voting for a candidate was revealed in another country, where a voter was complaining that the recent rule changes had prevented payment for a vote. The explanation was that payment could be seen as a form of bribery! The potential voter was complaining that the new system does not even value the voters any more. 'There used to be a time when we were of value! Now my vote is worth nothing.' This is a complete reversal of the intention of the system, where the group members have the vote in order to engage in the process of helping to define and communicate who the group leader should be, based on the values they represent.

The intention of voting is that this will give people some element of control in their leadership and thereby the Gp and therefore their future. The previous two examples are a demonstration of how powerful the direct bond between an action and a direct benefit result is, once the link is made. To break this bond is difficult. It is only questioned by the voter if the alternative provided is another extrinsic value. In terms of a group's interaction and the relationship between the leader and follower, the bond between action and benefits is short and provides a leader with a simple option. This is done at the expense of the long-term benefits of participation and engagement in the system. The leader has in effect bought the vote and the intention of the vote is invalidated. The leaders have a moral *carte blanche* to change and re-write the Gp to suit their own needs, as the voter has traded his choice for an amount of money.

In Australia it is illegal not to vote, and this explains the high turn out in elections there. In other countries that vote, a low turn out may be indicative of apathy towards the selection of candidates or a choice of actively not participating in the system because one believes the system is incorrect. It displays a lack of engagement with the group as a whole. The politicians as a whole are not addressing the perceived challenges that would motivate the voter into action.

If the voters perceive that there are no challenges, then the candidates have no intrinsic motivators that will move them to vote. They appeal to extrinsic and simple offers to link the vote directly to the voter receiving physical benefits of some sort. Could it be that the candidates are so busy talking about them that it overshadows that the important part of the whole process is that the followers should be contributing to the Gp? The purpose of the vote has become one in which the leaders are more concerned with getting the benefits of the position and title rather than the engagement of the people. They have short cut the system and the voters are not engaging.

Like all groups it is a big hurdle to move from one Gp to another. For example, changing a state-owned enterprise (SOE) in China to a management by objective and profit organisation. In order to get access to the growing market, and the knowledge and understanding needed to meet that new market's SC, the SOE can join another group that has these abilities and expertise in management by objective and profit focus. This is the format of some joint venture contracts with partners in China. One group is joining another to create a whole new group with a new SC and therefore a new decision equation and DAS chain must be forged. Both groups have no understanding of the other group's previous SC or decision equation process. This is a typical challenge being faced by many SOEs in China. This is a considerable leadership dilemma and requires the newly formed larger group to redefine the decision equation in the light of the new SC and other components it is presented with.

To some group leaders, this is one way to break the short cut direct link that the SOE group has with the benefits. There are many different models being tried and developed all across China at the moment. Those that joined the SOEs a long time ago are now getting the Gp changed completely and it will require a whole new assessment before making a decision. The physical as well as intellectual section components may be completely different and the emotional ties to the old group are still real.

Changing the Gp is fundamental and perhaps going back against obligations that were made many years ago. Conversely, the message could be one that provides welcome change and an opportunity for improvement. How the message is received and processed very much depends on how the leader and group members define the Gp. The SC of meeting the demand from external and domestic markets is now higher on the priority list. The group members have made or are in the process of making their decisions. The long-term results have yet to be seen, although China's GDP is still growing.

Chapter 17: The terms of the relationship

'At the heart of leadership is the leader's relationship with followers. People will entrust their hopes and dreams to another
person only if they think the other is a reliable vessel.'

David Gergan

The relationship that is commonly described as leadership is focused on a message that is passed between the leader and the follower. The decision equation represents the final message that
represents the group decision and there are stages in the process of
creating the whole equation to the point where a decision is taken
into action and ultimately a solution found. The DAS chain is often
not as straightforward when it is first being established in the MBA
case study, and there are stages in the decision process even before
the actions start.

The first stage in the decision process is an appreciation by the
leader of the followers: who are they, and what they are capable of,
and what their likely motivators are. The second stage is the leader
initiating an engagement with the followers in the form of a message or proposal. The third stage is facilitating a response from the
followers and further defining the message and components. If the
acceptance and decision are not forthcoming at the first presentation of the message or proposal then the process may return to
stages one and two for further redefining of the message before the
full complete decision equation is formed. These stages are often
overlapped and done simultaneously in a meeting or a series of
meetings, with certain aspects of the components being defined
and cemented into their place in the equation. Then again the proposal could be simple enough to just be accepted and acted on right
away.

Whether the process is short, sharp and simple or is a lengthy
drawn-out negotiation, the process of facilitating an equa-
tion/plan/strategy to a decision happens in each group. If the followers' actions are positive and in the direction of the purpose

proposed then this is an indication that a relationship has formed or been maintained, and the relationship remains in place. If the responding action from the followers is not in the direction that the leader intended then the relationship has been questioned and may result in a redefining of the components or the relationship breaking off. Like the decision process itself, the breaking of a relationship does not have a defined time period. Some will slowly dissolve and others abruptly terminate.

The long-term result of a relationship dissolving could be a new leader being elected or appointed to the group or a new group of followers being found, or possibly a combination of both these actions. Often there is a meeting of minds somewhere to balance the needs of both sides and they agree to a new Gp with a short-term focus, subject to periodic review. This general overview of the relationship demonstrates that there are many possibilities and that the relationship is by no means permanent.

Whether by election, agreed appointments, persuasion or coercion, a leader's position is created and maintained and the relationship needs constant attention and reinforcement. This is partly to do with the passage of time, which causes people to forget or become complacent in resolving the same challenge. It is also to do with the changing environment around them, such as a different challenge outside of their technical scope from a competitor, or suffering from a lack of challenges. Over time the group members change, and in parallel with this the group members need to change over time. Change appeals to the intrinsic motivators of individuals.

Providing change using intrinsic motivators can be done by challenging individuals on how the components are defined and communicated. Providing new extrinsic motivators in the form of benefits is another way to appeal to and continue challenging the individuals, but it may be resisted by individuals who perceive it as a threat to their extrinsic benefits.

It may be necessary to change the Gp as the SC has been permanently resolved and a new challenge is being sought. This will cause the relationship to be re-examined by both parties. A definition of leadership needs to include reference to this constant need for review of the leadership relationship. The leader must be sure that the benefits and purpose are not confused by the individuals in the group. Benefits come as a result of resolving the SC and are not the basis for the reason why the group is formed in the first place.

The decision equation allows the motivators to be looked at in isolation, and therefore the equation allows a detailed examination of the relationship between the leader, the group and the followers. The equation represents the components needed to give a complete package of information to allow a decision to be made. The components cover both the intrinsic and extrinsic motivators of the co-constituents. Each component corresponds to motivators, as an individual's understanding, interpretation of the message and the components values system is unique to the individual.

How the components are combined and how many are used will provide identifiers for the types of relationships that are formed. The combinations of the components that can be used provide a range of variances and understandings. Using the decision equation and its five components simplifies the analysis of the communications mechanism between the co-constituents that are represented in the group. This relationship needs attention to maintain it over the duration of the SC. The needs of the group are balanced within the Gp and the relationship. How the message of the balance of needs and the decision equation are used in the process of creating the relationship is the focus of the next part of the book.

Below are listed the answers that have revealed themselves so far.

1. The leader is a position in a group, as are the followers. They are co-constituents in the group. The group is a separate entity and it is implicit in the other two terms. They are interdependent and do not exist without each other. The three are co-constituents in a relationship.
2. The general term 'leadership' is a catch-all general phrase that applies to a relationship between the three parties ra-

ther than describing the one position of 'leader' in the group. It is incorrect to assume that a person in a leader's position automatically forms a relationship that can be described as leadership purely because they occupy the position of a leader in a group. The leader could create another type of relationship, such as a coercive relationship.

3. Leadership is a type of relationship between three parties: the group as a whole, the followers and the leader. Any accurate definition must reference the parties in the relationship to be clear.

4. The relationship is formed on the basis of the perceived value that one party adds to the other. Each of the three parties makes a decision to belong to the group based on the perceived advantages of belonging to the group. The group's members require information before deciding to act in favour of the group's intention. The group's needs must be defined and communicated to the group's members in order to effect the positive action decision from the group's members.

5. The information needed by all parties can be grouped into a series of components that correspond to human motivators. These five components are included in the decision equation and cover the range of commonly accepted human motivators.

6. The decision equation represents the five information package as components and the process to get a decision into action. The decision equation is a tool to help analyse, understand, demonstrate and plan relationships.

7. The decision equation represents the functions of the group members. There is a need to initiate and facilitate the defining of the Gp and communicate it to the group members to help them make a decision to take action in the direction of the Gp. The function of initiating and facilitating the defining and communicating is often done by the leader, although it is not limited to his position.

8. The relationship will change as the group changes in terms of its members and as the components of the decision equation change.

There is a need to initiate and facilitate the defining of the components and to communicate them to the group members. These are functions that are often allocated to the position of leader. The followers in the group need to understand these components as they represent the needs of the group. Often it is the function of a leader to represent the group and be prepared to define and communicate the Gp. The reason why this is done is to get a decision to take action in the direction of that Gp. These logical conclusions allow a draft definition of leadership to be drawn up in order to test and build on. It is not fully developed and will serve as a framework to add to the theory is developed.

'The ability to initiate and facilitate the defining and communication of the Group purpose in order to get a decision from the group members to take action in the direction of that Group purpose.'

Table 17.1 consolidates the terms that have been used in the earlier chapters. The table will be added to in future in order to build a more complete understanding and interpretation of the terms used in the theory of leadership and in forming a definition of leadership. The terms of Maslow's motivators and Herzberg's dual structure theory have been grouped into intrinsic (internal) and extrinsic (external) sections. Terms like *intellectual* and *physical* have been used to further simplify these subgroups section names.

The decision equation is based on the components derived from practical experience and compared to the studies of Maslow and Herzberg. The components also correspond to the subgroup section names. The names of the sections, such as *purpose* and *Group* convey added meaning to the combined components as these are words that are in common use. Using the decision equation as the base, all terms used in future are shown in Table 17.1 in order to clarify what they correspond to in the decision equation.

Table 17.1 A table of terms

Specific Challenge + Reason Why? + Support + Proposed Actions +
Benefits Balance => decision

SC + RY? + SP + PA + BB => d *

The Group purpose (the five components alone) (Gp)

SC + RY?   SP + PA + BB

Purpose (p)   **Group (G)**

Intellectual   Physical

Conceptual   Material assets and actions

Intrinsic   Extrinsic

Frederick Herzberg's Dual structure Theory

Motivators   Hygienic

Abraham Maslow's Motivators

Self-actualisation + Esteem   Love and belonging, Safety, Physiological

Higher order   Lower order

---

*The equations use the directional equals sign (=>); when translated to
common prose it means 'in order to…' get, achieve, allow or commit, or
other verbs used to create the correct prose to explain the reason why the
action is being done. The direction of the arrow indicates the consecutive
nature of the actions of the words: A is done in order to get B. Other mathematical symbols used function as expected in common mathematical equations.

The decision equation components are abbreviated into capital
letters that are representative of the motivators of individuals in the
relationship. They are in capital letters as they can be subdivided
into smaller parts. The 'd' is a result that is specific to that equation
and its components and cannot be subdivided; therefore it is written in lower case, as is the 'p' in purpose.

The Venn diagram in Part 1 is used again as a foundation with added details to display graphically the co-constituents and the decision equation (Figure 17.1). The decision equation is included in order to help visualise the concept and how it all fits together. The decision equation is placed in the leader's position to reflect the generally accepted concept that it is the leader who in principle represents and communicates the group purpose.

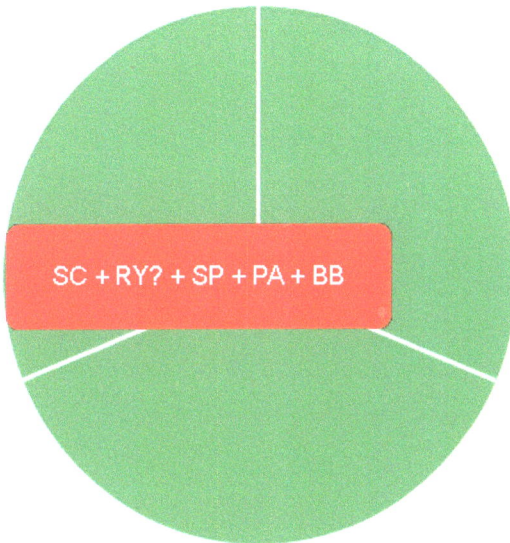

Figure 17.1 Venn diagram 2: inserting the decision equation into the group

The Group still consists of the three parties: the group, the leader and the followers. However, in this second Venn diagram there is a subdivision of the followers into three subgroups, and each subgroup has an element in the leader's group in red. The leader's group may consist of just himself or additional leaders for each of the subunits. This may be labelled in many ways, such as the 'team of leaders', 'the executive committee', 'the group elders' or whatever terms are used in the group. The Gp components are placed in the leaders' red areas in the assumption that it is the leader who usually communicates these components on behalf of the overall group.

PART 4: Communicating the message

Chapter 18: The start point

'The whole is other than the sum of the parts'
Kurt Koffka

Leadership currently goes on all around us, and therefore it should be possible to see how it is done. The component parts of the relationship message have been identified and we see that it is a relationship between the co-constituents. The functions of the leader and the followers have been identified and are explained in earlier chapters as:

'The ability to initiate and facilitate the defining and communication of the Group purpose in order to get a decision from the group members to take action in the direction of that Group purpose.'

It is the act of communicating that message that is the focus of study. Communications is a particularly rich field with a lot of literature in all aspects of human communications. Digital technology has greatly advanced the communications field in terms of efficiency – of that there is no doubt. Whether these technological advances have had such a proportionate difference in the effectiveness of our communications is not so certain.

In the case of boring repetitive messages, where the human was likely to make errors through poor handwriting and reading or tiredness there is no doubt that digital technology, such as the use of bar codes and high-speed digital transmission of data, has reduced the mistakes and increased the efficiency of the information flow. The message is now sent digitally, and in situations where previously a data entry mistake was made then technology is clearly making communication more effective. In contrast, mobile phones allow the individual to be reached almost immediately and repeatedly, but the message being sent may still not motivate. In communications, there is still room for increasing the effectiveness and not needing to rely so much on the efficiencies of digital communications. For example, in our lifetime the efficiency of communications has increased enormously in some types. This represents an efficiency: more information can be passed in a quicker amount of time. More people can be reached for opinions more quickly. A person with a mobile can be called immediately for an opinion and a decision can be taken far away, rather than the person on the ground resolving the challenge as would have had to happen before mobile phones.

In situations where time is important and linked to the venture then speed will also contribute to its effectiveness. Competition and efficient communications systems have led to a centralisation of decision making in some organisations rather than improving the individuals' skills and getting communications to be more effective. Often there is a tendency to move authorisation up the chain of command rather than down it. It would appear that this is the easier option. The speed and efficiency of communications has helped this trend.

There is a similar trend in the thought that business models supply all the necessary information. That this is enough to base decisions on for the group is an interesting and debatable idea. Following this path cuts out the need for intrinsic values to be considered in the process of getting ownership through designing the plan. When the numbers and trends derived from the physical actions and assets are seen as enough to base decisions on for the group from a distance, it creates a specific type of relationship that is different from a daily face-to-face one.

The way in which messages are communications will help determine the nature of the group's relationship. Business plans tend toward graphs, and the focus is on numbers, numbers, numbers. It is easy to become de-linked from the customer, the operations, and any area where the SC and the RY? are important. In order for the effectiveness of the group to improve it is the content of the message that must improve, not necessarily the efficiency of its transmission.

The receiver must be able to derive more meaning and information from the message, both explicit and implicit. The more explicit and complete the better. To ensure that the full message can be conveyed it should be said explicitly, rather than being left to implication and guesswork. To be more effective it must include details of the purpose, and any of the Group section components adds to the knowledge of the proposed actions to be done. The resolving of the SC is the goal and the receiver would need to know this before being to be able to proceed towards the goal. By leaving it to guesswork there is room for interpretation and misunderstanding.

Part of the challenge lies within the human brain and its incredible abilities. It has the ability to assume, to piece things together and to make a whole picture from a few random bits of information. This ability is both friend and foe of the communicator. It is best explained by demonstrating a phenomenon that relates to images to explain it. An image is made up of colours and structures. With a few of the colours or outline structures some can imagine the rest of the picture. This is known as the Gestalt effect. It is well known to most, because they have experienced it even if they do not know its name. Gestalt psychology describes the phenomenon where the brain sees the complete image before the smaller parts are examined in detail. Some examples of Gestalt forms are shown here.

Figure 18.1 Gestalt forms demonstrating reification
Figure 18.2 Gestalt forms demonstrating the law of closure

In Figure 18.1, the triangle, rectangle, sphere and water level are seen by the brain before the brain examines the smaller objects that cause that effect to happen. This effect is known as reification. Similarly, in Figure 18.2 the brain sees the circle and rectangle before examining closely to see that it is not necessarily those shapes but a series of unconnected lines. This phenomenon is known as the law of closure.

These images demonstrate the power of the brain to see things that are not actually drawn. A similar phenomenon exists in language. Often the complete sentence or phrase is predicted ahead of completion and the meaning is understood before the question is complete. Some would say that the brain is jumping to conclusions that are not necessarily there. It does, however, point to a phenomenon that exists in the brain, which is the brain's need for completion or closure.

In Gestalt terms these phenomenon are know as reification and the law of closure only when applied to plans or the reasons why an action is taken. The human brain is filling in the missing components that allow them to make sense of why the actions are being proposed. They are completing the Gp section in order to process their decision in the DAS chain.

Some individuals see the shapes immediately and others will take more time to see them. If you uses your hand to cover the top half of the shape in the two figures, you can see that it will take longer to assume what the shape is. Admittedly once the shape has been seen it is difficult to erase this from the memory and start with a fresh slate, but it does demonstrate the brain's amazing capacity to assume the entire part.

The decision equation is a full assembly of components needed to make a decision. Similar to the Gestalt phenomenon there are individuals who are able to make a decision based on only a few components of the equation. They have experienced or very fast minds and will predict or fill in the gaps in order to move into action as fast as possible.

Some individuals will often be able to work out and assume some of the components of the decision equation without being told them. Some are capable through experience of seeing the whole equation and some are not. Others may not have this ability to predict and see the whole equation. Children often ask why something is being asked of them: they are expressing what they are thinking. Others have been trained, or have learned, not to assume or even ask why.

Gestalt psychologist Max Wertheimer (20) proposed the two main ways of problem solving. One is a 'productive' thinking process where the individual resolves a challenge with a quick reaction which is unplanned and insightful to the challenge presented. This requires practice and a good understanding of the SC and RY? Imagination, good knowledge of fundamental principles and creativity are needed and often prototyping is the only way to be certain of the resolving the SC.

The second way is by 'reproductive' thinking, using previous experiences and what is already known. Individuals often have several segments of information, such as purpose and concept, available to them. By deliberately examining the situation for similarities to other situations they come up with a solution by using solutions that they have experienced, seen or heard before. They are using reproductive thinking. This is a common way of thinking and many companies value this ability by focusing on hiring experienced individuals rather than having to develop productive thinking to solve problems and risk not getting it acceptable first time.

The segments of information the individual uses are based on previous experience or what they have heard or understood. The child has heard that when they are tired they should go to bed to sleep. When told to go to bed the child will respond 'But I am not tired'. The child is filling in the segments of understanding based on previous learning and is debating the need or logic for going to bed. The child wants to know why they are being sent to bed. They are assuming the remaining components in the equation. The human brain and its capacity to assume and create a full overall picture is sometimes helpful and sometimes a hindrance. When individuals are not given the SC and RY? they will often assume them and their brains will make up these segments of information to complete their own overall picture of the process.

The brain is proving to be an incredibly complex in its function and how it has developed to help us survive and thrive. Iain

McGilchrist writes to this effect in his 2009 book *The Mastery and his Emissary – The Divided Brain and the Making of the Western World* [25]. The right hemisphere of the brain will search to find the overall whole picture or situation, and the left hemisphere will then focus on the details of a particular aspect of the picture. It happens in that order as well. The overall situation is assessed first and then the specific parts are focused on.[30] Further understanding of the brain and how it works is progressing rapidly as psychology and neuroscience are revealing how complex the brain is.

Defining the message is very important, and clarity is the key to allowing the message to be understood effectively. The receiver will assess the overall situation and then focus on the specific components, such as the proposed actions or benefits balance. How the components are grouped together and arranged in speech patterns will create further meaning and implications that come from this. The components all relate to each other and this will effect priority, meaning and measurement of effectiveness and efficiencies, as well as lead to other indicators. Who defines and communicates which components will again help determine the specific types of relationships that are formed.

In an established organisation, the defining of the group message is usually performed by the appointed leader. Typically the leader or representative from the larger overall group will present the SC to the subgroup leader. It could alternatively be the customer that presents the challenge directly to the group. In some situations it is down to other group members, such as the sales team, to identify the SC and communicate it to the group leader. The person who has identified an SC to the group must initiate and define the SC in a manner that the group will understand and show how it effects the group and its members. Who does this defining of the SC will be influential on the position of leader and therefore the relationship in the group.

The process of defining and communicating the leadership message is an important one because it will influence the actions and solutions of the group. So far the components of the Gp have been extracted, initiated and defined, usually by the appointed leader in the group. The leader can use the components to define the Gp for his level. The examples used will be in a simple leader–follower positional group where the positional leader defines and communicates the Gp to the followers on behalf of the group.

The traditional hierarchy group, with the leader defining and communicating the Gp, is not always the case in reality. Often the positional leader does not have the technical expertise to define a specific procedure or PA. The components that are not in the area of the leader's technical expertise will be defined by someone who is better qualified. The positional leader, however, is able to represent the group and communicate the Gp. A more detailed look at the way in which the components are assembled and defined in practice will reveal the flexibility of the group in reality and how the decision equation can be used to reflect this application.

The message that is formed for the group is an overall picture and is the full Gp. The Gp is representative of the group entity itself and the thinking and intentions of the group. In theory the Gp explains each component of the group entity as understood by the individuals in the group. It is representative of the group and its members, the co-constituents in the relationship. The decision into action is taken by the individuals, and it is how they interpret and accept (or not) the meaning of the components of the Gp. In practice, team leaders often don't state the purpose and just issue tasks. The individuals receiving the tasks will assume what the purpose is in their own minds or just accept that their boss has already done so and is acting in their and the group's interests. The receiver will make a full Gp in his mind and decide.

The start point of the leader's message is to understand that each individual will have each component defined already in their own minds once the SC or another component is issued. For example, if the leader asks the team members if they would like US $1,000 each, the group members are already trying to work out what they have to do to get it: the PA and BB. The leader should create a full group purpose in order to replace the assumed components in the minds of the individuals in order to get action in a positive direction towards the group's defined purpose, not the individuals' assumed motivators.

Similarly, the Gp is not necessarily formed and completed in one communication or statement. It may take some negotiation and back and forth before a full plan and group purpose is prepared and formalised for the group. In the event that the positional leader is not the one who defines each component, initiation and facilitation in the defining and communication of the Gp will be his main focus, and must be allowed for in any substantial planning process.

The start point of the message will define the relationship in as much as the group members will have an idea of what they as individuals want and need when they join the group. The leaders may have the ability to change the group's needs and to define a path ahead based on how the SC and RY? are perceived. Specifically, how the Gp is created, maintained, defined, communicated and acted upon by the co-constituents is what defines the relationship. It is the process of making the Gp that is the relationship.

Chapter 19: Identifying the messages currently in use

'I couldn't help but be totally honest'

Bob Lutz

Leaders deliver their messages in a number of different ways. The common direct message is sent to complete a simple task. This can be seen in a simple instruction to tell someone or group to do something. 'You and you, take the equipment and chairs and move them to the conference room'. It is as simple in structure as the oft-repeated instruction; 'John, do your homework'. Phrases like these are simple and allow the individual to identify and equate them to the components used in the decision equation.

Example 19.1 Demonstration of translating a phrase into the components of the G section in the decision equation

'You and you, take the projector equipment and chairs and move them upstairs to the conference room'

[– Support – (people and materiel) –] [– Proposed Actions –]

SP + PA

So the support element and the proposed actions components are included in this simple task instruction message.

Example 19.2 A task instruction (G section equation)

'John, do your homework'

[– SP –] + [– PA –]

Example 19.3 has the same basic components as Examples 19.1 and 19.2, yet it adds an incentive to persuade and motivate the individual to make the decision into action.

Example 19.3 A task instruction with benefits as a persuasion (G section equation)

'John, do your homework, and then you can stay up late and watch the television'

[SP] [PA   ] [———— Benefits Balance ————]

SP + PA + BB

The SP and PA are there and the BB is easy to see. The task instruction has now be changed into a task instruction with benefits and it has an implied sequence of events or an order of priority of actions. The sequence, although not the focus of the intention or idea, gives the receiver no doubt as to how the events must unfold and there is also no doubt that the homework must be done. This is a positive persuasion because the action is something that they can do and there is a benefit reward if they do it.

John seems to have placed a higher priority on watching TV rather than learning. The parent controlling the situation has used his higher priority as a way of bribing or persuading John to do the homework. John still has to do the homework. The issue is now control of whether John is allowed to watch the TV. John now perceives to some extent that he is in control of what he can do after doing his homework. There is little change of the task or actual control of the TV and the extrinsic reward is still controlled by the parent.

By adding the word 'If' at the front of the task instruction with benefits, it changes the task instruction with benefits into a task challenge with benefits. There is a reward or extrinsic reward offered for doing the homework.

Example 19.4 A task challenge with benefits as a persuasion (G section equation)

'If you do your homework John, then you can stay up late and watch television'

SP + PA + BB

In Example 19.4 the word 'If' is added at the front and changes the task instruction into a task challenge and this challenge adds an intrinsic value for John. The challenge passes an amount of control of the situation over to John. John is able to control and most importantly engage in the decision process of the group of two as to whether he will be watching the television later or not. He may not know what is on TV, but is motivated just by the challenge of having some control over what he does if he completes his homework.

The task instruction and task challenge appear to be the same at this stage. This is because they are plans and G section equations with no involvement or acknowledgement of the followers. The difference cannot be seen at this stage. The message must be communicated to the group members. Moving it from the plan into a decision is represented by taking a (G or P) section equation into a decision equation.

None of the section equations above has been decided on yet, hence their form with no decision symbol in them. Once the decision is confirmed and made by verbal statement or physical signal, an agreement of some sort is made or more likely an action is taken by starting the homework, and the decision is made and moved into action. Changing it from a G section equation into a decision equation is just a matter of adding the decision symbols.

Example 19.5 Progressing a task instruction with benefits into a decision equation

SP + PA + BB processed into a decision
SP + PA + BB => decision

SP + PA + BB => d

In the case of the task instruction with benefits John was given no choice and was not involved in any defining of the components, just the decision. In the case of the task challenge he has an option of defining the course of action he takes in respect to the Benefit Balance of staying up late and watching TV. This can be shown by placing brackets around the component BB that is being challenged. The process from proposal to decision equation is shown below.

Example 19.6 Progressing a proposed task challenge with benefits into a decision equation

SP + PA + (BB) The Group section proposal with the BB challenge in brackets

Once John indicates through action or expression that he accepts the challenge and makes a decision it progresses to a decision equation, although John has decided the BB component. It is represented as shown below, with the decision that the follower has defined the component shown in brackets (in this case the BB).

SP + PA => d(BB)

Both the task instruction and challenge with benefits in Examples 19.3 and 19.4 are missing two components of the full decision equation created earlier, but they can still get the job done. If this process is used every time, the student may start to believe that the only purpose for doing homework is to stay up late to watch TV, rather than to learn and practice the lessons of the homework. They are equations with their own specific names. The different components and the mix identify the differences.

In Example 19.1, the task instruction of moving the equipment and chairs is a simple one issued to two individuals being referred to as 'you and you'. It is a common form of instruction and does not even refer to their names or titles. They are told to 'take the equipment and chairs upstairs into the conference room'. The SP and PA components are present, but the way in which the individuals are addressed suggests that the leader feels no need to use, or even know, their names or titles.

The implication and perhaps body language, although impossible to see, would indicate that the positional leader doesn't need or want to know them closely. Perhaps the instruction is issued in a rush or more likely the positional leader is so assured of his leadership position in the group that he doesn't doubt that they will unquestioningly follow his instructions.

There is no BB component issued with the task instruction in Example 5. The message's explicit content consists only of SP and PA components. The implied message is also revealing in terms of the relationship between the leader and followers; the respect and position the leader gives to the followers. Agreed there are many factors not known around these exact situations however these examples demonstrates the amount of information that can be gleaned even in a short, simple message. Understanding the explicit and implicit information contained in a message is not new however now it has context in leadership theory.

Much of the information presented in a message is done by implication and is in conjunction with and first seen in the body language. Often it is the body language message which is received first, interpreted and is then confirmed by the content in the leader's task instruction message. In each example 5-10, the leader's message is designed to get a decision from the followers. Specifically it is designed to get the followers to take action in the direction of the message the leader gives. The message is said with words and in a manner that expects agreement.

A message when presented as a task instruction similar to Examples 19.1–19.6 expects the followers to make decisions on the explicitly expressed PA. The followers will also interpret the way the message is delivered. The followers may choose to include whether they like the implication of the message regarding their perceived place in the group. Are they being adequately recognised? Are they placed in the group at a level they expect? How are they valued by the group and the leader?

In this situation where the leader only ever speaks to his followers in terms of actions and asset-based components in a task instruction, the message will get either compliance or non-compliance with his task. The leader may consider the messages are all the same no matter how it is sent. From a leader's point of view the response will be either positive or negative, as a non-action or delay in decision is not in the direction of the task requested. The response could be said to be binary in that it is positive (1) or negative (0).

This is a very simple overview, as humans have found many different ways of responding to demands, requests and challenges. The options will present themselves as a whole range between the binary position of positive (1) and negative or non-action (0). The degree of compliance and the amount of time the decision takes are variables, even though in the end the decision will be 1 or 0. The decision process will effect how the actions are done and this will affect the solution. The decision process and how it comes about is the start of the DAS chain. The decision needs to be a value of 1 in order to move forward into positive action and to obtain a solution to the SC initially presented.

In everyday tasks such as outlined in Examples 19.1–19.6 it may seem time-consuming and unnecessary for the leader to have to mention the SC and RY? The group is choosing to resolve the SC in a statement that reflects all five components of the decision equation. This is a choice the leader makes. This has been demonstrated earlier in the case of the Army orders formats: they do not reiterate all of the benefits each time they issue a set of orders. However, the Army orders format is very clear on what must be said and how it is said; the purpose is always stated, for example. A positional leader in other groups has the option of what to include, unless of course their procedures dictate otherwise.

Of course how leaders communicate the message in terms of words used and tone, pitch, speed and body language, will effect how it is interpreted. In the case of John doing his homework it is unlikely that each time John's parents set a new task they are doing so in this format in order to condition John to linking the PA directly to the BB, over time it just happens. By repeating this process of short-cutting to the BB the mind is trained and those who receive the message become like Pavlov's dog. Similar to Gestalt, where the complete equation is searched for, the first thought will be to look for the BB possible to them rather than the purpose behind it. If repeated in this format often enough, John is in effect being trained to link the proposed actions directly with the physical benefits. He is being conditioned.

Soon enough followers stop asking why and indeed may even stop thinking in terms of adding value to an action. Any actions that are proposed are seen as the only path to benefits and the benefits become the exclusive reason for taking any action. Effectively, the individuals become de-linked from any purpose and intrinsic concerns of the group. The DAS chain is weakened if not broken at the early stage of the decision-making process. Thinking patterns become habits and (as can be proven by experiment and experience) habits can be hard to break.

In companies and large organisations the BB component is represented partially by contracts, agreements and salaries, amongst other things. These are not renegotiated each time a task is set. To leave out the BB component is a common practice in the issue of a normal routine action proposal. Often already established benefits are only reiterated when a task of special risk or unusual circumstance presents itself, or when they are changed.

This is true in many groups, not just the military. It is not necessary to explicitly mention the component if this component remains unchanged. This is the advantage of long-term contracts and understandings established in the group. They are regarded as standard conditions that apply by the co-constituents. Indeed some conditions are considered so standardised that if they are mentioned in a routine briefing then the followers will be suspicious that they are being changed.

In the case of the SC and RY? components, leaders, by consistently linking the actions to resolving the SC of the customer, are focusing the group on the purpose. This repeated linking reminds all in the group of the Gp. If the leader links actions directly to BB the followers would have cause to question the leader's commitment to the Gp, and therefore so can they. A constant reminder to save costs and reduce expenditure will eventually prioritised over resolving the SC at the front end of the equation.

The components that form the Group section in the decision equation are important as they outline the actions being proposed and who is to carry out these actions, and what equipment and support they have to help the complete these actions. The three Group section components, however, do not make up the complete decision equation and therefore they are not the complete message, as it does not address the SC and RY? that the Group section components are based on. Decisions based on actions and assets are the short-cut message of a leader. The positional leader has decided for the followers that it is quicker to get action going and base a decision on trust in their boss and not have to include other tedious time-consuming intrinsic factors such as such as esteem and self-actualisation in the equation.

Bob Lutz, the former Vice President of General Motors (GM), has written about this extensively in numerous articles. His book, called *Car Guys vs Bean Counters* [26] is specifically devoted to this subject. The actions of the GM factory bosses during the 1990s focused directly on the BB that could be achieved by adjusting the PA in engineering and production rather than catering for the demand or SC presented by the customer. The cars they were making were designed with production cost savings and economies of scale in mind, such as using the same chassis and parts for different cars in order to get maximum economies of scale.

While cost control is very important in business, the design and appearance of the cars that GM produced at the time suited no group of customers, just a theoretical Mr Average (if there is such a thing). The market research had amalgamated all the market demands into an average and produced a 'jack of all trades' vehicle that nobody wanted. Bob Lutz contends that the GM organisation had changed and had become ruled by a group of bean counters who only looked at the numbers and forgot about the design appeal to the different market sectors.

The cars produced at GM during the 1990s were a strange hybrid stuck in the middle of the market demand sectors, and hence did not sell well. Under his leadership GM underwent a refocus to regain the link to the customer's SC and restructured itself to become the success story it once was. The refocus of the company, with a priority on the 'car guys' who linked the designs and therefore factory actions to the customers' demands, was his stated reason for GM's recovery at that time.

There are other automobile industry specialists who do not agree with this, and point to Alan Mulally a former executive with Boeing, who was hired by Ford as their president. They suggest that Ford survived the recent crisis precisely because they listened to the bean counters and were able to restructure their debt and work their way back out of the situation he inherited. The bean counters were able to slash and restore the balance of spending in line with the SC of the customers, represented by successful cars and the revenue they derived from them [27].

The broken business models in both cases were due to the same lack of focus on the SC and RY? Both components had been reduced in priority. In GM's case they were forgotten as the focal point for the actions or were just wrong and therefore ineffective for the market. In Ford's case they had been abandoned as a means to justify and focus the G section components on, and were therefore inefficient. In both cases the companies had become de-linked from the Group purpose. Both Bob Lutz and Alan Mulally[31] refocused their groups on the purpose and this focus was what led to the improvements in their situations.

Chapter 20: A more effective message

'To effectively communicate, we must realize that we are all different in the way we perceive the world and use this understanding as a guide to our communication with others.'

Anthony Robbins

In practice, the complete five-component decision equation message is not always used. It is not necessary in all situations, although it is important to ensure that the message does not become de-linked in the overall process. A leader has a number of different ways to do this in order to be effective at communicating his message. There are many situations that require the need for more information to be presented to the followers in order to allow them to make a decision into action in the direction of the group's purpose. Example 19.1 (copied below) is used to demonstrate the need for more than just the two group components in a simple task instruction:

Example 20.1 Repeated Example 19.1

'You and you, take the projector equipment and chairs and move them upstairs to the conference room'

[– Support – (people and materiel) –] [– Proposed Actions –]

This task instruction may be enough to get the chairs and equipment upstairs, and the leader may well at this stage leave to attend to another aspect of his work and trust the followers to get on and complete the proposed actions. Indeed, after issuing the task instruction the leader departs, and the followers may set about the task with enthusiasm. The scenarios below demonstrate the difference that stems from a different method.

Scenario 1 – The followers switch off the projector, pile it and the wires on the chairs, and start moving them out of the downstairs room, down the corridor and up the stairs. On reaching the upstairs conference room they find that the room is locked. They place the chairs with the projector equipment outside the door in the upstairs corridor. Thinking their task is complete they head off to lunch. The leader arrives an hour later with a VIP at the upstairs conference room to find the chairs and projector equipment placed neatly outside the conference room and the door locked. The VIP suggests that the time needed to get the presentation sorted would make him late for another appointment and they agree to postpone. Who was at fault? Both sides would like to blame the other in the heat of the moment, but the message that the leader gave the followers could have been more effective.

This example of how ineffective communications can be when situations change is deliberately simple and is set at a level that, while it may not seem that important, is typical of many situations that get put down to a miscommunication or that the blame lies with followers who do not think. The leader assumed that the upstairs conference room would be open or that the followers would appreciate the need to get it open and do so. The followers of course did what they were asked, and in their opinion, given the circumstances, they did the best they could.

The followers had no idea that the projector equipment was needed for a VIP presentation and of course had no idea of the time factors involved and therefore no sense of urgency was attached to the task, let alone having any ownership towards its completion as perceived by the leader. Without going into who is to blame for this result it is clear that a better solution exists – but how to achieve it?

A better solution for this typical situation already exists and can be found quickly using the decision equation. The SC has not been met because of a change in the predicted environment. The original assumption by the leader was that the room would not be locked, and when the door is found to be locked the assumed environment has changed, requiring a second corrective action to achieve the Gp. However, the leader is not present to make the decision and issue a new task instruction to resolve it. The result is Scenario 1.

Situations change, and when the consequences are much more serious the need for corrective action is often immediate, such as when lives are in danger. Unpredicted situations present themselves commonly in war, fires, car accidents, floods, tsunamis, earthquakes and many other similar events. There is a need for corrective action because of the change of circumstances, and the consequences of inaction place lives at further risk. The normal group leader is not always present to order that corrective action, lives are potentially at risk, and the situation has suddenly become much more serious.

The solution, fortunately, is the same and is already in use in some groups. Some groups plan ahead for changes in circumstances and give the information necessary to allow both followers and leaders to take decisions for corrective actions to happen, according to the situation. It is the leader's original message that must change to cope with this unexpected situation. The leader's message needs to be different from the example issued before to allow for the unexpected.

The SC and RY? components can help provide direction in this unexpected situation. The leader needs to define the purpose as a minimum. Although we have seen that while it is not necessary to state all of the components every time, in order to allow for changing circumstances it is necessary to state the purpose in the message that the leader gives. The earlier example must change to one that allows the followers to understand the leader's intentions more effectively.

In the military this is done in their battle orders. The formal orders set consists of at least four of the components of the decision equation, with an emphasis placed on the SC and RY? These components are stated explicitly, and in a sequence that each soldier commits to memory, developing a habit of using the terms. The decision equation follows a military orders sequence and the

Maslow's hierarchy order, and as a consequence ensures that the necessary components, and therefore the corresponding motivators, are covered.

This sequence of orders and levels of hierarchy, however, does not follow the normal sequence of human speech patterns. There are many different ways that humans communicate a message in everyday speech. The grammar and patterns are arranged such that when using the decision equation components it can appear cumbersome and not make sense, so the message is put in other formats. The components are rearranged to suit common speech patterns and can be identified in different ways, such as the already seen 'Task Instruction'.

Followers who are part of the military process are trained to receive instructions in the format of orders and to act on this type of message. Leaders of all groups have the option and already use a format of instruction in which they can identify the components of a decision equation.

Example 20.2 The standard decision equation based on patterns used in military orders formats

The decision equation is based on the orders sequence and is addressed to the whole group and therefore addresses the purpose of all group members first.

$$SC + RY? + SP + PA + BB = decision$$

Purpose section and a Group section added together
Purpose added to a Task instruction with a Benefits Balance

$$(SC + RY?) + (SP + PA + BB) \Rightarrow decision$$

The followers get used to the pattern and work with the existing system. Outlined in Example 20.3 is a format which is couched inside the orders format, called a mission statement. This format encompasses all of the necessary components of the decision equation, in particular the purpose components of SC and RY? However, the sequence is different. This is because it is designed to address individuals and be very specific in its focus for individuals. The purpose, SC + RY?, is inserted after the SP and PA components. BB is last as it only comes about after the SC is achieved.

The SP is placed first to ensure that all are listening and focused and the mission is designed to addresses the specific individual in the group as if the orders group were for them specifically. The PA of that group follows next, then the other components. The sequence has changed and therefore the individual is being reminded of the sequence of events and priorities.

Example 20.3 The mission statement format

SP + PA => SC => RY? => BB => decision

Below is the earlier Example 20.1 with the projector equipment being moved. As a Mission statement it would read like this:

'You and you are to take the projector equipment and chairs (SP) and move them upstairs to the conference room (PA), in order to allow me to give a VIP presentation at 1300 hours, in one hour's time (SC), in order to get their support for the changes we want to make to the communications systems (RY?), in order to help make it easier for us to work more effectively together and improve Internet access for everybody, including you (BB).'

This statement has used all five of the components of the decision equation. The phrase used to join the components is 'in order to…'.

The order of the components in this sentence starts with the SP and PA in order to get the attention of the individuals in the group being addressed. To put the SP and PA components at the beginning is in line with normal speech patterns used. These components are quickly followed by the SC, RY? and BB results. The SP and PA at the front helps reinforces what the leader wants them, as individuals in the group, to do specifically. Inserting the purpose into the task instruction is an act that links the PA to the purpose of the group. Only after these important components are stated is the final component, BB, added in to the statement to confirm sequence and priority.

The mission statement is very specific and explicit in its nature. A simple task instruction has been given purpose. By changing its sequence to have SP first it is making the actions and purpose specific to the individual in the group. The sentence has also given the whole process, by implication, a sequence that the follower should understand that will resolve the challenge first by the subsequent actions; then and only then can the benefits be achieved, in that order. As a decision equation it can now be recognised as a Group with a purpose.

The mission statement lists the target group tasked (SP) to complete an action (PA), with a reason why (RY?) the action is being proposed. This seems like repetition, perhaps, as within the orders format as the mission statement comes after the Situation, which has already mentioned these components. The situation paragraph already contains the SC and RY? the group is formed at the larger group levels. The mission statement is specific to the group of the leader listed in the mission statement and is a subgroup when compared to those covered in the Situation paragraph. These subunits are given their own tasks within this larger plan. This is a reinforcement of the hierarchy and value chain in the grouping system.

All groups and subgroups know their positions in the hierarchy and the part they play in the larger group's plan of action. This knowledge of the part they play imparts the value they have to the overall group; they feel that they are an important part in the plan. They know their larger group's names, resources and equipment that they can expect at the larger group levels, and that they could possibly receive or call upon if and when needed.

The mission statement in an orders format covers all five components again, but at the level specific to the group listed in the mission statement. It may seem over-elaborate to repeat this, but it is very specific for this particular group, whereas the Situation paragraph deals with their group but at a higher level. Placing the SP and PA at the front for the mission statement makes it individual to each member of the group at that level.

There is extra thought required to define the SC and RY? in order to make it specific to their level. The RY? explains why their subgroup is chosen to resolve the SC at their level. When a leader regularly states the SC and RY? components, it demonstrates that he is focused on the purpose of the actions and in turn can expect or even demand the followers to at the very least understand why they are being asked to perform the actions proposed.

The purpose can be seen by implication as a confirmation that the operation is a 'just' one, according to the group: it is justified or sanctioned by and is in the interests of the group. The whole group benefits by their actions. The Gp reinforces the group's needs and reminds the group members of their obligation to the group. This in turn places a value on their work in the group and therefore a value on them being in the group. Maslow's third level motivator of love and belonging is brought into play as well as reinforcing some of the safety and physiological levels that the group provides. There are additional and very significant advantages to including the purpose in an instruction.

The mission statement creates different additional options for actions in the event of the unexpected situation. Take, for example, the scenario with the projectors and equipment at the upstairs locked conference room door. When presented with the unpredicted situation of the locked door, the followers with a full mission statement, as given in Example 20.3, could well have taken a different course of action.

Scenario 2. The two followers, on arriving upstairs and finding the room locked, park the chairs and equipment beside the door and stop to assess their options, knowing they cannot reach the leader. One of the two quickly looks at his watch and states that lunch is being served in the canteen and looks at the new follower. The new follower, who had been listening carefully to the leader, suggests they had better quickly find the key and get the equipment set up before it gets too late for lunch. He quickly checks the administrator's office downstairs, but that door is also locked with a sign on the door that read 'Out to Lunch – Closed from 12:00 to

1:30'. They quickly work out that he won't be back before the VIP's conference will start. One follower opts to leave the equipment and goes for lunch. The second follower stays and decides that he will use the old room downstairs and set up the projectors and equipment ready for the VIP briefing, now due to start in 35 minutes.

At the appointed time the leader arrives at the upstairs conference room with the VIP. The leader reads a sign on the locked door that reads:

'Conference room locked, please use conference room downstairs Room 15'.

The leader ushers the VIP towards the stairs while putting on a big confident smile to the VIP, attempting to conceal the alarm bells that are starting to go off inside his head. On arriving at the downstairs conference room the second follower has the projector and equipment set up in the same place as before and is trying to transfer the picture from the computer to the connected projector. The follower, quickly realising that the leader has arrived, leaves the projector temporarily and states confidently that:

'This conference room was the only one available, and although I am having technical problems syncing the laptop with the projector, other than that, all is ready for the VIP briefing.'

Turning to the VIP he asks:

'Would you like a coffee or water sir, while the equipment setup is being sorted?'

The leader quickly assesses the situation, confirms with the VIP and orders two coffees. The leader then quickly follows up with a big smile, asks the name of the new follower (Mr Chen) and thanks him for his quick thinking and excellent work. He sets about pushing the appropriate buttons on the laptop to complete the presentation transfer to the screen and ready for the presentation to get under way.

The results are very different – the message was very different. The more complete message from the leader has allowed at least one follower to display his initiative because all the components he needed were included in the message. The components used are the explicit difference. The implicit difference is that the new follower, Mr Chen, was able to make decisions to take action in a direction that he knew would help achieve the aim of the leader making a presentation to the VIP without having been told what to do. It was not the desired conference room, and Mr Chen took a risk. Mr Chen went with a solution to the SC and RY? that he knew he could action and achieve.

The actions of Mr Chen were definitely counter to the proposed actions to put the equipment upstairs, as instructed by the leader, but they were in the direction of the leader's intention to give the VIP a briefing towards improving communications and thereby team effectiveness, at the appointed time. The message in the second scenario was certainly longer, but more importantly it had the essential ingredient of the purpose added to it. Mr Chen, when presented with an unpredicted situation, was able to take corrective action in the direction of the overall intention of the leader. The new situation was not expected and the leader was not there to give the corrective action instruction needed to be effective in the overall plan.

A situation in which someone is able to take action in the correct direction without being told what to do describes an action that is called an initiative. Mr Chen took the initiative when corrective action was needed. He took action in the direction of the Gp without having been told what to do. The Scenario 1 PA related to a very different location than that which was used to complete the overall plan. In Scenario 2 it was the SC and RY? the conference room was needed that made the instruction effective. The purpose of the actions was clear in Mr Chen's mind. He took initiative actions that were directed by the purpose rather than the original PA. It was not the location proposed, but it did resolve the specific challenge presented to the group. Well done Mr Chen – and the leader owes him lunch.

An initiative action without instructions is not without the risk of incorrect action being taken. It is possible that an individual might take action in the wrong direction, such as break the door open to achieve the Scenario 2 results in the originally planned conference room. The initiative taken would have achieved its objective, but would have shown the VIP the culture of the group in a different, perhaps less favourable light: a view of a broken door. The need to ensure that the initiative is taken in the right direction places further emphasis on why the leader should be explicit about the purpose of his plan. If the leader does not express the purpose of the plan, then it is left to the creative juices and assumptions of the followers to guess what the leader's intention behind the PA was; alternatively they do nothing except the explicitly stated PA of the task instruction.

The element that purpose introduces to the message of the leader can be seen in the actions taken by the followers. It is more than just playing with words. It is the implications for the Group section components, and in particular in this scenario the PA, that creates the environment for the higher level motivators, such as esteem, self-actualisation and problem solving, to take place. It creates the opportunity for those who do have the capacity and desire to fulfil their need for the higher level motivators, such as recognition and solving problems.

Some individuals have a path to aspire to achieve more than just extrinsic motivators. When these qualities are actively encouraged and rewarded, the followers have the potential to achieve these higher levels for the group and for themselves. It is in the process of decision making in the group that the positive or negative decision value can be reached more quickly and the action can be directed to a solution that is linked to the SC that the group was created to resolve. The group can be more effective in its purpose.

There are those who are dominated by intrinsic motivators. What they do must be seen by others as morally right. The driving force behind doing something is that it is the right or 'just' thing to do. Those who think like this are more focused on the SC and RY? itself rather than the PA and BB that are presented. The purpose of getting the best solution to the challenge is important.

Mr Chen's focus was on doing the right thing for the group and getting a solution to the SC as presented by the leader in his mission statement. The follower who went to lunch before resolving the SC was at that time dominated by extrinsic rewards and the call for lunch. This first follower was happy to merely complete the task. Scenario 2 presents a message where the behaviour of one of the followers was radically different than in Scenario 1. By a slight change in the message the opportunity can be created.

The indifference of the leader to the followers or inexperience of the leader does not excuse the leader from creating the environment for those who may or may have the capacity and confidence to act. For a leader to limit the potential of the group members is detrimental or even counter to the whole group performance, and therefore contrary to the purpose of the leader.

Chapter 21: Initiative and ownership

'Every child is an artist. The problem is how to remain an artist
once we grow up'

Pablo Picasso

Situations in which the circumstances change are frequent. When
they occur there are options open to the followers in the absence of
the leader. The simple option is no action beyond those proposed
by the leader in the original task instruction or mission statement.
This is a scene that plays itself out often in the work environment.
It is a reflection of the group and its leader–follower relationship.
This alone justifies the inclusion of the purpose in the message. It
allows some form of corrective action to be taken in the event of
change. It is not, however, the only reason for including the purpose in the message.

In a task instruction there is no explicit expectation for intrinsic
understanding or thought outside of the three Group section components. Children observe and copy, not fully understanding but
appreciating that these actions are done by their role models and
that these task instructions work (or at least they worked on them).
Task instructions are often the first type of PA that followers are
introduced to. They come first because they occur in the first group
that an individual ever belong to: the family. Parents of family
groups instruct their children; from there, individuals encounter
other groups, such as classrooms for education, teams for sports,
neighbourhood kids, school friends for social engagements, rela-
tives and parent's friend's children. Later, their main groups occur
at university and work, and there are other group memberships that
form the experience the individual has with group dynamics and
interactions between group constituents.

Even at an early age children will ask questions about all manner of things. There is an inbuilt desire to know why they are being
asked to do this or that. Humans seem hard wired to inquire about
the challenges that cause them to have to do a proposed action.

With such an inquiring mind one might question the need for teachers to tell children anything. Why not just answer and guide their questions to the point where they can learn the knowledge needed by society? Children seem to be constantly looking for the SC and RY? to complete the whole picture in their mind. It allows them to move forward in order to focus on the actions.

Herein lies the difference between learning by rote and learning through comprehension. By comprehension the challenge is understood and adjusted for in the actions. The group is taken into consideration when formulating the message. Complex problems, with purpose as a priority, present options for actions that will result in benefits if the challenges are resolved. The purpose creates a group-based sense of priorities and a way to evaluate whether the actions are appropriate or not.

When purpose is included a different reward and recognition system is in play. With purpose, explicitly stated intrinsic values become part of the expectation for recognition in the group. The lessons being learned are not the completion of the task, but the ability to solve the ethical or prioritised issue and the resolution of the challenge.

Task instructions work at all levels for simple situations, and while they may achieve the PA and benefits are awarded, the message is one way and the intrinsic and explicit group-related issues of specific challenge and reason why are not factored into the equation. The task may be so simple that it is not necessary to remind everyone of its importance to the group: it is an assumption on the part of those issuing the task instruction. The SC and RY? are group-related components with no implied depth for comprehension needed other than the self-esteem and recognition of knowing that the SC has been resolved.

The military spends a lot of time training soldiers' thinking processes to ensure that it is the SC that is being addressed, not just the PA. The orders format and the process of delivering the orders is the formalisation and structure for this process. The military constructs the format of orders and mission statements and teaches people how to extract, make and repeat them in the correct sequence, even demonstrating the pitch, tone and body language to use where possible. Assessments are done on the young leader's ability to present orders and the level of clarity they bring to those listening.

The procedures to extract a set of orders are learned, and while not studied with respect to how to motivate decisions, battle procedure is learned in order to extract orders correctly and issue good clear orders with the aim of getting the front line soldier into action with the minimum waste of time and fuss, knowing what they are required to do and how they are to do it. Few organisations dedicate the time to this level of training on the interaction of their groups. The process does change the way the individual thinks. Soldiers become purpose-driven rather than task-driven. It also creates the potential for initiative and creativity of solutions.

This statement may surprise those who only have a surface knowledge of the military and its processes. Few expect initiative when used in reference to the military: a perception so widely that held some believe it to be a contradiction in terms when the words 'military' and 'initiative' are in close proximity.

The definition of initiative is an action taken without having been told to do so. In the dictionary it is given a number of situations; for example, a legal initiative is to originate legislature without being prompted by others. Other examples given are 'a first step, origination'[32] and 'on one's own initiative without being prompted by others', and the phrase 'to take the initiative' is explained to be the first to take action. It is specific to an action taken before another has suggested or proposed it. This is a simple definition of what initiative is.

This simple definition of initiative does, however, present limitations in the theory of leadership. An individual can take action without being told what to do, such as steal a wallet or leave their workplace station in order to do something else and thereby cause the production line to stop. These are initiatives in the strict definition of the word, but would not be described as positive or in favour of the wallet owner or the factory production line team and customers they were producing for. This simple explanation needs further definition in order to be more applicable to the theory of leadership, which applies to groups not individuals. In leadership theory discussions the initiatives taken should be in the interests of the group being analysed. The initiatives being sought in groups are initiatives taken in the direction of the group's interests. Initiative taken in the direction of the group's interests can be defined as positive initiative actions. Many individuals want to possess the ability to take or create positive initiatives in the group, and recognition for it and the value it adds to the group is a desired goal. Like leadership, positive initiative actions are results. The challenge is in knowing what path must be followed to achieve this result. A second crossword solution has been entered, without the clues to finding the route to obtain it.

Using a similar approach to the one used for discovering the path to leadership, the foundation stones of positive initiative are in the basic building blocks of knowledge and bits of information now known as components. Initiative is linked to a term which Michael Polanyi called 'tacit knowledge'. His book *The Tacit Dimension* was published in 1966 and is based on his Terry Lectures delivered to Yale University some four years before [29]. He describes a situation in which 'we can know more than we can tell'[33] – a paradox it would seem. He calls this knowledge 'tacit knowing' or 'tacit knowledge' in his book. It is this knowledge that can be used to get initiative decisions and action.

Polanyi's lectures go into great depth on the nature of knowledge itself at a philosophical level and he details two types of knowledge that are known and understood. One is proximal knowledge, which we have in practical terms by experience of touch and direct contact, and the second is distal knowledge, which is based on knowledge gained through another party or extension, and yet to be directly experienced. These types of knowledge are very much linked to where one is positioned in the overall scheme of things.

The example he uses is the game of chess. The knowledge of the rules and the structure of the board and pieces is proximal knowledge. The knowledge of how to control the game of chess is distal knowledge and describes what it is to understand the comprehensive meaning and implications of the rules and how to apply these rules in a game.

The two types of knowledge are separate and within a relationship at different levels. There is a link between the two different types of knowledge, and that is the subject being analysed. Polanyi uses the difference to explain some of the situations that exist around us, such as the link between physics, chemistry and engineering. They are different sciences: from one point of view engineering includes the operational principles of machines and some knowledge of physics that is relevant to these machines. This is proximal knowledge where the purpose of the machine is understood and known by close contact with the design and purpose of the machine.[34]

When the machine breaks down, it is physics and chemistry that tell us why the parts have broken; this is distal knowledge for the engineer. By combining the two types of knowledge the engineer gains a tacit knowledge of the purpose of the machine, and the engineer's distal knowledge of the physics and chemistry of the parts will give him the ability to tell us if the parts are suitable in achieving the purpose of the machine. The two types of knowledge combine in the engineer to form the tacit knowledge needed, or the tacit knowing, as it is also referred to by Michael Polanyi.

It is this linking of the two types of knowledge, or tacit knowledge, that can be used to describe the knowledge needed in order to create positive initiatives. For the follower the knowledge of the actions to be done by the follower is proximal and the direction in which the action should be taken, otherwise known as the purpose of the group, is distal. It is this understanding of the link and relationship between the two sections, the Group and purpose, that creates the tacit knowledge that can be used to describe initiative. This tacit knowledge affects two levels in leadership theory.

An individual may have both the distal and proximal knowledge of a situation to form his own tacit knowledge of the situation. Simple tasks where the individual has both the distal and proximal knowledge can often be performed by the individual. To resolve the challenge of hunger the individual gets and eats some food. To get warm, the individual puts on more clothing, adds another log to the fire or simply turns up the heating. These challenges are resolved by the individual and the training in these challenges starts early. Parents train individuals to dress, feed, and look after themselves to varying degrees. This store of individual level tacit knowledge is added to as they become more experienced in managing themselves. The tacit knowledge learning curve is steep to begin with at home, and continues at university or in the first few years after leaving home, and further on as individuals join new groups and progress through life. This is called individual tacit knowledge.

The second level of tacit knowledge is where the individual has one type of knowledge (for example proximal knowledge) and they have a vague idea about further proximal knowledge and believe there should be an opportunity to link the two to achieve a new idea or solution to a challenge. It requires the one party with the proximal knowledge and minimal further proximal knowledge to believe it possible to resolve the challenge and go about finding those that know how to complete the tacit knowledge picture. Steve Jobs, the founder of Apple, understood the SC of the customers who used computers and devices. He knew it so well that he seemed to know it better than the customers themselves. He defined the SC and set about finding those with expertise to complete the Gp that combined his proximal and their proximal knowledge to make the group's tacit knowledge complete.

Jobs knew (or believed) that he could find people to finance and assemble equipment well enough to resolve the SC that he identified in the customers. He initiated and facilitated the defining and communicating of the Gp in order to achieve a solution for the SC and in the process achieved his dream of solving the SC: his dream. He founded an empire based on his ability to get others to understand his tacit knowledge, which allowed them to take the plan into action.

Henry Ford [24], the motor car magnate, was another individual who had was able to initiate and facilitate a situation where he created the group tacit knowledge required to resolve an SC that he defined. He is reported to have said of his customers (although there is no evidence to back this up):

'If I asked the customers what they wanted, they would have said they wanted a faster horse'[35]

It is, however, a common finding that customers do not necessarily know what they want specifically. Some do not know at all. Using the adage as a guide we will assume that it was said by Ford in order to provide a focal point, as he would have had to specify the challenge of the customers at some stage.

He was able to define the SC more specifically and communicate his ideas and plan to others well enough for them to contribute their expertise to get the individual from A to B more quickly (and at least as comfortably and economically) than a horse. As an economist, and knowing the customers' SC, he battled and gathered the necessary finance, engineering and marketing skills to achieve his dream of a Model T Ford car that was affordable to most. Both Jobs, and perhaps Ford, initiated and facilitated the tacit knowledge in the group to be able to define and communicate the Gp as an actionable plan to others in order to get the group to put them into action.

Group tacit knowledge, as demonstrated earlier in the case of moving the projector for the VIP presentation, can be created in everyday situations. The leader can create an opportunity where one party can possess a proximal knowledge of one type of knowledge and a partial knowledge of the other. Presenting it to the group co-constituents in the form of an idea may find other co-constituents in the group who can complete the partial knowledge type and form the group's tacit knowing. The group then possesses both types of knowledge, in the purpose and the actions needed to resolve that particular SC.

Perhaps at this stage it is better defined as a tacit belief until it becomes proven as tacit knowing or knowledge. This is the function of R&D teams working with a defined SC and combining it with their proximal knowledge of the product or service creation to form a solution. This process is not, however, limited to the R&D teams, as each team member will be deficient in one or more of the components in a DAS chain. It is something that every group must do to achieve the maximum from the group co-constituents in all groups.

Tacit knowledge acts on two levels. The first level is where both the distal and proximal are contained in the individual; the second is where the tacit knowledge, either distal or proximal, comes from different members of the group and combines in an individual to cause an initiative. The combination of the two types of knowledge creates the potential for positive initiatives towards a resolution of the SC. Individuals may or may not act in the group direction based on the individual and the situation. The situation may force an initiative action or they may have the confidence to do so based on the group relationship, or are inclined to do so because it is the 'right' thing to do for the group or individual depending on their priorities. These priorities are the results of experience, cultural conditioning and individual motivations within the group.

Leaders focus on creating and developing group tacit knowledge as leaders are fundamentally concerned with groups. They focus on ensuring that the group members focus their initiatives towards the resolution of the group's SC rather than their individual needs. Individuals who have experience of both types of knowledge are usually labelled 'experienced' and are capable of taking positive initiatives before they are told to do so. Once they do so they are more likely to be confident in taking another initiative. The key is that the leader chooses individuals who place the resolution of the group's SC above the individual's needs and is recognised for doing so, even if the initiative does not always result in the final solution. Creating and using tacit knowledge in groups is the basis for better solutions and discovery.

A positional leader in a group has the opportunity to create an environment in which the followers have a tacit knowledge of the overall situation by stating explicitly the purpose of the group. It is often the followers who already know the action aspects of the plan – they just need what for them is the distal knowledge of the SC and RY?

Ownership of a positive initiative action is often quickly claimed by the individuals themselves or others wanting the recognition. Whether it is described as a concept, idea, plan or tacit knowledge, it is the expression of the idea or putting into action of that idea that is proof of ownership. Trademarks, copyrights and intellectual property protection are much contended issues between groups. In some cases the goal is to create market entry barriers and financial benefits, while in others it is purely recognition that the group or individual is after. An initiative is a motivation in that it is a method of achieving recognition. Each initiative will have an ownership claim on it to some degree.

In motivational terms an initiative is the proof of ownership of that tacit knowledge. The individual or group that expressed the idea or took it into action is the owner of the tacit knowledge. This link between initiative and ownership in some cases is very personal and strong.

Michael Polanyi's SC is that 'we can know more than we can tell' and goes on to suggest that this statement would seem to be a paradox, and thus make it a challenge. In *Meno*, Plato explains that if all knowledge is explicit, i.e. capable of being clearly stated, then we cannot know a problem or look for its solution. Plato goes on to explain, logically, that if problems nevertheless exist, and discoveries can be made by solving them, we can know things, and important things, that we cannot tell [31]. In solving his this paradox Polanyi specified the different types of knowledge and identified the combination of the two as tacit knowledge, and the way to explain it.

Combining Gestalt psychology and tacit knowledge would lead one to understand that humans are naturally inclined to 'fill in the gaps'. This may be what causes curiosity and desire to know something. It leads to individuals accumulating knowledge of one type or another. Using that knowledge to good effect is about knowing which packets to combine and how to communicate them. The amount that is accumulated is phenomenal, as is the way in which we use it. The patterns of thought become habits and are unknown to us, and as these patterns are subsumed into our non-conscious thought framework and actions they become automatic responses.

Michael Polanyi's statement that 'we can know more than we can tell' is very true, and leadership is a good example of what seems to be a paradox. Leadership is recognised when it is seen, but is not possible to define. By using this knowledge and focusing on how the components are assembled it is possible to discover and define the different relationship. There, within, it will be more likely to be able to distinguish the relationship that best suits the common perception of leadership and prove that 'we can know more than we call tell'.

Chapter 22: Combining initiative, ownership and decisions

'Never tell people how to do things. Tell them what to do and they will surprise you with their ingenuity.'

General George Patton

Initiative and the path to it are understood as a combination of two types of knowledge, distal and proximal, which form tacit knowledge. This combination creates the potential for an initiative action to take place. How can this be put into practice, repeated, planned, analysed and taught to others? The decision equation can be used to plan and demonstrate the environment in which initiative can occur. The ability to create initiative will allow individuals to practice the process of taking the initiative and give them confidence to do so when unpredicted situations occur in future.

Practice and confidence in the process of using tacit knowledge-derived initiative abilities lead to greater experience in producing different actions and solutions. The benefits that come are seen in the form of trust, loyalty, confidence, innovation and creativity. All of these terms are results that are based on the nature of the relationship in the group. Practising and proving initiative builds these terms, which apply to the relationships between the leaders and followers.

Practice and planning for the situations can be done using the Gp components as a draft model, with the leader filling in the details of their particular situation as needed. To contrive an initiative the leader cannot tell the followers what to do – otherwise it would not be an initiative. The leader can just leave the task of defining a missing component up to the followers to volunteer options or he can actively encourage it by issuing component-specific challenges. In addition to this the follower must have distal knowledge of the purpose in order to know which direction to aim any actions in favour of.

Example 22.1 Transition from a Gp proposal to an initiative-owned decision equation

a. *Step 1: Preparation of the Gp*: The explicitly known components of the draft Gp are prepared by the leader, and in this case the leader subtracts the PA component heading from the draft Gp, as it is not known:

SC + RY? + SP + BB

b. *Step 2: Propose the Gp*: The leader has a choice of how to present the draft Gp to the followers and group as a separate entity.

Option 1: The leader presents to the followers a 'situational statement' which states all the proximal knowledge he has prepared in the hope (or expectation) that the followers will volunteer the PA information:

SC + RY? + SP + BB

or

Option 2: The leader creates a challenge focused on the PA component in the Gp and presents the knowledge as well as an 'initiative challenge' to the followers, specifying the PA component challenge:

SC + RY? + SP + (PA) + BB

As a result of the leader presenting the above Gp proposal, he can either hope the followers volunteer to define a PA to complete Option 1's Gp or that they will respond to the challenge presented by the leader in Option 2 and provide a PA or perhaps two or three different PAs for the group to decide upon.

The followers are being given a challenge to define the PA component and use their proximal knowledge of actions needed to complete the Gp and create the group tacit knowledge needed. This example demonstrates using the PA component; however, this exercise can be done with other components of the Gp and multiple components at the same challenge.

c. *Step 3: Counter and confirm the Gp*: The followers or group do nothing or engage with the leader in the form of a counter proposal to the component being focused on or question other components as defined by the leader in the draft Gp presented.

In this case it is assumed that both options receive positive engagement, as the followers use the distal knowledge they needed and that was provided by the leader to combine with their proximal knowledge of the actions. They define the PA component and express this to the leader as something that can be done. The followers and leaders have effectively made the plan. The leader will formalise it in a full Gp and agree it with the followers. They confirm and the decision is made.

The decision, though, is slightly different than earlier examples. It is a decision in which some of the components have been defined by group members other than the leader. The decision has changed in nature and reflects a multi-party decision process in which the followers have taken the initiative and defined the PA component. The decision has changed into an initiative-owned decision (iod), and this can be shown in the decision equation.

d. *Step 4: Move the confirmed Gp into a decision equation*: The full confirmed Gp is progressed into a decision equation. Once confirmation of the Gp and its components is understood and agreed by the co-constituents the decision is added and the Gp becomes a decision equation:

SC + RY? + SP + BB => iod(PA)

The component that the followers have defined (PA), representing their proximal knowledge, is added to the decision side of the equation in Step 3. Again the letters in 'iod' are lower case as they cannot be subdivided and are unique to that set of circumstances.

In Step 2, Option 1, the leader has issued a statement outlining the extent of his knowledge of the situation; it is known simply as a 'situational statement'. Option 2 describes when the leader specifically challenges the followers to define the missing component (PA) while stating the proximal knowledge he has. It is called an 'initiative challenge'. The leader needs to be explicit to his followers that they are challenged to define the component (PA in this case) or at least present options that will complete the Gp and resolve the specific challenge as defined by the leader.

The situation statement or initiative challenge delivered by the leader includes four defined components of the Gp and the followers have defined the fifth component PA by themselves as they have proximal knowledge of how the action should be done. Add to this the followers' distal knowledge of the purpose, and the SP and BB communicated by the leader, and it completes the tacit knowledge needed for completing the defining of the Gp. The counter proposal is sent to the leader with the defined PA component to complete the Gp.

The leader may accept it or send it back for redefining, and this process can go back and forth for some time in the form of a negotiation or a confirmed instruction, depending on the relationship formed. In this case the leader approves and the Gp is formed and formally proposed as completed as an initiative-owned decision. The followers have defined the PA as an act of initiative and helped the group form the full Gp with all five components present. The PA component, as now defined, is the followers' initiative and they have ownership of the PA component.

This is an example of an initiative-owned equation (io equation). This initiative ownership creation process can be done with any component in the same way. When the leader communicates the draft Gp or sections of it, with less than the full defined five components, the leader creates an opportunity to fill in the gaps. Some will see it and take the opportunity for recognition by volunteering options, while others may need the prompt of a challenge to make explicit the group's needs and focus the thinking of the followers. The draft Gp is exactly that: it is a start to the decision-making process, and the leader initiates and facilitates the defining and communicating of the components. He ensures that these components are communicated correctly in order to get others to define the needed components in order to complete the Gp in order to get a decision.

The leader's proximal knowledge of the SC and the RY? of the group will allow him to assess whether the situation and opportunity presented represent a challenge that is relevant to the group and whether action needs to be taken. This is when the leader initiates the defining and communicating process in the group in order to form the full Gp. This process will require facilitating, and the more complex the SC and subsequent plan the more effective the facilitation and communication of the purpose (or follower's distal knowledge) will need to be to ensure the engagement and decision of the followers and group.

Any one of the components can be defined by an individual in the group, or the defined component may come from outside the group. It is a necessary function of the leader to initiate and facilitate the forming of the Gp. It is detailing the needs of the group to the followers and the followers' needs to the group. The leader may offer up definitions himself, or another individual or team in the group may be specifically detailed to do this, such as the sales department. Similarly, it could be another individual who just volunteers notice of an SC facing the group in the form of an opportunity or a threat.

That follower-defined component is the initiative taken and it is owned by that specific creative follower. The overall Gp that results in a decision is described as an initiative-owned decision (iod). The component that is the follower-defined initiative-owned component is inserted in brackets behind the iod symbol. This indicates an initiative-owned decision expressly, and actions verify the ownership of the initiative. Initiative ownership indicates a situation in which the decision, action or solution has been arrived at using components defined by more than one member of the group. There is an initiative-defined component that has led to an initiative-based decision and it is owned by the individual who defined that component.

Example 22.2 Process flow of the creation of an initiative-owned decision equation

Step 1: Preparation of the draft Gp →

Step 2: Situational Statement or Initiative Challenges communicated along with known details of the draft Gp →

Step 3: Counter proposal of draft Gp →

Step 4: Gp confirmed and positive initiative owned decision taken → Action

The component of the iod belongs to the individual who defined it and expressed that decision in the action of expressing or physically moving into positive action as an expression to others in the group. It is important in developing a sense of ownership in the group of the purpose and recognising those who have it. The possessive nature of the decision gets intrinsic commitment and engagement from the individuals concerned. They have an ownership stake in the Group purpose and the relationship to the group and all other group members.

The leader has the opportunity to create the potential for initiative in the group. The leader has the choice of providing this or just telling group members what to do in the form of task instructions. Of course, in the latter situation the leader is required to be present whenever the situation changes and the followers cannot think of which way to take action; otherwise no action (or potentially the wrong actions) could be taken. By not stating the purpose explicitly, the positional leader creates more work for himself. This omission of purpose also prevents initiative from being readily possible. The level of experience that his followers have will also play a part. Hersey and Blanchard go into great depth on how to identify the nature of their followers, in terms of skills and attitude, with their situational leadership curve tool.[36]

The purpose section of the decision equation, when stated explicitly provides the intention of the group as defined by the leader. The purpose will also help the follower identify whether the plan is just or ethically right by the standards of his peers. The SC will be identified, and again the follower will be able to make quick judgements on whether the challenge is possible. There are many factors in the components that the group members will use to help make a decision.

The more experienced of the group members can quickly get some indications as to the SP or PA needed to resolve the SC identified. The purpose will indicate who will be important to helping resolve the SC and who may not be. Those with experience may know much more than the leader about the SP and PA needed to resolve the SC. It is this experience that will help the group if it is engaged properly by the group and leader. The Gp that the leader eventually defines and comes to represent may well be a mix of many individuals' ideas, thoughts and initiatives. The draft Gp sent out to initiate the whole process may, however, be limited to just the purpose components if it is the intention of the leader to create a team to work out the G section options for resolving the SC.

Using examples from active groups that practise these relationship processes, the military starts by using the mission statement. The mission statement has the purpose as well as the task instruction element combined to form the Gp. At lower levels, the leader issues all the components of the Gp himself. In the planning stages the leader has the option of getting the proximal knowledge of the SP, PA and any BB from his specialists and subordinates by issuing an initiative challenge process of proposal–counter-proposal to formulate the defined components of the Gp. The specialists, during the formal presentation of the confirmed decision equation or orders, may be required to present their component themselves rather than the leader.

In the mission statement and formal presentation of the group purpose the military are covering both bases and have created a mission statement format that has potential for initiative if the situation changes. However, to start with all must work to a pre-decided plan. It is important to note that it is designed to do this due to experience gained in battle. Tacit knowledge is created in all co-constituents as a prerequisite in formal orders. It ensures that those in the group could take the initiative in the event that it is required, such as after an unpredictable change in the situation.

To start with, the mission statement includes the PA and all five components being issued for the start of the operation. The mission tells the followers what they are doing and to some extent how to do the task. The leader also does not give ownership of the components to anybody but the leader, as the one responsible for and owning the confirmed plan. Given the size and complexity of many military operations this is not surprising. Getting off the start line in the right way is the foundation for the hoped-for success.

The mission statement is used at most levels within the military, but as the command level gets higher the senior officers can rely on greater experience, knowledge and a staff that is specifically formed to define the specialist factors of the different components in the decision equation. The purpose or intention of the group remains the property of the commander and can be the place where the leader demonstrates his character in the Gp (orders) as suggested by Field Marshall Viscount Slim in his book *Defeat into Victory* [32].

The book was required reading for all young aspiring officers attending Royal Military Academy Sandhurst. Having graduated from RMAS, any who were lucky enough to join the Brigade of Gurkhas were told to read it again! It is a great read, and it continues to reinforce lessons on leadership as well as giving an opportunity to spot new lessons missed the first time round. Field Marshall Viscount Slim specifically mentions the intention of the leader when discussing the processes used to communicate to the groups under his command:

'One part of the orders I did, however, draft myself – the intention. It is usually the shortest of all paragraphs, but it is always the most important, because it states – or it should – just what the commander intends to achieve. It is the one overriding expression of will by which everything in the order and every action by every commander and soldier in the army must be dominated. It should, therefore be worded by the commander himself.'[37]

This is strong and sound advice that is borne out in any group. This author has no intention to change the emphasis as issued. The intention statement or purpose is a another type of message and is a step on from the initiative challenge. It is issued in a situation when the group understands that it is part of their function to define the remaining components based on the purpose statement.

This is the case in the military and other large groups where organisations and teams have been created to perform the function of defining and communicating the components of the Gp. Often these teams are centrally based, such as HQ staff or the executive committee, and focused around the leader in order to support this function of defining and communicating.

Example 22.3 Field Marshall Viscount Slim's statement of intent or purpose statement as a draft message or initial Gp

a. SC + RY?

His group HQ staff are required to fill in the rest of the details pertaining to the remaining components. Even in the formal orders group the Field Marshall would stand up and deliver the purpose statement himself, ensuring that the message is conveyed with all his character, intent and passion. The orders themselves represent the subsequent initiative-owned equation, displaying the Field Marshall's HQ staff's initiatives in the confirmed initiative-owned decision equation.

b. SC + RY? => iod (SP, PA, BB)

Groups with more experienced members will be able, or even be expected, to draw on their experience and to take on initiative challenges and define the remaining components themselves based on the purpose alone. Whether initiative is taken in the planning and defining stage or in the execution stage it is best done with knowledge of the purpose. The leader therefore must communicate the purpose as a minimum.

The more experienced group members will already have a good idea of how to define the SP, PA and BB components, and how to go about resolving the challenge in the direction of the SC presented. Without the purpose it would be reduced to a task instruction. In experienced groups, if the leader did all the defining he would probably just be repeating what the followers already know – not a good use of the group members' time or knowledge. The balance is in knowing the group members' limits.

The leader, by introducing the purpose, has laid a solid foundation to create the potential for initiative and followers who can respond to intrinsic motivators. Without creating the environment for initiative the leader will not easily find it, or identify group members who have the capacity to develop and demonstrate tacit knowledge of the situation. By not creating the environment for initiative the leader is leaving to chance that an unpredicted situation will produce an opportunity for initiative guessing. Alternatively, with no purpose and therefore direction it will be an excuse to stall the operation. In this situation the leader can only hope that the group members will take action in the right direction.

The purpose is the intrinsic element that forms the core of the message. The Group section of the equation may well already be known or is yet to be defined, and is not as important as the purpose. The purpose is what leads to the formation and organisation of the Group. Therefore the purpose element is the vital element of the Gp. A clear strong purpose is like steroids for initiative, creativity and a whole range of intrinsic motivators.

Chapter 23: Engagement, and ownership, between the co-constituents

'Outstanding leaders go out of their way to boost the self-esteem of their personnel. If people believe in themselves, it's amazing what they can accomplish.'

Sam Walton

Earlier chapters have developed an understanding of the five components of the decision equation and combining the two different types of knowledge in the group to create opportunities for initiative in the resolution of the group's SC. The journey has been made in an effort to find a path from the basic foundations of the individual decision-making processes to the goal of defining types of relationships in order to clarify what is leadership and what is not.

The question is how is it different? This distinction is one that confuses leadership theory in terms of defining leadership and how to get it. Greater specification of the relationship is needed, and creating the decision equation is a tool designed to resolve this challenge.

Using the decision equation it is possible to describe the components used in the leader's message and to link the types of messages that are sent between the co-constituents in groups. Understanding the types of messages that can be delivered allows the group's representative (usually the appointed leader) to design a message to cater for the individual's needs for intrinsic as well as extrinsic motivators. The message at this stage is a plan in the leader's mind and will contain at least some or all of the components when communicated to the group.

Examples 19.1–19.4, task instructions, have demonstrated that this can be done as one-way communications that expect a positive action decision to be made in response. The later examples have also shown that there are different ways of presenting the message that will get better intrinsic engagement by challenging and including the purpose in the case of a mission statement. Inserting purpose will add more motivational factors for the co-constituents. With challenges, the process of engaging the followers in defining the components of the message presents an opportunity to create an environment for multi-party decisions and initiatives. This can lead to the situation where the leader only needs to issue a purpose statement, or less, and the group will respond accordingly to produce the full Gp and decision into action to resolve the SC, as if an automated process.

Using the decision equation the leader can get the followers to define the components of the equation. If this can be achieved then the co-constituents together have defined the Gp and can make the decision more easily. The co-constituents as a whole have defined the Gp rather than just the leader. The co-constituents are all engaged in the Gp's design and therefore in its ownership. They are co-authors of the Gp. The parties are less divided and more conceptually aligned to the group's needs than they are to their own individual needs.

This can be done and is based on the group experience and willingness of the co-constituents to participate in defining the overall Gp. The leader to some extent will dictate how and who defines which components and how they all come together. The leader has a function unlike any other in the group and that is the initiation and facilitation of the defining and communicating of the group purpose.

Whether the message is sent using a demand or task instruction and is delivered as an expected course of action with no rebuttal, or as an initiative challenge inviting the group members to contribute and own the Gp, is the leader's choice (unless in the military). As an exercise, an initiative challenge can be used to educate, as a training tool, or as a test of their skills and understanding of the planning process. It also creates the extrinsic motivator of an increased value of belonging to the individual. A technique of requesting that something be done is another way of giving the individual the perception of choice and respect, although it is rhetorical in its nature. Proposing a challenge to the individual or sub-group prompts thinking and intellectual engagement.

Different messages will get different results and it does depend on the amount of time the leader has in which to get a decision into action from the group. Any challenge creates potential for establishing an engagement between the co-constituents. The word 'engagement' here suggests more than a physical proximity; it describes an intellectual process entered into by two or more parties. There is the engagement between the parties, a bonding through a commitment or implied promise, moral, verbal, conceptual or otherwise, described by members of the group. That promise can be backed by actions and perhaps legal proof, such as employment contracts, advance payment or a marriage licence.

In the case of a group relationship and the parties involved there is expected to be some form of verbal, moral, or conceptual engagement and commitment between the co-constituents. This can be combined with any of the physical bonds represented in titles and contracts signed between the group and its members if they exist. Employment contracts are a physical representation of a commitment to a company and organisation. It may also be seen as a physical representation of an intellectual promise made by both parties.

Due to changes in situations and to the parties involved over the passage of time, it is not unreasonable to expect a regular review of these types of contracts as changes occur and time passes. The engagement between co-constituents needs to be set up so that the parties can prove, if required, that an agreed understanding was established.

Achieving challenges and problem solving are seen as intrinsic motivators. The satisfaction or pleasure gained from being able to solve the challenge and then get it right is the reward and a motivator in of itself. It is this value that Maslow identified as a higher level factor and Herzberg as a 'motivator' in individuals. By presenting the Group components as a challenge to the followers, the leader adds intrinsic motivating factors to what would otherwise only be an extrinsic motivator for the individual. The process of including the followers in defining the Group purpose is a way of not only getting options but also of adding intrinsic motivators, and achieves engagement and ownership. The key is to continue to feed the hunger for motivators and not allow it become sated or starved.

Clayton Alderfer proposed an extra interpretation that reinforced some factors of Maslow's hierarchy of needs in his Existence, Relatedness and Growth (ERG) theory published in 1972 [24]. Alderfer developed Maslow's theories into his ERG theory and related the *existence* needs of individuals to the first two levels, physiological and safety, of Maslow's hierarchy. The next two levels, belonging and the need for esteem, are contained in Alderfer's *relatedness* needs. He then isolated the term *growth* as a specific need that had not been mentioned by Maslow. Alderfer linked *growth* to both the fourth and fifth higher level orders of esteem and self-actualisation as a way to achieve both of the needs identified by Maslow.

Further in this work Alderfer went on to propose that if individuals do not achieve the *growth* that they desire, they revert to lower levels and increase their efforts in the areas that satisfied their lower level needs in the false hope that this will satiate their higher level needs. They will work harder, but still not achieve their personal goals of growth. This is often described as working harder but not smarter. This leads to frustration and burn-out. Leaders who want to keep individuals effective and efficient need to focus on the use of intrinsic higher level motivators to prevent this wasted effort.

Introducing intrinsic challenges into the Group components has the practical effect mentioned earlier: the sharing of the function of defining the Gp. By presenting the components as challenges to be solved the followers are given an opportunity to express themselves and start practising the skill of defining the components in the decision equation. This prepares them for future roles as a leader as well as meeting the intrinsic needs of the individual. Being asked to define components gives them practice as well as helping them realise their value in the group. They are getting more respect within the group. The parties are engaging and developing the group's functional maturity.

The practice that the group member gets in defining a specific component is important for future understanding of the Gp and developing the tacit knowledge that is needed to understand the relationship. Experience in how these components are defined and why they are shaped the way they are will lead to better understanding and the decision process will be easier in future. Whether a leader gets the group to perform a task through a highly collaborative effort with many technical aspects involved, or just to do a simple task, the key aim behind his communication is to get the group to make a decision into action to resolve the SC of the group.

Requesting the followers to define one or more of the components means that the followers no longer need to be persuaded of the details of that component, as they helped define it and understand it. It only needs to be checked. In the case where the followers may have more knowledge of the component than the leader, the collaborative approach is often the best and only way to resolve the defining of that component in the equation.

Larger companies and organisations are often set up to work like this, where the production manager, the technical specialists, the operations executive or account managers are the ones who provide the detailed plans for the components. When the plan and the message are sent the specialist may even be the ones who present that component of the plan in the briefing and confirmation of the Gp. It is this intellectual bond that is being drawn between the co-constituents. It is a commitment that is made at that time and with respect to that plan.

In larger organisations the function of defining a component may be written as part of the job description or is encompassed in their title and specialist role. In smaller groups and at lower levels of large groups it may be just a verbal confirmation; in a sports team a hand signal or action may signify unity with the team. The verbal bonds are important, as they are commitments and confirm a sense of ownership of the component and its role in the Gp. They have committed their thoughts and ideas towards the Group aspect of the plan; they are part of the Gp. This process of engagement in the decision process makes the next step of getting the group member's decision into actions smoother and more likely to get positive involvement from the group.

This engagement of the group members by the leader has three clear aims. One is to ensure involvement and thereby a greater degree of ownership of the Gp by individuals in the group. The second aim is to ensure that the most technically correct solution is found and that the group members are given all the facts and knowledge the group has at the time. The third aim is to smooth the transition into action and find an appropriate resolution to the SC of the group.

It is the leader who bears the responsibility for getting the group into action and the effectiveness of those actions. Even when the leader is dealing with an experienced group it is important to confirm that the plans are correct and that the action is in line with resolving the SC. Questions, challenges, discussion, training and preparation are a leader's friend and all serve to confirm if the message has been received and understood by the co-constituents. These confirmations are linked to that SC and they also lay the foundations for a longer-term relationship to be built. Transitioning from a task instruction environment to a purpose-led group that takes ownership of the SCs presented is a situation in which engagement between the co-constituents is of key importance.

The transition from being task-orientated to purpose-driven can be achieved first by moving from a Group section components-focused task instruction environment to injecting purpose wherever possible. Ensure that the group members are fully aware of the SC faced and the RY? that the group chooses to resolve that SC. It can be refined into a slogan, logo or sound bite as appropriate to that SC. It is a constant reminder of the group's overall purpose and the engagement and ownership that each have committed to. Each group member should be able to link their actions with the purpose, and in particular the SC.

In an ideal world the followers should be reminding the leader or asking the leader how their actions help achieve the Gp and SC of the customer. If the followers can quote the SC then the leader knows that the group's message is getting through and he has created a situation where there is the potential for initiative in the right direction.

In demands and task instruction situations the potential for initiative to be displayed is limited, and if it happens at all it is based on educated guesswork towards a perceived purpose rather than on a focused pursuit of resolving the SC. The more the situations change, the more potential there is for initiative to happen. In situations of emergency there is greater potential for initiatives to be taken because of the higher amount of unexpected situations. A good leader knows that it is better to prepare for these situations by creating an environment in which initiative can be taken in a focused direction of the Gp. Further to this, initiative can be practised and perfected before the emergency comes along.

Through Geert Hofstede's [17] studies and experience it is known that in some highly collective cultures there is a demotivation to stand out as an individual, and it is not encouraged. This does not mean initiative is not present or that these groups do not have potential for it in their ranks. Leaders need to be aware of this and learn how to get initiatives moving and forthcoming through better engagement.

The nature of the group will play a part, and the way in which the leader leads the group will effect whether that group will take initiatives. In groups that are risk-averse, reserved judgements dominate and changing procedures is discouraged by heavy penalties, which induce fear and reduce the chance for initiative to be displayed. The speed of change and knowledge uptake will present huge challenges in these groups.

Without purpose any initiatives are the result of guesswork and previous experience. In these faster-changing environments it will be even more important to emphasise the purpose rather than the just the proposed actions so that the followers can use the purpose to aim for when motivated and pressed to take the initiative.

Where groups are slow to pick up the idea of change, engagement is again the key. By engaging with questions on isolated components the leader can encourage individuals and subgroups to deliver, for example, three options for a specific component or a minor aspect of the component that affects them in the change. Competitions to find the most options and ideas are to be encouraged as group activities rather than being done as individuals in isolation from the group. In these situations the purpose is reinforced and the group members are taking are taking part in defining aspects of the Gp. The leader must lead the group or allow themselves to be reduced to task instructions with no potential for initiatives or intrinsic values in the group.

Any initiative is a indication at some level of engagement and ownership of a component of the Gp. Ownership is a very important result of initiative and is based on the individual's engagement in the component, which could easily be a result of the challenge put forward by a leader.

In the event that the group members ask questions of any component of the Gp message it must be seen as a question arising because there is a level of engagement with the SC and that component. It should be seen as an opportunity to engage them in the defining of that component of the Gp. Engagement leads to initiative and ownership of the decision, which leads to initiative-owned actions and ultimately initiative-owned solutions. The individual who owns the solution to the SC is more likely to produce a better solution than one driven by a task instruction.

When a question is asked, the leader is wise to listen for two things. Firstly, listen for the level of engagement being shown by the questioner. Which component are they addressing in the question? Is it purely questioning to confirm details of their BB, or is it to question the purpose section of the Gp. The focus component will indicate the dominant motivator in the questioner at the time.

It could be the fear and safety motivator wanting to preserve his position and title in the group rather than the purpose. Secondly, listen to the question itself in order to answer its explicit content. The aim of the initiative challenge statement or message is to get the intrinsic purpose-based values to dominate the individual as a priority, rather than their individual benefits, needs or results. The benefits and results will happen only after the Gp has been achieved. Typically the Gp is communicated and understood at the higher levels in an organisation; positional leaders often convert the mission or purpose statement to a task instruction because it is easier. These omissions may not harm the organisation immediately; however, in situations of competition and change they will make it more difficult to improve the group's ability to react, resolve challenges effectively and perhaps survive.

Knowing the different types of messages and when to use them will be highly advantageous to the leader of a group. Initiative challenges and purpose statements encourage those who want to achieve more and prove they can meet a challenge: they show a path ahead for those who want to grow. They are based on engagement and developing the relationships between the co-constituents focused on the SC.

Creating opportunity for initiative and ownership of an SC will be a catalyst in finding more options and more effective solutions. To be more effective, leaders need to know when and how to use the decision equation in defining and communicating the Gp. Generating tacit knowledge throughout the relationship is important in being an effective leader. Having others in the group owning that tacit knowledge and able to pass it on will only make the leaders more efficient in their function of making the group more effective.

Chapter 24: The relationship so far

'Leadership is not just the province of people at the top. Leadership can occur at all levels and by any individual. In fact, we see that it is important for leaders to develop leadership in those below them.'

Bernard M. Bass & Ronald E. Riggio

It is the leader's ability to create a bridge between the co-constituents of the relationship in order to get first decisions and from those decisions actions to produce effective solutions. All the time the leader has a metaphorical 'foot' in each party's camp and is acting as the bridge between them. Earlier, Chapter 17, 'The terms of the relationship' our understanding of leadership was outlined as follows:

'The ability to initiate and facilitate the defining and communication of the Group purpose in order to get a decision from the group members to take action in the direction of that Group purpose.'

Part 4 has developed a more detailed understanding of the Gp: that it is communicated in many different ways in practice and that its delivery will affect the results. The group purpose is a message that can be designed and delivered in expectation of compliance, or it can be first initiated as a proposal or a challenge. The message can be added to, counter-proposed back and forth and then finally completed by all parties as co-authors of the Gp. Any component can, in theory, be defined by any individual in the group, although usually the purpose components of SC and RY? are defined by the leader of each group. When the leader does this it creates the potential for engagement and initiative, and therefore ownership can occur.

Michael Polanyi's observation, that an understanding of tacit knowledge in solving the perceived paradox that we can know more than we can tell, has been used to analyse relationship messages and the component parts of the decision equation. How they interact to affect the motivators contained within the components and therefore influence decision making in the individual has introduced the link to *initiative*, a term often associated with leadership.

Specifying the type of knowledge of the subgroup sections in the decision equation and how they create the opportunity for initiative has led to two different types of decisions that can be the result of the decision process. The introduction of the purpose subsection can produce the potential for initiative and different decisions, and thence actions and solutions.

Table 24.1 Some of the many types of messages in a relationship

Message types	Group purposes, completed decision equations or initiative-owned decision equations
Demand	SP + PA
Task instruction with benefits	SP + PA + BB
Task challenge	SP + PA + (BB)
Group purpose	SC + RY? + SP + PA + BB
Mission statement	SP + PA => SC => RY? => BB
Situational statement	SC + RY? + SP + BB
Initiative challenge (1 component)	SP + (PA) => SC => RY? => BB
Initiative challenge (2 components)	SP + (PA) => SC => RY? => (BB)
Purpose statement/statement of intent	SC => RY?
Purpose challenge	SC => RY? + (SP) + (PA) + (BB)
Challenge (S, RY?, SP, PA, BB)	(S)C + (RY?) + (SP) + (PA) + (BB)
Demand decision equation	SP + PA = d
Task instruction with benefits decision equation	SP + PA + BB => d
Task challenge decision equation	SP + PA => d(BB)

Message types	Group purposes, completed decision equations or initiative-owned decision equations
Full decision equation	SC + RY? + SP + PA + BB => d
Mission statement decision equation	SP + PA => SC => RY? => BB = d
Initiative-owned decision equation (1 component)	SC + RY? + SP + BB => iod(PA)
Initiative-owned decision equation (2 components)	SC + RY? + SP => iod(PA, BB)
Initiative-owned decision equation (3 components)	SC => RY? => iod(SP, PA, BB)
Initiative-owned decision equation (S, RY, SP, PA, BB)	C = iod

The introduction of initiative to the study has added an aspect of time to the definition of leadership. The addition of purpose to the leader's message allows co-constituents to take a whole series of initiative-owned actions based on a purpose that needs to continue until it is resolved, which is as yet an undetermined time period. The individuals in this relationship and other influencing factors over time may change, so the leader not only needs to create a relationship, but also needs to maintain it in order to resolve the purposed specified for the group.

At this stage the definition of leadership has progressed and Part 4 has necessitated these additions to earlier versions of the definition to create a more accurate/advanced, but not yet complete, definition. This is an intermediate definition which details the function of the leader and outlines the purpose of the leader.

'The ability to initiate and facilitate the defining and communication of the Group purpose in order to create and maintain positive decisions from the group members to take action in the direction of that Group purpose.'

A more detailed Venn diagram is drawn up to reflect the increased participation in the Gp. Venn diagram 3 (Figure 24.1) shows that the three subgroups are defining the SP and PA components for each of their subgroups. The component SP (upper case) is subdivided into lower case (sp1, sp2 and sp3) to represent the SC at each sublevel as they perceive it. Similarly, the components of PA are subdivided into pa1, pa2 and pa3. The participation in the creation and defining of the Gp is shared.

The components SP and PA are owned by the subgroups who have taken the initiative to define and commit their ideas to the plan. Figure 24.1 demonstrates the more complex nature of the message and the options open to the leader in defining the Group purpose. The colours continue to represent the same parties: the leader and subleaders in red, with the followers in green; all are members of the third party: the overall group.

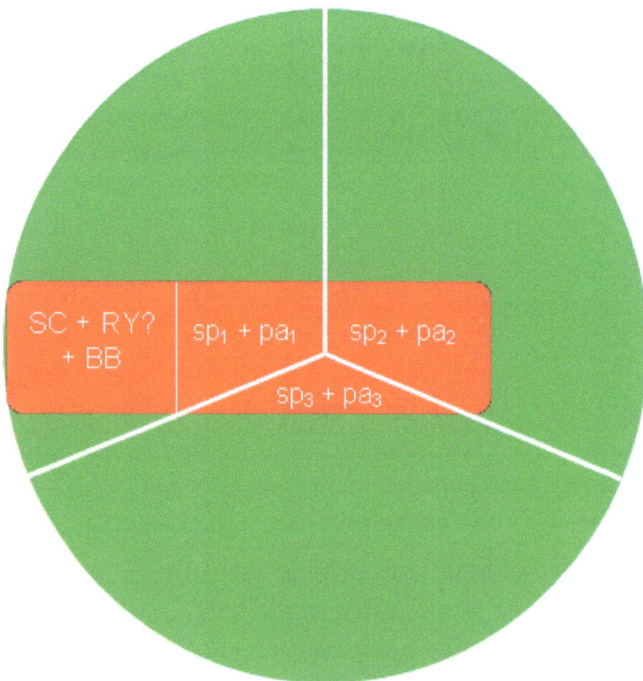

Figure 24.1 Venn diagram 3: the group purpose and its defining by subgroups

Part 4 has also further identified a number of areas which will need to be the subject of Part 5 in order to obtain further detail about the definition of leadership. The introduction of initiative into the decision equation tool has allowed relationships to be grouped into those that result in initiative ownership and those that do not. The decision equation tool will be used to help describe and further differentiate relationships in order to clarify some of the confusion that is present due to generalisations. This is caused by introducing words such as 'manager' into the study of leadership. A very common challenge presented in leadership forums is:

'What is the difference between a manager and a leader?'

The term *manager* is an example of a word being used in place of or alongside leadership. The word manager started to appear in the English language around 1600 and has become used in everyday terms to describe a position in an organisation. Management is perceived as different, but is equally difficult to define in terms of how it differs from leadership.

There are those who say that a manager is different from a leader and can point out this difference when they see it, but they cannot define the difference. It has become a paradox, like leadership. This describes the conditions needed for better definition. There is a common perception that leadership is a better quality to have than management. Why should this be so if we still cannot accurately define either? We have a gut feeling or a limited knowledge of what both leadership and management are, but not enough to define the two or differentiate them.

By defining the relationship and what leadership is more accurately there will be a clearer understanding of which terms relate to which relationships and which equations best demonstrate them. Most importantly, Part 5 will show the confirmation process of leadership. The term *confirmation* is used in order to describe the process of confirming that the followers have received the message, perceived an understanding of the message and lodged an acknowledgement with the leader to confirm the proposed message and decision made before going into action. The crossword puzzle is slowly getting more of the clues pencilled in. Black squares are being filled to create the boundaries and guidelines delineating the path to the solutions presented in the word 'leadership'. Initiatives, engagement and management all have an influence on the term. Their place in the crossword puzzle needs to be fixed in the process of answering the question 'What is leadership?' in order to clarify the final puzzle as a whole picture.

PART 5: Confirming the relationship

Chapter 25: The decision

'The task of leadership is not to put greatness into humanity, but
to elicit it, for the greatness is already there.'

John Buchan

The efforts made in defining and communicating the message are
done in order to get a decision from the group members to take action in the direction of the SC and RY? Using the five components
of the decision equation the leader can present the Gp to the point
when followers can make a decision. The leader has a choice of
how the message is defined and passed to the followers. Likewise,
the followers have a choice of actions to take.

The followers have the option on what their decision will be,
and how to demonstrate or express their decision. It can be in the
form of a positive action, a delay on the decision, or a negative expression of opinion or action contrary to the leader's and group's
proposed aims. Within each of these three options, there can be
differing ways of displaying or expressing their decisions. What
the followers decide and how they express their decision is the final step, and it confirms whether a relationship exists or not. The
followers are confirming that they have received and understood
what the message means, and what their decision is. There are
many different possible responses and they will confirm the type of
relationship that is formed between the co-constituents.

There are initiative challenges and purpose statements that will
appeal to individual intrinsic motivators and get maximum engagement and ownership from the aspects that create, form and
maintain a relationship in a group. The leader could issue a simple
task instruction with the expectation or demand that the followers
follow. By using initiative challenges and getting ownership in the
various components of the Gp, the leader creates a scenario in

which the decision is more likely to be made in favour of the Gp. The phrase 'more likely' is used, as it is not certain that all individuals in the group will action the commitments made in a plan, even after it is expressed. It is only certain when an action proves the commitment to the decision.

Confirmation of the proposed action by the followers can take a number of forms, starting with a nod of the head, a handshake or a verbal expression of commitment, right up to taking physical action towards the Gp. These are each steps in confirming the decision that has been made. The leader can prompt the confirmation process by asking questions of the followers that relate to the proposed Gp. Questions that deal with aspects of the purpose subsection of the Gp, firstly to ensure that the followers know the direction they are working towards, but also to establish their understanding, their link, and their commitment to that purpose.

Each individual may expect similar commitments to actions from other individuals in the group, including the leader, at the various stages in the overall plan. These expressions and continuous actions are confirming the relationship. Therefore it is necessary to add the phrase 'create and maintain a decision relationship' to the leadership definition to reflect this ongoing need for the process in the relationship.

It is the transition from the decision into the expression or actions taken in line with the Group purpose that is the focus of Part 5. This transition phase is known as the confirmation process of the relationship. With experience, the co-constituents will establish what level of expression of intention is needed to know that the action will be performed to completion. Until the appropriate expression or action is taken, the leader will not know the results of the decision process. It is important for group members to understand that trust and loyalty are the results of this process and not something to be assumed merely because a positional hierarchy is in place.

Once the group member has taken action, it confirms the decision made and that a relationship has been established or confirmed. The leader must wait until that confirmation before he knows whether the actions are being made in the direction of the Gp. Moving the decision from the point when the decision is made and into an action will depend a lot on what is in the message and how it is delivered. The leader can affect what the message includes and how it is delivered. It will provide an indication of the type of relationship that the leader hopes to establish.

These relationships describe the way in which the elements at the disposal of the group are used to get the group members to do what the group wants them to do. In order to get the group members to make a decision into action in the direction of the Gp they must perceive that it is worth their while to do so. The requirements of the group are met and at the same time the group can meet the requirements of the individual group members. The group members will make an assessment of all the information they have on the situation presented in the leader's message and balance it against the alternative options that are open to them.

In some cases, the option to do nothing may be more in their favour and their decision is therefore to take no action in the direction of the Gp as proposed. In some situations the leader will resort to using force (coercion) or threats, penalties and reductions to the benefits previously offered (coercion/persuasion) in order to make the option of 'doing nothing' towards the Gp a worse option than the one proposed. In general terms the balance of benefits has been swung in the favour of the Gp action and away from the 'do nothing' option. The BB value is forced or persuaded to the positive value by reductions and penalties enforced on the BB factors.

When all the elements in the Gp present themselves as positive, a move into action is an easy decision to make with the willing engagement of the Gp. When the purpose is explicit and intrinsically good, it motivates and appeals to the followers. In situations in which membership and belonging to the group gives them titles, respect and work that is stable and challenging, while not too difficult, with salaries, pensions and benefits that they are comfortable with, the decision to take action is easier: it is done willingly.

Belonging to the group is a motivator and has advantages as well as disadvantages; it is down to the perception of the individual. For example, few join the Army to get financially rich. Some perceive that there are no alternative jobs in the area, but they do not expect to achieve what is commonly considered rich. Membership of the military has a different appeal; things such as advancement, recognition, travel, growth and life experience feature very highly as motivators. The financial counter-balance is a guaranteed index-linked pension which is important to some. This is dependent on the military one joins, and different military groups have different appeals for soldiers and officers alike.

The military discipline system is often seen as a disadvantage, as is going to war, with all its implied risks to life and limb, but even this possibility has its appeal to some as a rite of passage to potentially greater recognition. Many make the decision to join based on the balance of information and their needs at the time. As they age and gain these experiences they become seen as normal, and individuals look for more motivators over and above the ones already experienced. Some of the motivators and variety cannot be found elsewhere, and the group members may elect to stay, or re-join after a short exit period.

Similarly, in many different walks of life it is the balance that is created and defined by the individual's peer groups that influences the individual perception and his decision to join or not. This decision must then be communicated to that group in order to confirm that a relationship can be created and started. It is this action, such as submitting an application form to apply for a group place and to agree to the terms and conditions of that group, that confirms the relationship has been started and is on its way to being established.

The different types of decision equations outlined in Part 4 and the components that make up a leader's message to form the Gp is a useful indicator of the different relationships that can be formed. When words and phrases such as *coercion, persuasion* and *willing engagement* are used, it becomes apparent that the general term 'leadership' does not necessarily suit all of these types of relationships. More detail and definition is needed to be accurate to allow more effective study and to prevent confusion in the understanding and application of leadership.

As Socrates and later Michael Polanyi pointed out: 'we can know more then we can tell'. This is demonstrated when some well-known leaders are compared: Joseph Stalin and Mohandas Gandhi; Mao Ze Dong and Franklin D. Roosevelt; Kim Jong Il and Nelson Mandela. All were leaders in a leader–follower hierarchy or positional sense of the term. They did, however, demonstrate very different relationships with their followers. The term *manager* adds further confusion to the term, as the distinction between a leader and a manager is often difficult to define. Again, the relationship is different, and this difference is often easy to perceive, even if it is not possible to point to a consistent, defining difference that is applicable across many types of relationships.

As to the difference between leaders and managers, Warren Bennis provided a long list of the differentials between management and leadership as he saw them. Table 25.1 highlights a number of Warren Bennis's [8] comparisons of leaders and managers. These comparisons serve to confirm a tacit knowledge of where the differences lie. Bennis was differentiated from his peers in the academic study of leadership in that he is perceived to have maintained a bias towards trait theory study long after mainstream academics had moved on to other areas of focus. He studied under, and later alongside, Douglas McGregor at MIT Sloan School of Management and was a well-published and respected academic in the field of leadership theory [33]. Bennis went on to say in his book:

'a leader must be authentic, i.e. author of one's own creation'[38]

Bennis later developed this theory as the foundation of his concept of the authentic leadership approach. The revealing observation of his study and comparatives is that they are often based on the relationship rather than the traditional traits or characteristics of the leader in isolation, as is often done in trait theory.

In a number of Bennis's comparatives, the difference between a manager and a leader are based on the leader's or manager's relationship with their followers in the group, not the situational focus often adopted by others. He was ahead of his time perhaps, and in hindsight perceptions may have been incorrect, but his comparisons are often quoted and used as good interpretations of what many feel is the difference between a leader and a manager.

Table 25.1 Warren Bennis's comparative terms for leadership and management[39]

The Leader	The Manager
The leader develops	The manager maintains
Leaders conquer the context	Managers surrender to it
The leader innovates	The manager administrates
The leader is an original	The manager is a copy
The leader focuses on people	The manager focuses on systems and structure
The leader inspires trust	The manager relies on control
The leader has a long-range perspective	The manager has a short-range view
The leader asks what and why	The manager asks how and when
The leader has his eye on the horizon	The manager has an eye on the bottom line
The leader originates	The manager imitates
The leader challenges the status quo	The manager accepts the status quo
Leaders do the right things	Managers do things right

The terms *coercion*, *persuasion* and *willing engagement* go some way towards differentiating the relationships as descriptions. A leader is a position in a group hierarchy, as is the position of a follower. Leadership describes a relationship between three parties and is different from the term *leader* in a positional hierarchy sense.

The specific nature of the relationship and what differentiates it from other relationships can be demonstrated using the decision equation. The different formats can be seen and will define each relationship. The relationships can be differentiated in terms of the process by which the leader gets the decisions to be taken in the group and further by the components used to do so. It is the nature of decisions that they have a large effect on the actions and solutions of the group. The different types of decision are the most obvious differentiator.

Chapter 26: Comparing the different decision equations

'People ask the difference between a leader and a boss... The leader works in the open, and the boss in covert. The leader leads, and the boss drives'

Theodore Roosevelt

For an individual to take a decision into action it requires the Gp components to add up to a positive balance in the perception of the individual. The decision equation tool displays the components used, and can demonstrate the Gp formation process. Initially it is the number of components used that differentiates the nature of the decisions. From there, how they are assembled further refines the nature of the relationships within the overall decision differences.

Before attaching relationship labels to the decision equations it is important to be clear on the types of equations that can result from the decision process. These are messages that define the decision process between the co-constituents in the relationship they belong to. These are fewer than presented in Table 24.1; in that table there are examples of Gp proposals in the form of a task challenge, a situation statement and an initiative challenge, which are all proposals prior to any relationship being created or confirmed. This only happens when the decision equation is formed, and even then action is not always guaranteed, but the decision at least represents an intention or commitment.

Type 1: A demand or task instruction without Benefits Balance

$$SP + PA => d$$

$$(\text{group}) => d$$

$$g => d$$

Type 2: A task instruction with the Benefits Balance stated explicitly.

$$SP + PA + BB => d$$

(Group) => d

G => d

There is no BB component being used by the leader in Type 1. This is a demand or task instruction with only two components of the Group subsection; therefore a lower case g is used to label the Group subsection in brackets below, as it is not a full three-component Group subsection. The hierarchy or perceived hierarchy, or implied threat of force, penalty etc. is expected to coerce the decision from the individual and affect the subsequent action.

In Type 2, the BB component is added to be part of the decision process. The difference is one component and can be seen in the equation by using the upper case G rather than the lower case g used in Type 1. The difference in application is that the BB is used as a measure of persuasion to make the decision process easier. It does not change the PA or SP.

Which form the leader chooses to use will determine the nature of the relationship over time. It is not possible to be certain of the type of relationship in one isolated message, but in this instance there is no expectation of engagement with the follower on this issue of the SP and PA. This is true of all messages in isolation: they merely indicate the nature of the relationship at that instance.

Type 3: A mission statement – in this case with Benefits Balance stated explicitly along with all the other components.

SP + PA + SC + RY + BB => d

(Group (incl. BB)) + (purpose) => d

Gp => d

Typically a mission statement is used as standard practice in the military and it states all the components, which provides potential for initiative, but does not give initiative free rein until the situation has changed. Only beyond the prepared plan can initiative action can be taken in order to meet the overall purpose of the group. Within the components the subgroup leaders have some flexibility about which individuals to use and how within the overall group plan. This flexibility gives some sense of control or recognition to the subgroup leader and individuals chosen, which adds an element of intrinsic motivation. However, this is below subgroup level and remains limited at that level.

The mission statement is a safe option to use as a leader, as it covers all the details (to avoid making the mistake of assuming too much knowledge in the followers), yet at the same time it provides the potential for initiative. This can be and is used outside of the military as well, and to good effect when new groups are formed and the experience in the team is not known or limited. This format is often used when a leader is explaining to those outside the group the function and purpose of the group.

It is important to note that initiative is allowed where and when the situation changes or when there are no details in the orders to cover that specific situation. So there is potential for initiative, but it still has a normal lower case 'd' as potential is no guarantee that initiative will actually be taken or that it will be in the right direction.

Type 4: An initiative-owned decision equation as the result of a challenge

a. $SC + RY? + SP + BB \Rightarrow iod\ (PA)$
(purpose) + (group) $\Rightarrow iod\ (PA)$

or

b. $SC + RY? + PA + BB \Rightarrow iod\ (SP)$
(purpose) + (group) $\Rightarrow iod\ (SP)$

or

c. $SC + RY? + SP \Rightarrow iod\ (PA, BB)$
(purpose) + (group) $\Rightarrow iod\ (PA, BB)$

All reduce to this fourth type of equation, an initiative-owned equation:

$pg \Rightarrow iod\ (g)$

This format is often used when technical specialists are needed to define the technical details of the Group subsection. The important difference here is that one or more of the Group subsection components is not detailed by the leader, but is intentionally presented as a challenge for the co-constituents (usually the followers) to work out. The leader explains the other components and then asks for options or the completed Gp from the co-constituents or their subgroup representatives. The component that is the focus of the challenge, which becomes the initiative-owned component, is represented in brackets on the initiative-owned decision side of the equation.

This bracketing after the iod demonstrates that the component was defined by other co-constituents in the relationship. In the final equation of this type the (g) represents one or two of the three components in the Group section. It is not specific to a component, but it represents one or two of the Group components have been defined by the second or third party. Any equation with iod in it has been made by more than one co-constituent, group, leader or follower. The content in the brackets displays which components of the equation were made by those parties other than the leader.

Type 5: A purpose statement, sometimes called a statement of intent

$$SC + RY? => iod (G)$$

$$(purpose) => iod(G)$$

$$p => iod(G)$$

This form of decision equation is typically used by an end user to a supplier, or a leader who is in an established team that has specialists to complete the rest of the Group section of the message. It can also be used within groups or to attract new group members to the purpose of a group. This is often the process used in the political process, for example in order to gain membership and votes. To the young and uninitiated, the name of the group may not mean anything, and it is only when the group's purpose is explained that it takes any shape or form as a virtual or real entity, cause or activity.

Type 6: An initiative-owned equation based on a challenge only.

C => iod (Gp)

(a challenge – a purpose initiator) => iod(Gp)

p => iod (Gp)

This final type of equation also demonstrates an important point in the difference between a group and an individual motivator. A challenge in isolation is not related to the group until it is specified and the RY? component is added to it to form a purpose for the group. In Table 24.1 there is listed a challenge statement. A leader may use this type of message as a motivator to individuals in the team or to subgroups to see how volunteers take up the challenge. Which person or group can define all of the components? The challenge only becomes the SC once it has been specified, and similarly only once the RY? is added to it can it become a purpose specifically owned by that group. Potential leaders can use this method to practise defining components and Gp. It also helps the leader identify those with the attitude towards prioritising individual and group targets and a desire to grow themselves and the group.

When the challenge is defined and specified this again is an individual motivator without the RY? component added to it. Once the RY? is added it belongs to the group identified and they have decided to define why they choose to resolve this specific challenge. Only when the SC is linked to RY? does it become a group-related specified challenge. It is included in leadership theory as motivation applies to individuals, not groups, and leaders need to know how to get decisions from the followers: a specific challenge is one type of message that can achieve this.

When the six different forms of decision equation are placed in close proximity the different nature of the resulting decisions, as well as the components used to get them, becomes clearer.

Example 26.1 Short forms of the six different types of equations

1. g => d (g)
2. G => d (G)
3. Gp => d (Gp)
4. pg=> iod (g)
5. p => iod (G)
6. C => iod (Gp)

The difference between the decisions is obvious as there are two clearly identified groups. Those decisions taken without any initiative or follower or group input are Types 1–3 and those taken as a result of initiative ownership by a follower or group element are types 4–6. Those without initiative demonstrate a process that involves only the leader and his interpretation of the group's needs. Those with initiative ownership are the result of the process of engagement by the leader between the co-constituents. In the equations with no group engagement the group and followers are view as physical assets and resources with no need for their opinions or concerns.

The differences are at two levels. The first is in the decision and the second is the component patterns within those equations represented in the brackets. The component patterns effect the decisions and are therefore subsets of the different decision sets. The decision differences are small and very significant in terms of relationships.

Understanding the nature of the two different decision types without referencing the brackets is a start point before looking at the multiple component pattern differences within the brackets and expanded equations. Types 1, 2 and 3 – the demand, task instruction with benefits, and mission statement – have the defining of the components in common. All components are defined according to the perception of the leader. Access to the components' details is controlled and in the case of Types 1 and 2 is restricted by the leader. The defining and communicating of the components is done in order to get tasks into action.

The second type of decision is initiative-owned decisions: Types 4–6. These decisions are owned by more than one of the co-constituents in the group, usually the leader (as the group's representative) and the followers. All three are co-authors in the decision. Specifically, the defining of components is done by the co-constituents based on access to the purpose subsection and the challenge that causes the formation and actions of the group.

The significant difference between the two decisions is the ownership of the Gp. In Types 1–3 the components are owned by the leader alone. In Types 4–6 the decision is co-owned by the group's constituents, unlike the non-initiative-based decisions in Types 1–3. In this group's case the defining and communicating of the components is done by co-constituents in order for all to achieve ownership of the Gp.

At the second more detailed level within the equations there are multiple differences which cause the decision differences. There are three key differences, as displayed in the brackets attached to the decisions. When combined with the two different types of decisions it makes a total of six types of equations. These differences not only lead to the different decisions, but have significant knock on effects in the subsequent actions and solutions produced in these DAS chains.

In Types 1 and 2 there is no reference to the larger group, the challenge or the RY? the group is performing the actions. In these two types of equations, coming from the demand and task instruction with benefits messages, if the situation changes and the leader and co-constituents cannot communicate and discuss the new situation, the possibility of a positive corrective action being made depends on the followers' decision processing experience and guesswork. Their decision will be taken with no knowledge of the group's needs and can result in no action or even counterproductive actions. The individuals in this situation will have little option but to think as individuals, as there is no group-based direction to guide them.

If the followers have earlier experience of similar challenges, of the group level plans and aims, they may guess at the group's needs; this becomes one option for resolving the new situation. Any corrective action, if taken at all, will be based on a mix of experienced guesswork, with the right priorities and confidence of the followers in that new situation. This is true of demands and task instruction-based types of message.

In the case of Type 3 equations, the mission statement, there is the potential for positive initiative-owned decisions to be taken, as the message does include the group's needs in the SC and RY? components. The followers have been given the purpose subsection and have this direction as a guide and as an explicitly stated option, as well as any other options they may have figured out in resolving the new situation.

The mission statement does still retain the PA, and this could reduce the effectiveness of the potential solution as there is a possibility for confusion. Three options present themselves in the new situation. One is to repeat the PA, another is to change and align a new PA with the purpose (SC + RY?) as a guide, and the third option is to do nothing until a new PA is issued by a leader.

In light of the new situation, these options sometimes may appear to contradict each other. Which option has priority? Do the followers know which has priority, and do they accept that priority assessment? Giving both PA and purpose may appear to be a safe bet with a well-trained team, but if changes happen without a well-trained team the new situation soon reverts to the same need for a new leader to make decisions or have the original leader permanently present.

The mission statement has potential for initiative, but does not demand it. This type of equation is one that allows for initiative but also needs an understanding of the group's priorities understood by the followers. It covers all the components and implies adherence to the details of all of the components. To be effective it must cater for the abilities, training and experience of the followers in order to enable the potential for initiative thought and action. It is a catch-all for leaders and followers who do not necessarily know each other well enough, and therefore assumptions are not made.

There is another use for the mission statement: it can be used when transitioning individuals from an environment of task instructions to one in which initiative ownership is expected. Setting this as a halfway stage in developing initiative is useful for those groups whose members may be reluctant or not confident enough to leap to single or multiple component initiative challenges in one bound. As group members get to know each other and develop a firm understanding of the process in this type of equation, a new relationship establishes itself and the co-constituents may adopt a different equation pattern and therefore a different relationship. As such, the mission statement can be used to transition groups to the next level of group engagement, the initiative challenge, and beyond to reach for the occasional purpose statement.

Types 4–6 are initiative-owned decision equations, which include the purpose and challenge, and therefore the group's needs or the purpose initiator. In the event of a situation change after the leader is separated from the co-constituents, the followers will usually already have knowledge of the group's needs. More than that, they are already practised in defining one or more components, so to do so again will be easier and they will have an element of confidence born from their earlier experience. Initiative challenges, purpose statements and challenges are used to get engagement, initiatives and ownership in the Gp in order to produce the actions needed to get better solutions. The wise leader prepares and practises the group before the need arises to do so in order to be sure that the group stands a better chance of performing effectively when the need arises.

The initiative challenge is the first occasion where there is an explicit and focused requirement for initiative. This requirement is unencumbered by a potentially conflicting PA and it is an initiative-owned decision that results. The decision has been made by the co-constituents and by implication this shows an element of conscious choice taken and ownership of the decision. The co-constituents are engaged in the process of defining the Gp and there is a shared ownership in that Gp.

Type 5, the purpose statement, defined by the SC and RY?, has no elements of the Group section components. It results in an initiative-owned decision that, when confirmed by actions, proves engagement, initiative and ownership. The purpose statement indicates a large element of the followers' exclusive involvement in the Gp. This is typical of, but not limited to, senior levels in the military and larger groups with experienced, established relationships and is typically based on functionally mature and practised relationships. The direction is given by the leader. While the leader may have a detailed understanding of the requirements of some of the Group components, the leader also knows that the subgroup members have that knowledge and recent practice as well as the dedicated time to define them.

Similarly, the leader may initiate and issue only a challenge that results in a Type 6 decision equation. The challenge with an implied RY?, invites reply and engagement of all components. The challenge may involve many different disciplines, and the leader cannot be expected to have the specialist knowledge needed to define these components himself, but he has a tacit belief or perhaps knowledge that it is possible and worthy of pursuit. In this case the leader is initiating and implying the reason why the challenge should be taken by the group.

An example of this was when President John F. Kennedy challenged the American people at Rice Stadium on 12 September 1962:

'We choose to go to the moon, in this decade and do the other things, not because they are easy but because they are hard.'[40]

John F. Kennedy

Although Kennedy was a very able man individually, he did not have the technical knowledge to define the Gp himself. He tacitly believed (or had the tacit knowledge) that the administration could find the technical support needed to do it. He committed to help in the facilitation and ensure that the SP was there when the leader was appointed to a group designated to complete the Gp, specifying the group's needs. The American people (as well as many others hoping they would succeed), were inspired to tacitly believe and act in favour of this challenge laid down in that speech. The difference in the resulting decisions is one of no initiative, or a decision based on initiative ownership. The leader has six options to use to get a Gp and a decision for the group to follow into action. Whether he chooses to involve the co-constituents or not in the decision process is his choice. The form he uses will establish the level of engagement in the decision process and define the relationship.

The decision in its formation is still an intellectual concept. The expressions and actions taken by the group members will confirm this decision and determine whether they will act and perform as proposed and expressed. Over time a relationship will establish itself and reflect the type of relationship. Moving the group from the decision stage into action is the start of confirming that the relationship is being formed or maintained.

Chapter 27: From decisions into action

'Thinking is easy, acting is difficult, and to put one's thoughts into action is the most difficult thing in the world.'

Johann Wolfgang von Goethe

Decision making is initiating the search for and assembly of facts, creating options, making comparisons, balancing of positives and negatives as perceived within the individual's remembered experiences, defining solutions, and having the confidence to chose one option. Learning and practising the process of decision making and leadership starts as soon as children become aware of themselves as individuals, and perhaps before.

From childhood onwards, an individual's interaction with the group is behaviour that becomes so ingrained that it is difficult to see it as separate from the group. All its thoughts and actions are done in respect of the knowledge that others are or may be present, and this influences thinking and behaviour. This behaviour is defined by the group and it defines the individuals in the group. It is so ingrained in behaviour patterns that it is sometimes difficult to identify it unless a different way of thinking or behaving is presented. The relationship between the group members is one of these patterns that is difficult to see unless a contrasting pattern is brought into comparison to highlight the difference and the alternatives open to the individuals.

Moving from a decision in the mind of an individual to the physical expression of that decision to another in the group is one of those behaviours that may be imperceptible to outsiders, but which group members just know to be so. Signals, actions, words and understandings are all a step in the process of confirmation of a relationship between the individual and the group. It signals that the message has been received and perceived to have been understood.

The response will contain a verdict on whether the co-constituents agree to act in favour of the leader's proposed action.

Do they need further explanation or will they be taking a position of resistance to the Gp? The process in terms of establishing the relationship is important, as it is the confirmation stage. The actions taken by the followers at this stage will confirm, maintain, delay or even break up the relationship in the group.

When a decision is taken it is described as an intention. At this stage it is still an intellectual concept in the mind of the followers as individuals. Within the group, the individual may ask others for their opinions and discuss the options available, forming their own temporary subgroups to make or confirm their decision. Once the individuals have expressed these intentions to their peers and group leaders, the group's next step will be to change that intention into an expression of an action to confirm the decision.

An intention may not be enough and often it is only actions that are proof that a relationship has at least started. It is the action expression of this decision that gives the co-constituents a confirmed sense of their position in the relationship and therefore their value in the group. It also confirms a degree of ownership of the needs, concepts and values of the group.

As individuals, these expressions of commitments can be made many times a day. They are often used to confirm current hierarchies within established or perceived groups and relationships. Simply by expressing an individual's title, giving a salute or other glances, bowing, smiling or signalling deference we reaffirm our group hierarchies. These expressions and acts can be very subtle and implied, or they can be stated bluntly through very obvious actions and explicit statements of group allegiance or resistance.

Decisions expressed by actions are an obvious confirmation of the hierarchy. An acceptance gesture can be signalled by a positive action (+A) such as a smile, wave or salute; a rejection gesture is a negative action (−A). There are, as always, levels or degrees of acceptance and rejection. Permanent rejection can prevent a relationship from ever being established. The subtle questioning of some aspects of the components being presented in the proposed message can bring the relationship into question or just delay the action temporarily, depending on the component being redefined and agreed. The process from a decision to an action can encompass all of these possibilities and more. It is the expressed actions that prove the decision and intentions.

Each positive expression or action (+A) demonstrating the positive decision in the direction of the purpose is a confirmation of the positive decision and is by implication a confirmation of the relationship. Over time, this relationship may get stronger or weaker and is demonstrated by the expressed intentions and actions towards the Gp in subsequent challenges. Positive actions confirm the leader's continued guarantee and provision of the group's commitment to the needs of the followers, and the leader's position in the group is confirmed by the followers' continuance of the relationship. Terms and phrases such as *loyalty*, *duty to* and *bond of allegiance* all come as a result of the developing relationship as challenges are actioned. These terms are the results of shared concepts, action experiences and the balance of needs.

If the all the components are positive then the decision into action will be easier to make; this is called a positive decision in favour of the Gp. It can be displayed in symbolic logic as a positive expression or action (+A). Logically any action not taken in the direction of the Gp will be seen as a negative action (–A). A typical example would be a child resisting and questioning the reason why they should comply with an order from a parent to go to bed.

In situations where the followers do not make a decision there is no expression of intention or action at all. This third situation is called a 'non-decision' situation. The leader has failed to define or communicate the Group purpose well enough for the followers to make a decision or the receiver is not capable of understanding or complying, and therefore delays the decision into action. A 'non-decision' situation, while intellectually different from an negative action (–A) is neither rejecting nor confirming the relationship in practice and is therefore treated as a negative action, as it does not represent a positive decision in favour of the Gp. The non-decision may also be seen as a failure to recognise and reaffirm or establish the leader–follower hierarchy relationship implied in the statement, and because of these two reasons a non-decision is also displayed as the same symbol, –A.

A non-decision situation can be a challenging moment for the group as it represents a possible pause or even a breakdown in the relationship. From the leader's perspective any action taken that does not express itself in the direction of the Gp can be viewed as a negative value action (–A). With a leader who understands the decision process it may represent a failure to define and communicate the Gp effectively or his position as a leader may be in question.

In practice a 'non-decision' is usually temporary and is followed by some sort of question from the leader to appeal to the followers as to whether the order was heard or understood. The leader has to go back one step in the decision process to the confirmation stage and start it again by rephrasing or repeating the Gp or asking for confirmation of the receivers' understanding of the Gp. The process of confirmation is an important one in the decision process of the group as it could be questioning the relationship in the group.

Understanding the decision process and using the decision equation's components to establish where the breakdown is gives the leader an option to restart the decision process and redefine the Gp. These symbols + or – can be added to the decision equation to provide a more detailed expression of the process. Giving each component in the decision equation a positive (+) or negative (–) value will help demonstrate the process.

Before adding these details to the decision equation, here is a revision of the simple mathematical rules that apply to the addition and subtraction of positive and negative values within an equation. The rules for addition and subtraction are simpler to understand than multiplication or division functions, which are not used in the decision equation. When two positive values are added together, a positive value is the result. When two negative values are added together a negative value is the result. When a positive and a negative value are added together the outcome may be positive or negative, depending on the unit values involved. The examples below demonstrate these principles.

Example 27.1 Rules applying to addition and subtraction of values

−1 combined with − 2 = −3
−1 combined with +2 = +1
+1 combined with −2 = −1
+1 combined with +2 = +3

−3	−2	−1	0	+1	+2	+3

|___|___|___|___|___|___|___|

← Subtraction ←   → Addition →

Each result depends on the value it is combined with. Addition goes right along the scale and up in value. Subtraction goes left along the scale and down in value. Each component in the equation is given a positive or negative value and subsequent decisions and actions will reflect these positive or negative values as well.

The individual follower is the one who decides the value of each component in their own decision equation. Once the components are given their values the individual will make an overall balance of positives against negatives. One individual will have motivators that feature highly and dominate the equation, while others will not see them as important or of high value. Each individual has their own decision equations and components, which are inserted by the individual. The individual is motivated by different things and will give different factors, and therefore components, a different positive or negative weighting. The sequence of components may be able to influence this weighting process as the individual compiles their decision equation. The decision equation is now expanded to include the action phase. From its base, ending in the decision, the equation will now include the next step beyond the making of the decision. The next step into an expression or action progression of that decision is shown by adding the symbols => and the letter 'A' for Action, with the appropriate positive or negative values.

Examples of this expanded detail applied to the six forms of the decision equation, including the positive (+) or negative (–) values and the action (A) symbol as a result of the decision made are given below.

Type 1: A demand or task instruction with values

+SP + +PA => +d

+(Group has 2 positives) => +d

+g => +d => +A

Type 2: A task instruction with benefits with values

+SP + +PA + +BB => +d

+(Group with 3 positives) => +d

+G => +d => +A

The positive or negative value of the decision will automatically tender to the action symbol. For example, the Group section components are positive, which leads to a positive decision and is expressed in a positive Action done. The co-constituents feel that the SP, PA and BB are all positive for completing the decision into action.

Type 3: A mission statement with values

+SP + +PA+ –SC + –RY? + –BB => d

+(Group (incl. BB), 2 pos & 1 neg) + –(purpose, with 2 neg) => –d

–Gp => –d => –A

Three of the five components of the Gp are negative leading to a negative decision, which is expressed in no Action at all or Action against the Gp. In this case the SC is negative, suggesting something that is not viewed as a legal, just, viable or relevant challenge or to have any reason for the group concerned to be resolving. This is reinforced by a negative RY?

Perhaps the challenge presented to them is not ethically correct or is something they are opposed to in practice. This principle, ethical, legal standard or just plain disinterest is created by the group that they or their group belongs to. In this case the leader and or co-constituents decide to reject the challenge, and this is expressed by the negative Action result (–A) shown in the decision. The leader needs to rethink his position and proposal.

Type 4: An initiative-owned decision equation with values

$$+SC + +RY? + +SP + +BB => +iod(PA)$$

$$+(purpose, 2 pos) + +(group, 2 pos) => +iod(PA)$$

$$+gp => +iod(PA) => +ioA(PA)$$

Type 5: A purpose statement with values

$$+SC + –RY? => –iod$$

$$–(purpose, 1 pos \& 1 neg) => –iod$$

$$–p => –iod => –ioA$$

Although the followers are positive about the SC they are negative to the RY? the group should be resolving it. This can be due to many reasons and has caused a negative decision and therefore no action, rejecting the purpose for the group to be involved. In reality the process would stop there and the remaining components would not be defined. The person presenting the challenge may be approached by the group's leader or representative with a request for more information on why the group should be involved. The leader has the chance to redefine and start the decision process again.

The sequence of the full decision equation starting with the SC gives an additional level of weighting to the value of the component in the sequence, with the higher value being placed on the group-related components compared to the individually related factors and components. For the leader the focus and priority weighting are often done in this fashion, focusing towards the group-based components.

Type 6: A challenge with values

+C => +iod

(challenge, 1 pos) => +iod(S,RY?, SP,PA,BB)

+C => +iod => +ioA

The six equation examples are placed in close proximity to demonstrate the different possibilities of decisions and the resulting actions more clearly.

Example 27.2 Short forms of equation types with values

1. +g => +d => +A
2. +G => +d => +A
3. –Gp => –d => –A
4. +Gp => +iod => +ioA
5. –p => –iod => –ioA
6. +C => +iod => +ioA

The examples are relatively simple ones. The equations above all conform to mathematical norms and logical conclusions. Negative decisions leading to negative actions will often, in practice, result in the leader redefining the Gp and starting the decision process again.

When analysing situations in hindsight the situation may arise where an equation would not normally add up to a positive value decision, except that a single component has been given a high positive by the group's followers. Honour, sacrifice and the afterlife may be what motivates some individuals to place such a high value on one component of BB, or perhaps the RY? is given a positive value rather than the negative one usually attached to it, creating a positive BB. This creates what is seemingly an illogical equation. Logic dictates that this is not possible, but what happens when it does occur?

Chapter 28: Illogical equations cannot be!

'If a man expresses his opinion in a forest and no woman hears, is he still wrong?'

Joke repeated by Sir Ken Robinson

Sir Ken Robinson repeated this statement above during one of his revolution-inspiring talks on education. The joke, which he saw on a T-shirt in the USA, displays a creative method known as conceptual blending. At first it is just a confusing wordplay following the form of a philosophical thought experiment: 'If a tree falls in a forest and no one is there to hear, does it make a noise?'. It takes a bit of time to disentangle the joke from the original statement. To some it is initially a confusing mix of concepts, but as the brain puts it all into context and detail, it quickly reveals the clever humour of its author. The decision equation also suffers from occasional states of confusion where what appears to be a true reflection of the situation but the equation does not display logical values. The situation needs sorting and clarity.

The six examples of decisions shown in earlier chapters relate to decision equations that have positive and negative values attached them to help work out the expressed action value. The examples used follow a logical pattern. When retroactively forming equation models from the patterns of behaviour that have already happened, the component values are inserted into the equation and then added up. The decisions do not always match the actual results. The results are seen as mathematically illogical, and the standard rules of mathematics do not seem to apply. A pair of examples is given below:

Example 28.1 A pair of incorrect equations with values

Case 1

–G => +d => +A

Case 2

$+g => -d => -A$

The equations in Cases 1 and 2 reflect the results or actual behaviours. In Case 1, the G is a negative value and yet the decision and actions are positive. In Case 2 we have the opposite values. What is going on here? Something is not right. When these situations are described and the equations above are drawn up to analyse the situations, they appear as illogical equations. They describe situations that can arise around us and they defy logical explanation. To analyse these equations further, the full expanded decision equations are needed.

Example 28.2 A decision equation when a seemingly illogical challenge is presented

$-SP + -PA + +BB => +d => +A$

Two negative values and one positive value demand that when combined a negative decision should be taken. Yet a positive decision and subsequent positive action has taken place. The situation could be as follows: soldiers received an order from their group leader 'to shoot prisoners in their care'. At the same time they are also aware that their government has signed the Geneva Convention, which forbids this PA. They are in conflict with their bosses' instructions and their knowledge gained in basic training about the Geneva Convention and its rules.

They attempted to delay the PA while they questioned the boss to reassign the task to another day, or even get another group of people to do it. The boss reinforced the order and threatened that if they failed to comply with the order they would not face court martial for disobeying an order. On the second occasion, when they attempted to delay the decision and action the boss told them they would be shot themselves if they did not carry out the orders instantly. The soldiers perceived that as a consequence of disobeying their superior's orders they would be executed by the boss and the group to which they belong.

The soldiers receiving the orders are in conflict with different groups' rules. On one side there is the larger group of their national government, the ethics of the culture and the military that they belong to, which also does not condone the shooting of prisoners. In this case their subgroup leader is defining his own interpretation of the rules and defining who are prisoners or otherwise and demanding they be shot. The equation displays the hindsight assessment of the actions taken when the prisoners were in the end shot by the soldiers following the orders of their boss.

The equation, when drawn up in hindsight by investigators, is using values they know and also values that they know have been taught to the soldiers and the boss, who all stand accused of crimes against humanity. The SP component is assessed as negative: they did not want to do this. They also assessed the PA as negative, as the soldiers admitted to knowing the PA was illegal. Yet they still did the act after the boss added the threat and the BB element to the equation. The equation is drawn up in hindsight and it appears that the values create an illogical equation.

The action is taken as the result of the threat of a severe penalty of losing their own lives imposed on the individual soldiers in the group by the leaders. The soldiers perceived that they had no other options open to them other than to obey the orders and survive. In this instance there are two mistakes in the assessment of the components. The first is that the PA component is negative. The action was agreed by the soldiers and the order carried out in the end. The PA is therefore +PA. Similarly, the SP element is not reflecting the actual happenings just the intentions. Despite their attempts to delay and reassign because they did not want to do the shooting, the soldiers did actually do it, so the SP component is therefore +SP.

In this revised equation there are three positives in the group section of the equation and the action was carried out. The +BB was created by the boss who created an alternative punishment scenario of killing the soldiers if they did not carry out the orders so the BB value is positive for the soldiers if they perform the PA. By creating no alternative the individuals choose their immediate needs over any distant memories of Geneva Convention training.

The important difference is the timing of the situation and the threat. Coercion is used by creating an alternative that is worse than the outcome of the PA.

During the investigation the soldiers must prove that the threat to them was real and that they can prove beyond reasonable doubt that there was no alternative. The soldiers decided to action the option which preserved their lives. The soldiers 'chose' the lesser of the two evils. In the hindsight equation analysis the investigators' values for the soldiers' components were incorrect. The component values in the decision equation must reflect the actual actions taken, as this is the only true reflection of the decisions taken. Assessment of the Gp proposed by the boss before the decision and actions were taken is relevant to the investigation, but is not to be mixed up with the eventual decision equation, its confirming actions and the solution in the overall DAS chain.

Example 28.3 An illogical decision equation when an ethical challenge is presented

$$+SP + +PA + -BB => -d => -A$$

When an ethical challenge is presented, two positive values and one negative value should lead to a positive decision and action, but here it does not. Given the opportunity for one (person A) of two people to escape a sinking ship and live, the individual chooses not to. The one who could escape refuses to evacuate and stays with person B knowing that the probable result will be death for both A and B, rather than only for person B. In this case, to the investigator it seems illogical that person A would chose death over the option of life, and the investigator's hindsight equation appears to be illogical. In this case it is the assessment of the component's values that is in question.

The assessment must be done from the point of view of the individual, not the assessor. In the assessor's mind it is logical that the value of PA where person A leaves person B, who could not leave, so that A would live is seen as a positive. In the event that the individual in question (person A) had an opportunity to leave but chose not to. Person A assesses the PA to abandon the other and leave as negative. Person A may interpret the situation that the option of life without the other would be a greater negative than that of dying together.

Both the assessor and the individual are correct in seeing the BB of dying as negative, but in the mind of person A the alternative of living apart from person B is a greater negative, and this means that the PA of A leaving B is not an option. The PA should be negative, not positive. The individual perceives the PA as not a viable alternative and the assessor has given the PA component an incorrect value.

The two examples show the same cause behind the illogical equations: incorrect assessments of component values. There is confusion over the component values caused by mixing the intentions with the actual actions or by not assessing from the original individual's point of view. On occasion it is the interests of the assessors, and the traditions and rules of the group that sway these assessments. However, the equation must work out as logical. It is a process that a detective goes through each time they investigate a case: reconstruction of the decision equation and filling in all the factors to reflect what actually happened and thereby deduce the logical decision that also reflect the actual events.

When using the formula as a tool in planning and real-time situations the illogical equation also represents an incorrect assessment of a component. When the Gp is proposed and comes back differently from what is expected and is illogical there is cause for concern. One of the components is being interpreted differently from what is proposed. It is a difference of opinion and the decision equation has not yet been completed or confirmed.

The individual takes action in favour of the components they see and interpret at the time. They may choose to place their loyalty in a higher set of principles or priorities not detailed in the components proposed by the leader. Alternatively, the leader may be expecting too much commitment to the Gp from the followers. In the event of neither party compromising, one of the individuals has a decision to make: to leave the group. The individuals are electing themselves out of the relationship and group through their actions.

All groups consist of a balance of group needs and individual needs. The balance is based on the alternatives available to both the individuals and the group. Simple examples, such as groups requesting a different headdress, have led the UK police and armed forces to change their rules with respect to uniforms in the UK. France has been embroiled in a debate over the wearing of religious symbols in schools in order to keep the secular environment preserved.

Playing sports on a holy day has caused many individuals not to compete if the competition is scheduled for a sacred day forbidding sport. Hindu soldiers required to travel overseas during the First World War were given special approval and protection to do so from the appropriate Hindu priests. In each of these cases, and many others where there is an initial conflict, either the group or the individual has compromised and the decision equation has been completed with a decision over group membership on the activities of the group in question, such as sports competitions being held during religious holidays or periods such as Ramadan. Where there is no compromise, group membership is not achieved.

When these situations present themselves the individuals can express their opinion and decide not to take action in favour of the Gp. If their inclusion in the activity is needed by both parties, the leader and other followers will engage and communicate with the individual to re-establish the relationship in a positive direction if there is time.

When a unit of Gurkha soldiers, legendary for their loyalty, courage and discipline, were asked 'Who volunteers to jump out of a plane for the next operation?', most of the 100 soldiers present immediately volunteered. Those who did not volunteer were asked the question 'Why don't you want to parachute on the next operation?'. On hearing this, the remaining worried Gurkhas looked at each other, then broke out into a wave of relief and huge smiles, saying 'Ahh saheb, now that you say parachutes, we volunteer'. A redefining of the misunderstood component can sometimes make all the difference.

Illogical equations demonstrate incorrect component value assessments. The assessment and defining process must be started again. When a Gp's component values are being redefined it is also the nature of the relationship that is being redefined. It is necessary to examine all the component values of the Gp in order to obtain an accurate understanding of the relationship. Illogical equations do not exist when all components are correctly defined and understood by both parties.

The values of the components allow an individual to glimpse the relationship at that instance. The relationship is created or confirmed when a decision is expressed as a positive action towards the stated Gp. The value of the action results will indicate whether the relationship will survive over time. The nature of the relationship will reveal itself over a period of time and the assessor can gain a more accurate overview of that relationship based on the prevailing type of decision equation used in the group over time. There are no illogical equations, only incorrect component assessments.

Chapter 29: Relationships and labels

'Divide and rule, the politician cries; unite and lead are watch-
words of the wise'
Johann Wolfgang von Goethe

Using the formulas and mapping the decision process into action
has identified a series of differences in the relationships between
the co-constituents; most recently the difference between positive a
negative decisions. Positive decision and then action equations represent positive relationships. These decisions and relationships are
confirmed by their actions. The positive relationship is confirmed
and progresses to the next challenge. It is in its infancy, but it is a
relationship. These relationships will need to be strengthened by
more challenges and experience. They may grow to develop long-
term relationships over time based on the challenges and the balance of their interactions.

Negative decision equations which are not in the direction of
the Gp rarely progress to the action stage. By not confirming the
relationship with actions the group cannot be describe as a proven
relationship. The group is in transition to a relationship, meaning
that it is not yet stable, not yet confirmed by action, relationships.
One or more of the co-constituents' needs are not being met and
the group relationship is threatened. This can happen in an established relationship, marking the beginning of the end of the relationship, or it may be a new relationship, as explained earlier. A
negative decision identifies a transitional relationship.

Negative decisions will need to be reviewed and redefined. Perhaps the co-constituents need to compromise or be adjusted, and
then the new Gp must be confirmed as positive, otherwise it will
not last the test of time. If the co-constituents have better alternatives to choose, the group will dissolve or reform as a different
group of co-constituents and needs. A constantly changing group of
co-constituents will reduce the effectiveness of a group, as will a
lack of purpose and direction. It is a period of change and redefin-

ing of the relationship.

Relationships are those with positive decisions and actions. Any relationship can revert to a negative or transitional relationship. For the study, the focus remains the search for the answer to the question 'What is leadership?'. The earlier conclusion is that it is a type of relationship, and for this reason the focus will be on what is now labelled a positive relationship rather than one in transition in order to simplify the search. It is assumed that when referring to a relationship in future the assumption is made that it is a positive relationship unless specifically stated otherwise.

The second key difference in the decision equations is at the decision level, where there are two different types. There are decisions, and there are initiative-owned decisions, which lead to actions and initiative-owned actions respectively. In Chapter 26 the significant difference between the two decisions is the ownership of the Gp. In the first type, decision equations, the components are owned and controlled by the leader alone. The leader does this in order to achieve a task with little or no reference to the group-related challenge. In the second type, initiative-owned decisions, there is co-ownership by the group's co-constituents and it is done in order to gain co-constituents' ownership of the Gp.

This difference allows a grouping to be made. However, the label that is attached to those groups must be one that matches the actions and behavioural differences defined in the decisions. A group or relationship label, or descriptor, must be relevant to the group in order to make it easy to remember and link to the action and group that it describes. In order to do this it is worth identifying and describing the current and commonly used phrases and terms for groups and relationships. Once some labels are identified it should be possible to choose and match them to the activities and patterns of the decision equations.

Both leadership and management have been identified as terms without adequate definition. Current perception is that the leadership relationship is valued more highly than management. Many would give ostensive descriptions of leadership by contrasting it to management. Along with many other comparisons he made of the manager and leader, as seen in Table 25.1, Warren Bennis stated 'Managers are people who do things right and leaders are people who do the right thing'.[41] In this phrase, for example, leaders are linked to higher ethical standards and things that are 'right' morally or ethically. Socrates is attributed to have said 'All souls are immortal, but the souls of the righteous are immortal and divine'. This quote is repeated because it provides a priority and a standard for other to aspire to. Righteousness is often linked to leadership and is at the highest level in Maslow's hierarchy of needs.

Further refinement of the differences of leadership and management was provided by Rear Admiral Grace Hopper [34] when she stated that 'you manage things, you lead people'.[42] Here is a distinction between people and things when comparing the terms *management* and *leadership*. General (and then later President) Eisenhower said of leadership 'it is the ability to get people to want to do, what you want them to do'.[43] There is a clear indication that leadership is to do with the willingness of people indicated by the phrase 'to want to do, what you want them to do'. The implication is relationship is something that takes many instances to form and it is done over a period of time not in one instance in isolation.

The two types of decision lend themselves to fitting with the descriptors in the last two paragraphs. The Gp and therefore the decision equation can be linked to a higher and lower order of motivators; Admiral Grace Hooper's phrase would suggest that management deals with the assets rather than the people. While not an exact match, the element of willingness could match the concept of initiative-owned decisions. Similarly, the defining and control of components could be compared to controlling the restricted ownership and management of assets and actions rather than the leading of people.

By contrast, the initiative-owned decisions are the result of the inclusion of purpose in a Gp. This act is a deliberate and conscious attempt to engage with the co-constituents of the relationship. The Gp is appealing to all the individual's motivators and makes it possible to create the environment for initiative, creative thought and commitment to the group's cause rather than having only the hygienic factors of motivation to focus on.

Initiative-owned decisions are firmly linked to a willingness factor, while management is not associated with this factor or descriptor at all. Management relationships are a better match for the behaviour of controlling and managing the components of the Gp to the restriction of the co-constituents. Decisions indicate a managed relationship and initiative-owned decisions indicate a leadership relationship.

There are, however, more differences to be noted in the decision equations and those that lead to the six different decision equations. The component patterns in these equations represent further refinement of detail and therefore present the opportunity to further define different relationships. More terms are needed to match the different options where the behaviours match colloquial speech terms.

The Royal Military Academy Sandhurst views the act of leadership as a mix of being able to lead others by example, persuasion and discipline. These terms can be interpreted to mean that willingness in the case of example as co-constituents will follow if an example has been shown and expected. The word 'persuasion' is used in regular speech and therefore needs no interpretation, but readers are reminded that that persuasion should be viewed as a positive addition to an individual's lot rather than persuading through punishment of reductive measures. Penalties, reductive measures and force fall under the military heading of discipline. A synonym for discipline would be coercion or coercive measures.

The three different labels – willingness, persuasion and coercive – adequately describe a relationship and at the same time describe a behaviour pattern in respect to the decision process that has been examined. These are, however, ostensive descriptions and not logical proofs. It is to the logical proofs of the positive decision equations that the focus turns in order to match the behaviour patterns of these descriptors against.

Proving willingness is difficult; however, by using the decision equation it is becomes much easier to see indicative proof of willingness. The word 'persuasion' is a term like 'management' that is difficult to tie down to a specific definition. Where it stops being willingness and becomes persuasion is a fine dividing line. Again, coercion is in most cases easy to define, but the dividing line between coercion and persuasion is something that labour laws and courts will spend some time debating and passing judgement on.

To gain the logical proof of willingness only positive relationships that reflect a positive decision and action are used, as these at least start with a relationship that is established or maintaining itself. To prove willingness independent of persuasion or coercion is the focus, not the strength of the willingness.

The six types of equations used earlier to identify the process of matching them to relationship labels. The first step is to identify the decision equations and their names. The second step is to match the difference between a decision or initiative-owned decision with management or leadership respectively. The final step is identifying the three types of relationships that match willingness, persuasion and coercion.

Table 29.1 Step 1: List of the types of action equations with names

1. $g \Rightarrow d \Rightarrow A$	A demand or task instruction-derived action equation
2. $G \Rightarrow d \Rightarrow A$	Task instruction with benefits-derived action equation
3. $Gp \Rightarrow d \Rightarrow A$	A mission statement-derived action equation
4. $pg \Rightarrow iod \Rightarrow ioA$	An initiative challenge-derived initiative-owned action equation
5. $p \Rightarrow iod \Rightarrow ioA$	A purpose statement-derived initiative-owned action equation
6. $C \Rightarrow iod \Rightarrow ioA$	A challenge-derived initiative-owned action equation

The difference in the decisions and action results is the presence of initiative ownership or lack of it. The equations present a logical representation of the leadership and management difference. Those formats with initiative ownership are leadership relationships and those without are management. The equations are tools used to help demonstrate and define the differences in the types of leadership. The equations could be summarised as in Table 29.2.

Table 29.2 Step 2: List of equations matched with management or leadership labels

1. g => d => A	Management
2. G => d => A	Management
3. Gp => d => A	Management
4. pg => iod => ioA	Leadership
5. p => iod => ioA	Leadership
6. C => iod => ioA	Leadership

The final step applies the three relationship descriptors – willingness, persuasion and coercion – to the equations and the overall differences of the decisions. There is a direct correlation with terms such as willingness and leadership, as one is used to define the other, but is not so easy to identify terms such as management and coercion, as they are defined by different parts of the decision equations. One, such as coercion, fits within management, but not all management relationships are coercive, so it becomes a subset of the management group as does persuasion.

Equations 1–3 have no initiative ownership, while those from 4–6 do. Looking in detail at the expanded forms of these equations will reveal the differences at the component level. This is done in order to find a suitable match for the descriptors willingness, persuasion and coercion. Below are the first two expanded task instruction action equations.

Example 29.1 A demand and a task instruction with benefits-derived action equations

Type 1: SP + PA => d => A
Type 2: SP + PA + BB => d => A

The difference between both of these formats and all the other decision equation formats is the lack of the purpose section in the task instruction. The followers are only being given the extrinsic motivators or physical assets and actions components of the Group section. This places them both in the management relationship group.

The expanded equations additional reveal a difference in that equation 2 has the BB component included. The BB indicates that an element of persuasion is being used in this situation, whereas there is no attempt at persuasion in equation 1. It is a level of difference which marks equation 1 as a management by coercion relationship compared with equation 2, which is a management by persuasion relationship.

The BB may be a penalty or it may be a reward. This is a detail that cannot be seen in the formulas and the investigator must go through the message proposal phase to determine those details. Whenever the BB component is present this is a consideration, as the formula cannot display it.

Example 29.2 A mission statement-derived action equation

Type 3: SP + PA + SC + RY? + BB => d => A

The mission statement action equation does have purpose included in it and there is therefore the potential for taking initiative action while still being a management equation, because all the components are defined and controlled by the leader. The presence of BB confirms that this relationship has the component required for persuasion. It is a management by persuasion relationship with potential for leadership due to the addition of purpose.

The fourth equation, the initiative challenge-derived initiative-owned action equation is a leadership relationship as there is engagement in the defining and ownership of the components. Because this type of equation could potentially have BB still included in it there is the potential for it to be a leadership by persuasion relationship. There is, however, proof of willingness in the presence of the challenge and resulting initiative-owned component which the co-constituents have defined. Four examples are listed below.

Example 29.3 Some initiative challenge-derived initiative-owned action equations

Type 4a: SC + RY? + SP + BB => iod (PA) => ioA (PA)

or

Type 4b: SC + RY? + PA + BB => iod (SP) => ioA (SP)

or

Type 5: SC + RY? + BB => iod (SP, PA) => ioA (SP, PA)

or

Type 6: SC + RY? + SP => iod (PA, BB) => ioA (PA, BB)

In equation Types 4–6 the group is able to take positive initiative-owned actions. Equation types 4a and 4b have an element of persuasion added as there may still be the component SP & BB in the Gp; however, there is a resulting positive initiative-owned action. The initiative-owned action indicates the willingness of the individuals in the group. It is a 'leadership by the willing' relationship. Rather than term the relationship as 'leadership by the willing' which is awkward English, the relationship is called an initiative-owned leadership relationship, and Types 5 and 6 both fall under this relationship label.

Equation Types 5 and 6 have no BB involved and it is the purpose components that provide the motivation. The equation patterns and the presence of initiative-owned actions prove individual willingness. The final step in listing the relationship labels alongside the equations is in Table 29.3.

Table 29.3 Step 3: A list matching equations to relationships

1. g => d => A	Management	Coercion
2. G => d => A	Management	Persuasion
3. Gp => d => A	Management	Persuasion

4. pg => iod => ioA	Leadership	Willingness/persuasion
5. p => iod => ioA	Leadership	Willingness
6. C => iod => ioA	Leadership	Willingness

The relationship labels are applied to the equations, which can be used to distinguish them in detail. There is a degree of overlap and subgrouping to apply. It is not unlike the Sandhurst description of the act of leadership, being a mix; however, to be correct in the progression of the equations from coercion to willingness there is an element of overlap, where our language is not so specific yet the equations can differentiate. This table is shown in a Venn diagram form (Figure 29.1) which demonstrates the overlap.

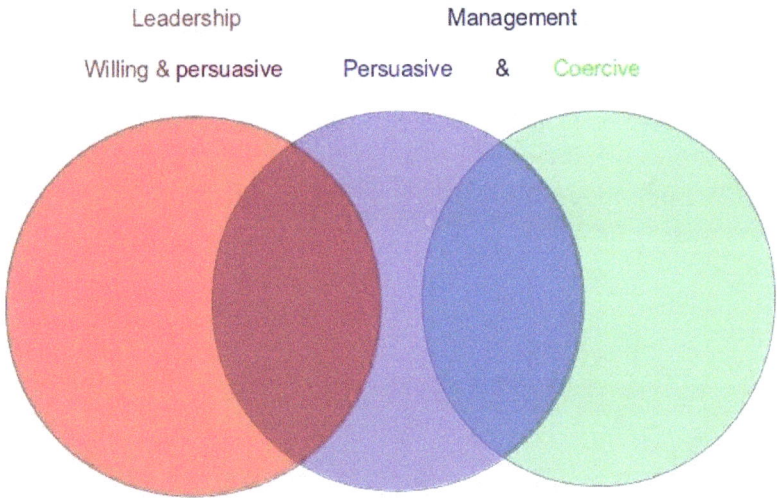

Leadership   Management

Willing & persuasive   Persuasive   &   Coercive

Leader – Follower hierarchical relationships

Figure 29.1 Venn diagram 4: leader–follower hierarchical relationships

Misunderstanding and confusion reign, partly because of poor definitions, but also because humans are capable of all of these relationships, and as they age they experience and develop them all in one form or another. They are able to, and often do, change the type of message they use depending on the co-constituents they are addressing at the time. Sandhurst states that a leader needs the ability to generate all these types of relationships. This is to be effective, or efficient, or to be good: no specific term is used by Sandhurst to qualify the leader. It is a statement designed for the positional leader in all situations; however, this also highlights the confusion. The positional leader needs these types of relationships, but the leader in question does not represent leadership exclusively. Often it is the resulting blend of relationships that makes a positional leader effective or efficient, but again there is no exclusivity of effectiveness and efficiency to one type of relationship or another.

A relationship is clear in the formula, but over time an individual may range from one to another type of message and get decisions or initiative-owned decisions from all groups. The relationship needs to be measured over time and labelled after the predominant form that is exercised between the co-constituents is established. At different levels of a large group it will vary. It is possible to audit all levels of an organisation and determine the prevailing relationships at different levels and overall.

Chapter 30: Overlapping relationships and final definitions

'Whether individuals or organizations, we follow those who lead not because we have to, but because we want to. We follow those who lead not for them, but for ourselves.'

Simon Sinek

The relationships have been differentiated into two main types: initiative-owned decisions and normal decisions. The labels attached to them are 'leadership' and 'management', with a further distinction under the management relationship label between persuasive and coercive relationships. The terms are commonly understood and describe the behaviours reflected in the equations and their patterns. They are similar to ones used earlier from the Royal Military Academy Sandhurst, where they teach the three types of leadership: first lead by example, then by persuasion, and then if necessary by discipline.

The purpose of these three different types of ability in the positional leader is to be effective in their role and position. The actions, to be effective, do not necessarily describe the leadership relationship or the ability itself. To be effective in the leader's position it may well be necessary for a leader to have knowledge or all three types of relationships.

In practice individuals will recognise the speech patterns in everyday use in all groups and subgroups. The individual looking to assume a leader's position will do so by focusing on one or more of these types of relationships. RMAS suggests that the ideal type of relationship to use, to which many aspire, is to lead by example or get willing engagement from the co-constituents.

This specific type of relationship is called 'initiative-owned leadership' in order to distinguish it from the general non-specific use of the word 'leadership' which applies more to a word that describes any action done by an individual in the leader's position. The leader must convince the followers to be co-authors and co-owners of the Group purpose.

When Warren Bennis proposed that leaders needed to be authentic, he was using another term that has been used to label leadership without differentiating it easily. 'Authentic' implies that the leader must have obvious ownership of the position, resolving the SC and the plan to be authentic. The leader creates or maintains ownership in the group members through accurate defining, co-authoring and communicating the Gp.

Simon Sinek in his global bestselling book *Start with Why* [35], identified that it is what he calls 'the reason why' that is the motivator behind great leaders and causes. People follow these leaders and causes because it is right. Those that start with the reason why will build their relationships on much stronger foundations than those who don't. The quote from Simon Sinek at the beginning of this chapter is most important when it states in the final sentence: 'We follow those who lead not for them, but for ourselves'. He goes on to design his 'Golden circle' in order to demonstrate his concept of how some leaders inspire rather than manipulate in order to motivate people.

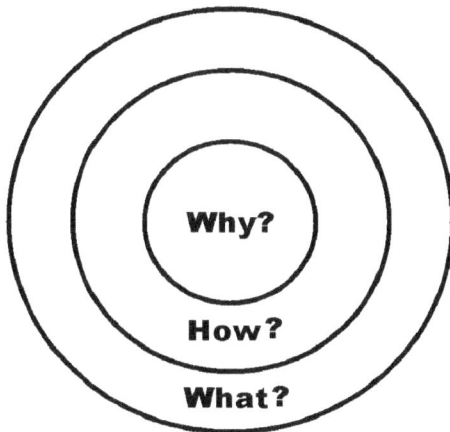

Figure 30.1 Simon Sinek's Golden circle

The terms in Simon Sinek's Golden Circle are as follows:[44]

'WHAT' applies to what the organisation does. Every organisation knows what services or products they sell.

'HOW' they do what they do. Some organisations know how they make themselves more valuable to the customer than other competitors. How do they make theirs unique and different in order to get the customer to buy them?

'WHY' means what is the purpose behind making the product or service, what specific challenge is it answering?

The sequence within the ring, moving from outside to inside, is the path that most people take. The path that great leaders and causes communicate is from the inside out.

It is not dissimilar from the decision equation in that it is providing a tool to help identify a common path in an individual's decision making process. Using this knowledge a similar circle can be drawn to give focus to the key components that result in a leadership relationship being possible. Purpose is in the centre, support and benefits are in the middle, and the task is on the outside.

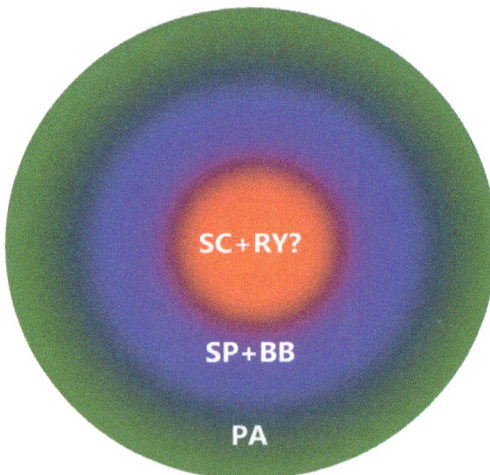

Figure 30.2 The relationship target

The relationship target combines the components of the Gp and places them in the circle at different corresponding levels to the

Why, How and What terms used by Simon Sinek. The relationship target uses the circle concept in order to draw a parallel in the focus on the centre, like that of a bull's eye in a target, yet it places the decision equation components at the corresponding levels away from the centre.

The colours representing each ring or component focus area are indicative of the relationships. SC + RY? relate to purpose and initiative-owned leadership, Sp and BB are the elements used to persuade, and the PA component in isolation would be a coercive relationship. There is no specific boundary in the colouring to signify the fact that there is often overlap in the relationships used over time.

The components and equation are placed in three different rings to demonstrate the priority of each level in parallel to Simon Sinek's golden circle. The three relationships are: initiative-owned leadership (the inner bull's eye, red, Why and purpose-focused), management by persuasion (middle ring, blue) and management by coercion (outer ring, green). Relationships build on the outer rings, and as the co-constituents become more knowledgeable the more they transition toward the inner bull's eye. The inner bull's eye, based on purpose, which allows for initiative-owned actions and initiative-owned solutions, is the target of most groups.

As such it specifies that initiative-owned actions are the key difference between an effective relationship and others. To define leadership itself the definition must include not only the function, but also the reason why it is done. Why is leadership done, what or who is it done to, and how is it done? All these questions must be answered within the definition. The description of the function and purpose of a leader from Part 4 is brought forward for further refinement:

'The leader initiates and facilitates the defining and communication of the group purpose in order to create and maintain initiative ownership in that group purpose.'

Part 5 introduced the confirmation stage of the relationship, and that action expressed is needed to demonstrate that the decision that has been made. A leader must create the environment for positive initiative-owned actions to take place in order for leadership relationship to be started. The leader must create tacit knowledge in the followers in order to achieve the possibility for initiative ownership to resolve the SC presented to the group. Only after consistently achieving positive initiative-owned actions can a leadership relationship be established and maintained. In each case the term *leadership* is referring to

'Leadership is a relationship where a leader initiates and facilitates the defining and communicating of the group purpose in order to create or maintain positive initiative-owned actions of the group purpose by the group.'

This is specifically called an initiative-owned leadership relationship:

+ioA => ioLR

'Management is a relationship where a leader defines and controls the group purpose and uses persuasion or coercion in order to create and maintain the ability of the group to achieve task related actions.'

+A => MR

'A persuasive relationship is where a leader defines and controls access to the benefits and support for the group in order to create and maintain the ability of the group to achieve a positive action which may or may not be resolving the group purpose.'

This is specifically called a management by persuasion relationship:

+A => M(persu)R

'A coercive relationship is where a leader defines, demands and instructs the group in order to create and maintain the ability of the group to achieve a positive action with no reference to the group purpose'.

This is specifically called a management by coercion relationship:

+A => M(coerc)R

The definition of leadership is the result of following through a group's decision-making process using the decision equation as a tool to analyse and match accepted terms for relationships. The relationships have been labelled where it is possible to differentiate the pattern as well as use terms that describe the behaviour displayed by the relationship. This is done to identify and define the relationship. There are areas of overlap, although with expanded decision equations it is possible to specify the relationship.

To verify whether the group actions are the result of an act of leadership, or whether the leadership is effective, or even measurable, again the decision equation can also be used as a guide. Part 6 covers these aspects of leadership verification and measurement.

PART 6: Verifying and measuring leadership

Chapter 31: The DAS chain and de-linked groups

'Management is of the mind, more a matter of accurate calcula-
tion, of statistics, of methods, timetables and routine; its practice
is a science. Managers are necessary; leaders are essential.'

Field Marshall Viscount Slim

Once a challenge is identified and specified the individual starts a
process of thought that can lead to actions and ultimately the successful resolution of the specified challenge. This is the case for all
challenges, from very simple ones that involve just one person or a
small group to those that engage whole nations. There is a chain of
events that happen once the challenge is identified and defined. A
complete chain is one that starts from a challenge to launch the decision process into action and provides a solution to that challenge.
This process is known as the Decision $\rightarrow$ Action $\rightarrow$ Solution chain
and each link is vital to maintaining the chain.

Example 31.1 The Decision $\rightarrow$ Action $\rightarrow$ Solution chain

$$\text{Decision} \rightarrow \text{Action} \rightarrow \text{Solution (DAS)}$$

$$D => A => S$$

DAS chains occur everywhere and all the time, from individuals
who feel hunger and somehow feed themselves to groups that are
threatened and that resolve, delay or eliminate the threat. How this
is done in groups has been the study of leadership as a general
term. This book has focused on the specific definition of leadership
in groups and the resolution of DAS chains. The decision equation
forms the start of the chain and uses the components to create the
decisions that lead to the actions and solutions.

As seen earlier, defining the components of the equation shapes
the message and the relationship in the group. The types of relationships made will to a large extent determine the efforts of the

group. The accurate definition of the SC will have a bearing on the effectiveness as a factor in the determination of motivation in the group. Once additional components, such as RY?, are added, they not only make the decision equation unique to that group, they also introduce potential for conflicting interests or correct linkage and alignment.

Each component must play its part and be aligned to resolving the SC to motivate others to join their group and to do so on a regular basis. When competing groups are present it can increase the options open to resolving the SC, improving effectiveness and driving efficiencies in the groups responding to that challenge.

Some will say that the reason why a commercial business exists is to make a profit. Remembering that motivation is specific to the individual, to claim that all co-constituents in the group are motivated by making a profit can only be the case if all can be convinced that they will individually benefit from the profit somehow. Many group members are not able to see any evidence of the link between company group profits and their individual BB. Not surprisingly, they fail to be motivated to work harder and provide the owner with another swimming pool or help put more money into the shareholders' pockets. Group members are rarely ever allowed access to the detailed accounts where future allocations of any profit might go. Any perceived link between profit and their individual benefit is just that: a perception or assumption, not based on fact.

If the business can receive sufficient revenue and be efficient with the use of its resources it will make a profit. Investors will invest. If they cannot do so then investors will not invest. Profit is a result of the Decision → Action → Solution chain, not a reason for the group to be created. This is deductive reasoning and based on results produced. The new investment is made based on inductive reasoning that over time the model will continue. Inductive thinking is based on knowledge, which Michael Polanyi labelled tacit knowledge or even tacit belief, that the model can continue if all stays the same.

Getting a profit from this particular DAS chain depends on having the right mix of people, capital and market access to be able to resolve the SC. Shareholders and owners of the company provide finance to the business. The provision of finance is a resource and should be listed in the Support component. Finance is a resource in the decision equation. The group as an entity will be engage in defining the RY? as well as supplying the finance in the SP component. A renewed injection of capital is done based on results gained previously and the tacit belief, hope or tacit knowledge and inductive reasoning that it is possible to get profit from the group.

There is an assumption that if the factors all remain the same why shouldn't the resulting profits continue? Because things change, people and ideas change, challenges change, and seasons change, and if they didn't things would remain the same – but they don't, and history has shown this. By using the same inductive reasoning used to encourage the investment the investors will understand that the factors will not stay the same.

Any profit comes as a result of the whole DAS chain process after the solution. In the case of Lincoln Electric, for example, James Lincoln was very clear in his priority listing of the DAS chain and what level of priority the investors had in the DAS chain. The definition of the components of the equation is of great importance to the group and its members. The terms laid out in the employment agreement are there to protect both the group and the group members. Employment agreements rarely reveal the split of resources across the whole group. The agreements usually only detail the benefits coming to the individual who is signing the agreement. Few are in possession of the tacit knowledge needed to be motivated by profit. Any assumptions to the contrary are just that: assumptions.

Profit is often used as an indication of the success of the group. Is it a reliable measure of the leadership in a group? As a measure of the use of all of the resources in that DAS chain, profit is an indicator. Profit as a measure of the relationship and how the human resources were motivated to use those resources is perhaps not the best indicator. The profit numbers are often used to attract further investment, and the numbers are based on many factors. The relationship in the group is just one influencing factor.

Few individuals are motivated to work to get profit for another individual or group of individuals unless the benefits are spread proportionally according to input, or their needs are already adequately met. What an individual determines is adequate for his needs will often depend on comparisons with peers in their groups, and on cultural and group norms. Some will place higher values on the Gp than others. Some individuals, when compared to others, will demand less from the group than others. This is a measure of the individual's commitment to a purpose or cause in comparison to others in the group, but only if the individual's hygienic needs are already met or assured in the future.

Leadership is the ability to initiate and facilitate the defining and communication of the Gp in order to create or maintain initiative ownership in the Gp by the group. If in the process of communicating with the co-constituents no components of the purpose are included, then it is not possible to consistently get initiative ownership over time. The Group section of the equation has become de-linked from the purpose section of the Gp. The DAS chain has been broken and the group is de-linked.

In cases of de-linking, solutions do not resolve the SC at all. A task instruction to block a gap in a doorway can be done by a wire mesh across the gap, but if the SC is to block the gap in order to prevent water from seeping in, the wire mesh solution is ineffective. The task instruction message from the leader is de-linked from the SC. In this case the solution is ineffective.

This is a very simple demonstration of de-linking. As has been demonstrated with relationships the cases are often not so clear-cut. There are differing levels of de-linking and products may meet 90% of the challenge but fail on 10%. If there are no alternatives to fill that gap, the customer has to accept it until an alternative can better that level of linkage and resolve the remaining 10% as well. There is an opportunity, but a new decision equation is needed first and the customer may not agree to the price. The new DAS chain is stopped before it reaches the action stage.

There are levels to de-linking and the customer will constantly be looking to get 100%, whereas many companies will only provide what is necessary to beat the competition, such as 91%. They are more efficient, perhaps, but most important for the customer is whether the 1% increase in effectiveness is worth the increase in price if there is one.

Many groups suffer from a level of de-linking when they produce solutions that are not fit for task. Groups that exist to resolve a SC can evaluate their SP, PA and BB against the SC. When they do not resolve they SC, they are de-linked with the SC they were formed to resolve but they might be accepted as the best option in the market. This is the customer's choice to accept a substandard service. The supplier may advertise itself as the world's best solution provider, and claim is true, at the time, as the supplier beats the competition and is the only 91% solution provider on offer. The laws of supply and demand have always affected, and will continue to affect, future solutions. It does not mean the supplier is de-linked or linked; to find this out the assessor must know the DAS chain from SC to solutions.

The financial crisis in 2008 highlighted a number of cases of de-linking. When customers placed their money in a building society or commercial bank, they did so on the understanding that it would be safe. This is a concept that has prevailed over the collective memory of those cultures with experience of the banking industry. The money was expected to be secure. The customer's money would get protection and the customer would be afforded a degree of convenience in access to and use of their money.

The customer was attracted by the safety and the level of personal service. The customer knew the bank would use the money to invest and gain a profit, and in return the customer could expect to be paid some interest on their savings to keep up with inflation. Competition between different commercial banks and building societies created different types of services with different interest rates, charges, accessibility and levels of credit.

There were, however, a smaller group of customers, usually companies, whose needs were very different, and much larger sums were required than standard mortgages and common personal loans. International trade and global market access created the need for much larger amounts of capital and firms stepped up to provide this capital, at a price, to these special customers. The high-volume capital companies needed much larger assets to offset the risks and act as securities against these higher volumes. The securities firms established themselves in this niche with corresponding interest rates, systems and gearings that attracted this type of corporate customer.

The SC of these two types of customer was measurably different in the risk and securities needed to balance against that volume of capital and risk. In the aftermath of the 1929 crash it was perceived that the difference should be enforced and the 1933 Banking Act (Glass–Steagall) was passed to restrict affiliations between the commercial banks and securities firms, amongst other provisions. This segregated the two very different DAS chains with their very different initiating SC components.

Over the passing years, different interpretations of the 1933 Banking Act were permitted and they succeeded in neutralising the effect of the segregation to the point where it was repealed by Congress in the 1999 Gramm–Leach–Bliley Act. While the exact market conditions of 1929 did not exist in 2008, the repeal of the laws and provisions that separated the commercial banks and the securities firms was viewed by many experts as a factor which engaged the retail level customer assets with the high-risk environment of the securities firms without informing them of the change, or giving them any of the advantages of that service.

When the 2008 crisis unfolded, the customers of the commercial bank model felt entrapped and cheated. Little clarity on where the commercial banking customers' money was being invested and improper practices in the sale of policies led to the widespread involvement of all users of money and credit systems in the USA and across the global financial markets as a whole. A long-term solution has still yet to be provided to prevent this from happening again.

The merging of commercial banks and securities firms had caused the firms to become de-linked from the commercial banking customers. The actions of the merged firms no longer had any relations with the SC as defined by the commercial banking customers. The leaders of the newly merged or formed financial companies did not redefine the DAS chain and did not engage with the commercial banking and mortgage-based customers to redefine the new DAS chain. Instead, the new companies used securities firm service advantages to sell new policies without backing the risk, as previously expected by the commercial banking customers.

There is also a case for the regulators being flat footed in their reaction to the new situation. Commercial banking regulators were ill equipped to cope with the new securities firms' processes and concepts. Sometimes even the securities firms themselves could not unravel the defined risk for adequate due diligence and analysis until after it had been accepted and was too late.

If we look at history to gain an insight into the potential inductive reasoning of the regulators at the time, the number of banks and securities firms that were failing leading up to 2008 had been growing both in frequency and in the volume of losses per failure. The trend was there, yet no requirement was made to prove that the industry was providing adequate measures or whether they linked service in line with the SC of the customers. The checks required up until then were only to prove that they were meeting a ratio based on historical data that was inconsistent with new debt and crediting systems.

With 20/20 hindsight it is easy to point fingers and make accusations. What is more difficult is to provide useful solutions. Increased regulations and procedures will deny initiative and thereby dull the beneficial effects of competition to give better solutions to the customers. That is, of course, if all the customers' needs are being met. Regulations may provide stability and reduced risk for those who define that as their SC. The balance is not easy to find, but it should not be the case that a small minority is able to benefit when the hygienic needs of the majority are being used and lost to provide these benefits. When the group co-constituents change and the SC is no longer as previously defined, then the whole decision equation needs to be rewritten, component by component. Regulators can use the decision equation as a guide to evaluate whether the provider is committing fraud or not and whether it is providing resolution as advertised or is just incompetent.

The process of linking is often not addressed by leaders and purpose is not considered a priority for all of the co-constituents in an organisation. Leaders often wrongly assume that the purpose is obvious and they choose not to re-examine the SC or RY? the group is created in the first place. As time goes by the parties must regularly review and redefine when needed. This is often considered a function of the leader in the group, even though all co-constituents are involved in the DAS chain. The purpose may well change from the original situation for reasons such as an alternative becoming available, or the challenge ceasing to exist.

Relationships are challenging because change exists. The faster the change the greater the need for leaders to reassess, re-engage and create or maintain the environment for positive group-based initiative actions to be possible. Typically, as markets change and new challenges present themselves the change requires a new decision equation and evaluations to be made. The short cut is to reassess and then just issue the demand or task instruction. It is quicker, even though it makes the next change more difficult.

In the case of the 1933 Banking Act (Glass–Steagall) it was a hindsight action designed to segregate the more high-risk needs into a separate category. The commercial banking organisations were clearly not fit to deal with the new levels of SC presented. The need and demand for capital or credit is clear and for the most part understood. Its source should not be at the expense of other unrelated groups and outside individuals' hygienic needs.

Leaders in the build-up to the 1929 crash had failed to reassess the risk potential, or were ignored in favour of the minority group's or individuals' profit potential. As situations develop the need to monitor the risk is as great as the need to cover the shortfall. The potential for a firm to corner the benefits while passing the risk to the majority or a separate group with no penalty undermines the concept of the larger group membership benefits.

Subgroups are de-linked from the larger financial industry's reason for existing. The options are to isolate the risk from the main group; prevent the risk in the interests of the larger group by better monitoring and regulation to reduce the risks; or finally to introduce penalties to outweigh the benefits to the minority that act outside the interests of the larger group.

When de-linking occurs it is the leaders of those groups who are responsible, as they have failed to maintain an effective relationship. There is either a lack of an explicitly defined decision equation or the original definitions are not explicit enough to cope with the changed environment and need updating. Typically this situation presents itself when the expectation from the customer is still there, demanding accountability, but it is increasingly difficult without clear definition. There is a lack of explicit definition and it makes the measurement of the relationship, particularly effectiveness, more difficult. Constant evaluation and redefining is needed in order to ensure that the group is effective in its purpose.

An example is taken from the UK's National Health Service (NHS). The Secretary of State for the Department of Health's remit is taken from the National Health Service Act, originally enacted in 1948 and updated in 2006.[45] As an act of parliament it details the task of the Secretary of State for the Department of Health. The PA is listed in great detail, which is helpful and at the same time limiting.

Nowhere in the Act or the constitution, which is extracted from the Act, is there an explicit statement of the SC or the RY? the Act was proposed. To find details of the purpose one has to go back to the history books and immerse oneself in the politics and emotions of the Second World War and its immediate aftermath in the UK when the first National Health Act was designed and enacted in 1946.

The Act and the reforms it brought about were based on William Beveridge's 1942 report.[46] The report argued that universal access to healthcare was necessary in order to fight the 'five giants': want, disease, squalor, ignorance and idleness. Beveridge believed that the government should provide its citizens with social security 'from the cradle to the grave'. In the case of the NHS, the SC had been identified to address the challenge of disease, the second of the five giants. To some extent squalor and ignorance had been identified in the report as being within the remit of the health service, although this was not explicitly stated.

No levels of prevention or lists of the types of diseases were outlined or included, as no SC was ever explicitly defined. The RY? the government believed UK should have this was assumed and again not clearly stated, defined or irrevocably attached to the National Health Service Act in order to provide clear and easy reference for those looking for direction and purpose. The challenge remained general and all-encompassing. This may well have been the intention, but it is extremely difficult to measure or provide for a general, open to definition and interpretation, goal as politicians know only too well.

Politicians at the time stated that there were a number of reasons for the establishment of the NHS. Aneurin Bevan, the first Secretary of State for Health, said:

'The collective principle asserts that... no society can legitimately call itself civilised if a sick person is denied medical aid because of lack of means.'[47]

Mr Bevin later stated in his resignation letter to Clement Atlee that the welfare services, of which the NHS was one corner stone, gave:

'...Britain the moral leadership of the world'[48]

From this letter one might extract that the RY? the Health Service was created was to establish moral leadership of the world in terms of healthcare for its people, in order to define the UK as a civilised country? Perhaps, as the past tense in the letter suggests, this moral leadership was a result of the 1946 National Health Service Act and its implementation in 1948. This may appear a cynical analysis of the situation, but it is done only in light of currently reported criticism of the NHS. To measure the NHS's effectiveness or efficiency and prevent further misdirection of the Health Service's actions, a more explicit SC needs to be defined to keep up with the times and demands of the UK people to whom the health service belongs, according to the NHS constitution.

The NHS and the global financial institutions are both examples of groups that suffer from a lack of current explicit definition of the SC. As a consequence of this, the groups' effectiveness, and whether they are fit for purpose, becomes more difficult to assess. As the customers become more demanding and earlier targets are reached, new ones need to be made. At the outset it was deemed enough to get the NHS system up and running. The system has been up and running for a long time now and it needs to be made effective, more specific for its purpose. Greater efficiencies are also demanded, and this is a different measurement from effectiveness. Again, it too needs well-defined components and they should either be subsumed in the purpose of the group or the purpose should be redefined.

In the financial markets the SC of the customer has changed as well as the instruments used to provide for that need. New equations need to be written to update and provide for new demands and ensure that the DAS chain is positive towards the customers and group rather than just the isolated group of individuals within it.

De-linking occurs by separation of the SC from the other components of the Gp. Effective relationships are often based on correct identification of the SC and RY? The purpose will influence and motivate the group members and how they use and allocate resources. The leader represents the group entity and ensures that the focus of the co-constituents is positive, towards the group rather than the individual.

Group structure can influence the leaders' ability to engage and ensure linking across the whole Gp with all the group members. Traditional multiple level groups are common. The organisation creates these limitations on defining components as deemed necessary to allow for engagement and functional controls within the group. The defining of both the Purpose and Group sections of the positional leader's message is linked to each level of the group all the way down. The traditional group structure in theory allows the co-constituents engagement, throughout the overall group, of all the components used in the Gp.

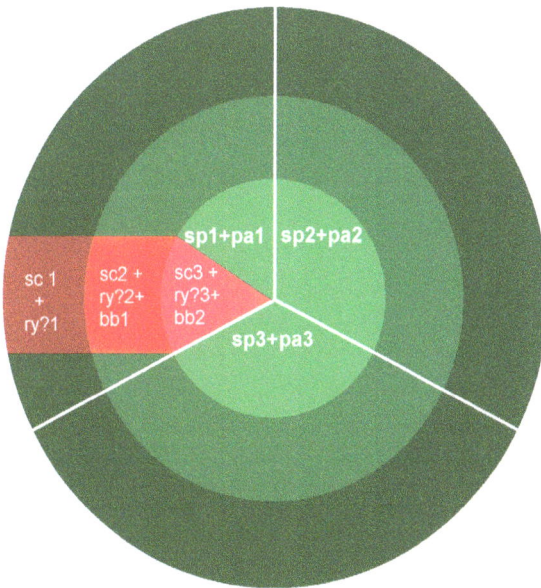

Figure 31.1 Venn diagram 5: a traditional multi layered group with Gp co-authors

In Figure 31.1 the multiple layers of the group are shown in different shades of green. The party of leaders at each level is contained within the red areas. The components of the decision equation are broken down into smaller elements of the component at each group level. Each group level leader is able to define all components and engage with the co-constituents from the larger group message and decide what not to include in the subgroup level message in order to create the environment for initiative or not. The functions within each level can be linked to the overall group's SC; in this example three functions are identified and are consistent throughout all levels of the group, and subgroups.

In some large groups the organisational structure may add to the difficulty of ensuring that the customer and overall group-agreed SC gets all the way down to the operators and achieves complete penetration and linking. Some organisations impose limitations on component engagement internal to their group by restricting authorities, creating multiple checks and balances to minimise risk and safeguard the interests of that subgroup. Some subgroups have limitations imposed upon them by seemingly unrelated outside groups, such as national level legal structures which differ between countries. Some examples are labour laws, copyright rules, financial laws, company licensing laws and environmental, health and safety laws. The matrix of component restrictions is overlaid on the group structure from outside, or the group self imposes it.

A matrix organisation is created at a level when the group imposes internal rules to prevent any engagement in some or all components between the parties in the group. Figure 31.2 shows a matrix structure overlaid onto the inner group in a traditional multilevel structure of groups. The blue areas denote the matrix areas focused on a particular component or aspect of the component in order to allow the subgroup members to focus on it: for example, production (PA), finance (SP fin), logistics SP(log), customer service SP(maint) or similar division of labour based on the nature of the resource or function. Within the matrix the subgroups reverts to traditional subsubgroupings in the shape of their circles (yellow, orange, and pink) for engagement on their specific function. The structure limits the components that can be defined by the subsubgroups.

The matrix structure explained above overlays limitations on defining certain components of the group purpose to the larger groups in the organisation. This could be due to functional specialisation or national level legal restrictions. It gains efficiencies in resource use, specialisation and functional focus, but introduces longer lines of communications. The efficiencies that a matrix structure is designed to improve are communications between layers, standard practices, new concepts, ideas, specialised knowledge, and approval processes in specialist fields.

It can be seen to help build relationships, loyalty and a sense of belonging and value to an organisation of peers within the organisation, creating a sense of competition. It helps reduce the distraction that other components might cause in the decision process and focuses individuals on the specific component field they are trained in.

Figure 31.2 Venn diagram 6: a matrix within in a traditional structure

This type of structure can be seen in many companies where the new concepts and skills in, for example, sales and marketing or R&D need to be communicated to all sales or R&D team members at every level of the overall group. The training, communications, procedures and support for that new concept can be put in place quickly and take effect hopefully faster than the competition can do it. Similarly, in theory the response to the SC presented by customers in demand for a product can be met by production teams all over the group as fast as possible.

This need for effectiveness and efficiency gives rise to matrix structure overlays within traditional structures. The difference between the two is which structure takes priority in terms of the Gp engagement and sequence of priorities. If the group structure is imposed from outside the group as a law of the country then it must be applied or the group risks conviction and penalties for operating against the interests of that country grouping.

The authority and levels of responsibility should match corresponding levels of definition within the appropriate group level. Where the group leaders are expected to take responsibility for the results without any ability to define the factors in the components that could affect the results it ends in frustration.

When the component relates to the function, exclusivity is given to that subgroup organisation, and at that level it is a matrix organisation. The matrix organisation focuses the expertise of a function or component in one area. The component is its function and that task completion becomes the priority. As long as the component function is still linked to and evaluated against the SC of the overall group's DAS chain the matrix can potentially achieve its effectiveness. Where the two are separated by long lines of ineffective communications the efficiencies are lost.

For example, take the case when the production unit of a multinational company in one country is told by a customer in that same country that they need a modification to be made to the product that the unit supplies. This sounds simple enough. The multinational in question has a matrix overlay that places limitation of engagement of production matters outside and above the country level of the group. The request from the customer is no longer a local matter.

The production unit is prevented from changing anything due to internal rules until the sales and marketing unit, which is a different unit and perhaps legal entity, and is responsible for defining and confirming the SC with the customer, authorises this change. If this message needs to go through many different layers of the organisation above and only then be transferred to the production (PA) component at a higher level before going through production approvals, such as R&D and engineering, and then returning to sales before finally returning to country level, it will take longer.

In addition, the message will change as it filters back and forth from customer to the higher level then across to production before a possible approval and instruction down the production chain to the in-country production unit. If the bosses of both of these production and sales components of the company are in different countries and at different levels of the larger group it adds more time and possibility for the message to change in ways that may be detrimental. The need for efficiencies in the organisation has created the potential for inefficiencies across the decision equation.

The advantages and disadvantages of a matrix organisation can be maximised using the decision equation to ensure efficiencies across DAS chains. The key point is the group's ability to link to all of the components of the equation in the interests of effectiveness and efficiencies. There will at some stage be a balance struck between these two factors which will become the priority ranking and can be expressed throughout the relationship.

Within organisations there are differing levels of authority to define the components, but all levels should have access to and have as a focal point the specific challenge of the group. Matrix structures are designed in the interests of efficiency and balanced against many factors, ranging from a simple one, like whether the customer's SC changes regularly or not, to other factors, such as how technical the product or service is. How regulated the market is and the risks involved should not be the cause for a leader to de-link the co-constituents from the Gp; indeed, there is more reason to strengthen the tacit knowledge of the group members to get better solutions.

Within both types of structures it is still possible for the lowest level group member to know and understand the SC of the overall larger group and the RW? at the highest level. Where the SC is ignored or specifically not included on the priority list in one subgroup, it will conflict with another group's priority ranking of effectiveness above efficiency. This is often seen in practice as the conflict between cost reduction versus any measure of quality, or in operations versus finance, or subgroup against subgroup. The overall Gp has been ignored or not defined and communicated effectively.

As the message and SC get passed they may go through two, three or more layers, each time possibly being translated and reinterpretation. The more layers, the greater the likelihood that the exact message may not be received in full, and the process of delinking starts.

Mottos and logos are commonly used by marketing teams to appeal to external groups. These are also used as ways of ensuring that the internal co-constituents of the group are linked to the customer and Gp. For a motto to have the desired affect the SC needs to be included. A well-constructed motto serves to link both the co-constituents and customers. It reminds them both of the initiating SC and RY? of the group and its priority towards the SC of the customer. Linking is the way to tacit knowledge. Tacit knowledge is the basis for initiative and initiative-owned decisions, actions and ultimately solutions that resolve the customer's initiating challenge.

Chapter 32: The verification of leadership

> 'Good is the enemy of great'
>
> *Jim Collins*

Proving leadership, without a clearly defined understanding of what leadership is provides the paradox. How can leadership be proved? In practice it is down to the interpretation of the assessor. For many in the past, it was enough to display the traits of a leader to qualify. Being in the leader's position in a group was also a very general way to prove leadership based on a positional definition of leadership. Academics, when asked to prove leadership, defensively highlight the lack of a suitable definition to be able to do so. After all what is the motivation for an academic to prove leadership? If any real motivator exists it would be the recognition of just having resolved the challenge, a purely intrinsic motivator.

Fortunately applicators are motivated to prove leadership by more than just the intrinsic factors. Resolving the SC of a group and achieving consistent positive initiatives, by developing individuals into a strong confident team and achieving solutions previously thought not possible have benefits that are practical in application. The group may achieve growth and greater revenue and possibly profits. The results of the group build a reputation which may be linked to the positional leader and individuals in the group. This recognition gains the leader respect and status among those who recognise this as a talent.

The recognition and reputation would create a need for this talent where there is a perceived or real lack of leadership. The leader's extrinsic value would increase due to the laws of supply and demand for this ability to create a more effective group and garner what is considered success from his team. Position, contractual agreements and rewards are offered for this ability to create successful teams. The extrinsic values will come as a result of a successful group, but they are not necessarily an indicator of leadership, just of the ability to be successful as a group. This is a common confusion, to link and assume a 'successful group' with good leadership.

While good leadership can lead to success, a successful group is not always the result of good leadership. The initiative-owned leadership relationship can be realised during the process of planning and action. 'Success', on the other hand is a loose term and is open to interpretation and based on many contributing factors, such as revenue, costs of materials, weather and many others, all dependent on how the assessor chooses to define success. One of the contributing factors could also be good initiative-owned leadership.

Jim Collins, in his popular book *Built to Last: Successful Habits of Visionary Companies*', published in 1994 [7], and subsequent follow up books address the issues of success and leadership, reinforcing the implication that the two terms are inextricably linked. In *Built to Last*, Collins identifies the Big Hairy Audacious Goal (BHAG)[49] as the key focal point of the group, and this provides the glue which unites the group. A good BHAG is labelled as a motivator, something to pursue above the basic needs that go beyond the simple desire to make money.

In *Good to Great: Why Some Companies Make the Leap... and Others Don't*, published in 2001 [38], Collins focused on 11 companies that were successful in terms of consistent stock market returns. He stated how he and presumably the stock market defines the term success. Stock market returns are at least one way of measuring success. In that same book he identified traits that are possessed by the leaders of these companies and he has given them a ranking structure of five levels of leadership, with Level 5 leadership being the highest and most desirable level to achieve.

A sceptic would cry that correlation does not imply causation. There is a gut feeling that the two are connected, but it cannot be proven that the success is due to the positional leaders and not a combination of many other factors. Also, leadership relationships exist outside of stock market-listed groups everywhere in very large numbers. The success of the company is measurable, but the criteria he uses to measure leadership are different and do not include factors included by the stock markets. The measurements are different and the coincidence of membership of the leader in the company is not the exclusive factor for success.

As in many other trait-based studies, in the *Good to Great* Collins identifies many characteristics perceived to be needed in a leader but does not isolate the ones that are specific to the leader and not the other co-constituents. Some of the co-constituents may also have these traits. They were not in the position when these traits combined with the team of co-constituents at the time, along with outside factors like market forces and capital availability, to result in his definition of a successful company.

The success of a company is not always caused by great Level 5 combinations of traits, just as it is possible to have such a combination of traits but still not be successful as a group. What may have a marginally higher degree of predictability is that if the positional leader does not possess any of the traits then it is less likely the group will be successful when competing against another group which does have these Level 5 traits as well as similar levels of the many others factors including the different co-constituents in each group that influence the outcome. That situation of 'equal factors bar one' does not happen in reality.

Good to Great seems to be grasping for and missing a key motivational element of the group as a separate entity. It is, as mentioned before, something that provides a platform or hook for the Gp to base or hang from and be the focus of all group members. The good BHAG he refers to is loosely that purpose that unites them. In his hedgehog and fox parable he identifies the need for consistent direction and momentum. The purpose and a proof of actions from the history of the group are those motivators of direction and momentum for all group members. This is knowledge that leaders must learn and understand.

Collins identifies the need for a method by which the leader can evaluate people's performance and how to hire the right people. Scott Adams referred to this in his cartoon strip earlier as the 'circular reasoning' that Dilbert mentions as the key to success of the group. These are factors that make a group more effective and efficient, but to identify and recruit the right people the 'why' and 'how' of the group must be identified first in order to provide the motivation for an individual to elect to join and stay in the group in the first place.

The definition of initiative-owned leadership is detailed enough to provide a practical method to prove the existence of leadership. The presence of positive initiative-owned actions is proof of willing and therefore a leadership relationship, specifically an initiative-owned leadership relationship. Positive initiative-owned decisions and actions are the differentiating factor between leadership and management relationships. Positive initiative-owned actions are clearly defined and can be proven by analysing the messages between the co-constituents in a relationship.

Positive initiative-owned actions provide the proof of leadership and progress into initiative-owned solutions. Positive initiative-owned actions can be explained clearly using definitions rather than gut feeling and confusing general terms, as is currently the case. These positive initiative-owned actions prove the presence of leadership. It is not to be confused with other terms such as success.

Ideally the followers at all levels will have an understanding of the purpose of the group, at least in concept, all the way to the highest level of the group. When operators in factories are asked why they do what they do, their answers will reveal whether there is the potential to take action in the direction of the group purpose. Some may even describe what they do in terms of solving the SC rather than stating their job title or function. A leadership assessor could compare this answer to the leaders of the groups at higher and higher levels and they will reveal what relationship environment has been created and whether it is by design, chance or experience-based guesswork.

By using this approach in a small isolated group it is relatively easy to prove leadership. They may know all the components of the Gp and it is possible to assess relatively quickly. In larger groups it will take more time, depending on the depth of the study. The level of penetration of the SC link and the relationships throughout the organisation can be assessed. Multiple layers of hierarchy increase the amount of time and planning needed to infuse the Gp into a large organisation. An assessor needs the overall group-level SC in order to search at lower levels for its presence in the subgroup positional leaders' messages. This is done to verify and assess the level of leadership penetration.

In matrix organisations, with their formal component limited engagement between the co-constituents, there is still the potential for co-constituents to create positive initiative-owned actions based on the components allowed and not the whole equation. The initiative actions will be based on the subgroup's component that has become the focus of the initiative challenge Gp. This will indicate positive initiative actions being present on that one component.

The subgroup could be creating products not fit to meet the SC that originated in another very distant part of the organisation. The subgroup has become de-linked from the overall SC while displaying positive initiative-owned action based on a task rather than the SC. The task could even have been issued by the customer in the form of a Request For Tender (RFT) document detailing the specifications of the product in order to get the same product from a number of sources so as to do comparison pricing. This task instruction, being issued by the customer, does not include why the product is needed and the specified challenge that it is supposed to resolve. The supplier is being denied the tacit knowledge needed for a good initiative-owned solution that exceeds the expectations of the customer.

Commercial industry is not the only area where groups strive for products and services that are fit for purpose. In research and development, the provision of services to save lives is an area which has a clear purpose identified and assumed, if not explicitly stated, as in the NHS. In the case where there is no competition to win these services the purpose is the standard.

The particle accelerator at CERN in Europe is an example of physicists setting out to discover and prove or disprove a theory. Fermilab in the USA could be labelled as a competitor to CERN for bragging rights, but the goal is the same for mankind, as the knowledge gained will be shared. These groups are driven by the challenge to get it right and resolve it, not just to beat the competition. The drive to beat the competition is what creates a good standard, or just a 'better then the competition' standard. 'Great' does not look at the competition: it focuses on the SC. The statement by Jim Collins that good is the enemy of great is correct: there is a noticeable difference in producing to beat the competition, if you have any, and getting it right.

This alludes to the mass market approach versus the tailored approach, producing consumables as they generate better revenues rather than everlasting products that reduce waste and resolve the challenge perhaps forever. These are choices made by the co-constituents of groups and can be driven by principle. Groups motivated by purpose can be very influential if the principle is motivating enough. It is the defining and control of the Gp that affects the individuals in these groups. The type of relationship does matter and the commercial industries are just one area in which groups are present. The competition for benefits derived from it is not always focused on the SC, but is often towards the Group section components, the right end of the equation, rather than flowing from left to right in the DAS chain.

Verification of leadership relationships can be done in two ways: within a single group level, known as horizontal verification, or across all the levels in a group. This second method is known as vertical verification and is assessing the relationship penetration in the group. Horizontal verification identifies the relationships at one level and is used to compare relationships and individuals at that level. The presence of leadership at one level does not mean that it is present at all levels. It is the vertical verification in large groups that will prove whether the group is still linked to the overall group's SC and purpose.

Organisation-wide verification of leadership involves all parties in the group and needs access to the SC of the overall group. The pattern of the Gp and decision equations used will determine the type of relationship and prove the environment potential for leadership relationships. Only positive initiative-owned actions as a result of co-authorship and ownership of the Gp by the co-constituents of the group will verify that initiative-owned leadership exists throughout the group.

Even in very large groups it is still possible for individuals in the smallest subgroup can define, and own components. It is the presence of positive initiative-owned decisions and actions that proves a leadership relationship. It needs effective and efficient communications systems to do so. The structure of the organisation and access to the defining and communicating of the components will affect the accuracy of the message and the time taken to pass the message. These issues are the logistics of leadership and relate to the penetration and measurement of the relationship.

Chapter 33: Measuring leadership, penetration and effectiveness

'Effective leadership is not about making speeches or being liked, leadership is defined by results not attributes.'

Peter Drucker

The reason for measuring a relationship is to find out whether the group is effective or not in resolving the challenge and whether the solution can be improved. It is different from identifying the type of relationship, or whether the current leaders in place are effective at creating the best relationship in the group for the best long-term results or a different leader or relationship type would be better.

Often, if the SC is being met the relationship is not questioned. The questioning usually starts when competition is present. The competition provides an alternative option for the customer and if the SC is not being met by one group the customer will choose another group to supply them. The group needs to find out why the challenge is not being met, as it places the effectiveness and existence of the group in doubt. The relationship in the group is one factor which could be affecting the solutions being produced by the group.

Measuring the effectiveness of the group is something that is done on a regular basis. Commercial business is an obvious area where competition to meet the customers' needs, or better define them, pushes groups to improve the solutions and products created. Whilst obvious, commercial business does not represent the largest groups by number of group members that are in competition.

The competition between the species provides the battleground for large amounts of government and commercial research. The pharmaceutical industry, health organisations and food-related industries are all engaged in the survival of the species and the effectiveness of groups just to feed themselves. There are many areas where governments and other groups work towards the purpose of the nation and the species as a whole.

The terms *nation*, *gender*, *religion* or *human race* effectively provide an overlay on top of everyday groups that individuals are usually more directly involved with, such as work, social, local communities and family. All of these groups need to be provided for and this creates a further need to prioritise the solutions that are possible and most effective. Again, this challenge alone needs specifying and defining. Commonly prioritisation of solutions is done at an individual level.

As individuals grow up and develop, lessons are learnt about where to place loyalties and priorities. The more groups, the more the list of priorities is needed and the picture becomes more complex. When the full extent of group affinities is added to the picture it is easy to see how competition arises for the individual's attention and the limited resources of their time, thoughts and efforts. Priorities are needed to make sense of the options.

In groups where individuals perceive that their needs have not been met they will be out of balance with the group or just other individuals in the group. When an individual in the group perceives that another in their group, or even in another group, is getting more than them they question it, especially if they are performing the same task. Often it is just down to the same title and recognition comparison. It is a common occurrence and can affect the balance between the co-constituents in the group. Often the leader is appealed to by the group members to redress this imbalance; if not the membership in the group will be at stake. The leader needs to initiate and facilitate a rebalance of the relationship as they have knowledge of the co-constituents' needs.

As highlighted by Maslow, it is at an individual level that priorities are worked out. Each individual will have a set of SC that they will choose to prioritise for action according to their needs in the five levels of motivation. Groups, as individual entities, also have their priorities, defined based on DAS chain processes, the priority being focused in the SC & RY? components of that DAS chain. These can be broken down into short- or long-term, financial, technical etc., however the overriding purpose of the overall group starts to form. Once the SC is joined by an RY?, a DAS chain has started to grow and provide direction for others to follow the group is developing its virtual profile and persona. Knowing the components of DAS chains allows measurement of the group.

Groups are measured by many different criteria. This book has defined some of the group relationships by the content and arrangement of the interaction messages, the physical representation of the ideas, concepts and intentions. As Jim Collins pointed out, the stock market has different criteria. To bridge the gap between the numerical measurement of a group and the relationships in a group is extremely difficult and not entirely possible until an interactive relationship can be measured numerically. To start with, to define the customer's challenge numerically does not appear possible to this author, so another way is needed.

To measure across all types of groups, terms such as *effective* and *efficient* have been used in earlier chapters. These are general terms and readers may ask: effective or efficient in relation to what? Every group is created in response to the SC of that DAS chain. It is at the beginning of the DAS chain in every process in groups. It relates to both individuals and groups. The defined SC becomes the focal point of the measurement. Using the DAS chain to help guide the measurement of effectiveness or efficiency thereby allows individuals to more easily assess priorities and help them focus their actions towards the purpose of the group.

The terms *effective* and *efficient* are again often confused. Efficiency is something most are familiar with: it is often expressed in a symbolic logic formula, such as number of kilometres per hour (km/h), number of units produced per hour of production or actions/hour, and many other ways are used to measure material resources against time, cost or actions. These are efficiencies and are commonly used in business and other groups who want to measure them. As the group gets larger and more complex, ratios become more specific, such as labour turnover per month or staff per room (hotel industry), and quite commonly they are linked to costs such as revenue per month, costs against profit ratio or return on capital expenditure (ROCE). These are all efficiencies that measure one of the group section components against another or a combination of factors within the same component.

Table 33.1 Examples of the measurement of efficiencies

Symbolic logic if applicable	Explanation	Decision equation components
km/h	Kilometres per hour, actions (PA) per hour (SP)	PA/SP
Units/h	Units produced (sp1) per hour (sp2)	sp1/sp2
	Customers served (actions – PA) per hour (SP)	PA/SP
	Bonus paid (BB) per month worked (SP)	BB/SP
$/h	Dollars (BB) per hour (SP)	BB/SP
ROCE	Return over capital expenditure	BB/SP
	Functions and procedures learned (PA) per month (SP)	PA/SP
	Group relationships established (PA) per time (SP)	PA/SP
	New initiatives taken per month	PA/SP

The measurement of efficiencies can be basic and simple, using the material resources against time or costs, or more esoteric measurements can be used, such as new functions learned per month. Being a quick learner is an important factor when competition is present and new challenges present themselves regularly. The ability to make decisions quickly, or to get others to make decisions quickly, is important is some situations. Efficiencies occur when the group section's components (SP, PA, BB), the physical components of decision equation, are compared to one another in order to achieve measurements that allows comparisons to be made and targets or standards to be set across the group or subgroups.

To be effective is different. For a group's PA to be effective it needs to be related to the SC of the group. For example 'Will the PA help towards resolving the SC'? This is true for all of the remaining four components of the equation (RY?, SP, PA, BB). To prove effectiveness the component needs to be compared against the SC component.

In the case of the RY? component, it is the function of the component to assess whether the group is correct or appropriate or will be effective in resolving the challenge as specified. The RY? component is there to assess whether the group would be effective at resolving the SC presented: it is a measure of the group's potential effectiveness. The individual who defines the RY? component is assessing whether the SC should, or can, be resolved by the group. The individual will use their tacit knowledge of the SC and Group section components and assess whether the group is fit to resolve that SC. In situations where there are other groups more capable then it is an assessment of whether the group can be effective and help resolve the SC, or whether it will hinder those already present or better equipped to do the job.

Table 33.2 contains examples of effectiveness. In the right-hand column the components are in a logical equation format to demonstrate the simple way to write it. For analysing and planning the decision equation components again make it simple to understand and apply to any DAS chain. In each it is very difficult to apply a component of the group section (SP, PA, BB) to the specific challenge without including the RY? component. As co-constituents (SC & RY?) they form the purpose and this gives rise to the SP, PA and BB.

Table 33.2 Example of measurement of effectiveness using Gp components

Situation explanation	Symbolic logic measurement
The break down of government and start of the Bosnian civil war threatened a large loss of life that could escalate to neighbouring countries (SC). The UN had the desire, will and means to intervene in order to save lives and preserve the stability of Europe (ry?1 & ry?2).	SC/RY?
The loss of life due to preventable disease – malaria and others like it – is not tackled by the affected individuals and governments due to lack of resources (SC). The Bill and Melinda Gates Foundation provides the resources (SP) to prevent further loss of life (RY?).	SC/RY? & SP
The need for metal to be joined together with strength to build large ships and machines in order to enable progress and a better standard of living (SC). Lincoln Electric formed a group and developed techniques to achieve this, benefiting all parties involved because it had the knowledge of how to do so better than other providers (RY?).	SC/RY?
A lack of support and resources to feed their families during a natural disaster (SC). Individuals donate money and time to organisations set up to provide this support (SP) in order to prevent loss of life, regardless of who the beneficiaries are, because they believe it is right and is a value they wish to be recognised for.	SC/SP & RY?
A new design is needed to meet the needs of a customer's customer (SC). A company commits extra materials to design and prototyping (SP) in order to achieve the design specifications of the customer in order to get the order for the future business (RY?)	SC/SP & RY?
The product will achieve the specifications listed to beat the competition, but not provide the long-term needs of the customer (SC). Operators spend extra time away from their other commitments such as families to get the product right (PA) in order to ensure the customer's success and their group's long-term future	SC/PA & RY?

Situation explanation	Symbolic logic measurement
partnership with the customer (RY?).	
The shortage of manpower has meant that the actions cannot be finished in time to meet the deadline (SC). The individual decides to stay and help, even though it is not his function (PA), in order to ensure the team gets the first success and gains experience and a second opportunity to bid again (RY?).	SC/PA & RY?
The company faces difficult economic times when the economy takes a downturn and orders fall off, threatening jobs at the company (SC). The boss insists on a pay cut for himself to maintain focus and reduce expenditure for the product creation (SP & BB) in order to demonstrate he is committed to the purpose (RY?).	SC/SP, BB & RY?

This method of evaluation and measurement of effectiveness can be done by anybody involved in the DAS chain or by third parties. The co-constituents can self-assess and can fix the situation if it is not right. The standard expected is challenge-related and is agreed in the defined SC by the customer and group. This defined SC standard means that leaders in the group are not the sole arbiters of the standards. It is the SC set by the customer and group. The leader is often the group's representative, there to ensure that the SC-derived standard is achieved by checking and supervision before it goes to the customer, as it is the group (and perhaps specifically the leader) who owns the SC definition and the customer expects him to deliver.

By communicating to others the SC standards required, it frees the co-constituents from needing the leader to be there 100% of the time to check, supervise and define the change if necessary. The leaders can use this SC standard as a way of developing the co-constituents as he gets them to confirm whether they think the product achieves the SC presented. The followers build focus on the group's SC and the group as an entity, not on the leader in isolation at the expense of the group entity. If the leader changes or is not present the followers can continue their work based on the group purpose and SC standard as defined.

For the customer it is important that the group is effective. The customer is not always concerned if the group is efficient. Efficiencies exist within the group, and while they may affect costs, the prices may already be fixed with the customer in the originally agreed DAS chain plan. In this situation the balance between effectiveness and efficiency becomes clear and a choice of priorities must be made. The individual with complete tacit knowledge of the Gp is best suited for this function. The more co-constituents that have this tacit knowledge, the greater the likelihood of a better decision and revised DAS chain.

There are many examples of the differences between effective and efficient, which also remind applicators of the constant need to review and update the DAS chain as the demands from customers change. One example is the UK postal system. The Royal Mail [39], was established as early as 1516 and developed from a limited expensive service for government offices into a nationwide uniform service nicknamed 'the penny post' by 1840. The service was that, for the price of a penny, a letter would be delivered anywhere in Great Britain. Prior to this service the price was approximately four pennies, and complex payments systems prevailed. The uniform penny post system also introduced the postage stamp system as a method of proving postage had already been paid.

The penny post was created for two main reasons. The first was to continue the service to customers, in that the government understood that by increasing the communications network between people it would improve the flow of ideas and information for the benefit of commerce and the nation as a whole. The second main reason caused the payment of a standard charge and proof of its payment to be used. By establishing the one fee charge and the adhesive stamp it vastly simplified the payments structure and auditing system.

There were the two different drivers for these actions. One is focused on the co-constituents in the group located in 'Great Britain' to be able to communicate more effectively, and the second one is for them to be more efficient in doing so. It represented a better service for a cheaper price to the customers. It also presented great efficiencies in administering charging systems and economies of scale for the Royal Mail organisation. At the height of its effectiveness in the late 19th century it was possible to receive and send three or more times a day in London, allowing multiple correspondences in the same day.

The degree of effectiveness has changed since those times to the extent that now the Royal Mail only offers next-day delivery guaranteed, and even this is not always achieved. The priority has focused more on efficiency of resources and the cost of running the service. The focus is the internal group efficiencies for the benefit of the group, who also happen to be the consumers – the taxpayers. The service has been redefined in order to achieve greater efficiency. The Royal Mail now offers different fee structures for the service depending on the delivery time needed, as long as it is only next day with no time specified.

The customers were demanding better and in 2000 the UK parliament rescinded the government's monopoly on the service and allowed private commercial companies to compete in order to ensure that the level of service is maintained to those who pay for it. Customers now have the option of the service that they feel ensures the safety and appropriate delivery time including before the next working day where possible.

In the case of the UK postal services its monopoly position allowed its efficiency to be a secondary priority. The government has maintained limited competition and allowed only itself to define the service they will provide. That was the defined SC in the DAS chain that was available prior to 2000. The service was not defined by the end user's individual SCs. It effectiveness was questioned by some who felt it would be better provided by a group operating in the customers' interests and they were prepared to pay for it. With the introduction of competition, customers now have an alternative service provider.

Competitors now provide secure transport of letters and goods such as currency for customers who are prepared to pay for the better value service offered. The service effectiveness is defined by the customer, not the service provider. The customer chooses to use other service providers when transporting valuable goods that must arrive on time. For standard not so valuable or important packages they use the Royal Mail's standard services.

The Post Office has accepted that in some cases the customers define the SC component in the equation and the Royal Mail can perform the express service, even though it is not the RY? it was formed. The Royal Mail caters for the largest volume of business, which allows it to achieve the best efficiencies. The RY? dictates they must provide a minimum service across the whole country, which is not something its competitors are required to do. It is effective at providing a basic service. When express or higher than normal standards are required efficiencies have taken a priority, and while they can provide such services they are not at competitive prices. The purpose of the Royal Mail is to provide the nationwide service. The competitors are there to attempt to ensure a level of efficiency in the Royal Mail standard service system for the customers.

Competitors like the commercial groups have efficiency levels that dictate that they could not compete in the standard service areas of the Royal Mail at an acceptable level and get any profit or benefit to their group, which has a different RY? The competitors are formed based on a different SC, which is co-authored with the customer. The DAS chains of the two groups are different and therefore different values will be used to measure the different groups' effectiveness.

Any assessment of effectiveness relies on knowledge of the Gp. If the reason for the assessment is to assess a group's ability to be effective then this is an area where the defining terms in the DAS chain do match those used to define a relationship. Then the terms can be overlapped and comparisons made. Again, correlation still does not prove causation unless being assessed from the same viewpoint and defined terms. The stock market and shareholders have a very different point of view from the customer and the co-constituents.

A group that produces a solution that resolves the SC of the group is effective. Within large groups with multiple layers it is easy to foresee how the SC can become diluted, confused or even left out all together. Large groups and small groups have the potential for this as it only takes one positional leader in any subgroup to create a relationship that de-links the followers from the purpose.

The original gut feeling that leadership and success are connected somehow is correct but difficult to prove. The feeling can be turned from tacit knowledge to explicit knowledge with more accurately defined terms. This tacit knowledge is based on the assumption that de-linked groups are likely to be less effective at producing the most effective solution over time than linked groups. The term *success* should be replaced by *effective*, and the old term *leadership* replaced with *initiative-owned leadership* in order to be more accurate. As long as the assumption of the superiority of linked groups remains, the connection is solid and comparisons can be made using the specific terms.

By assessing the relationship types both vertically and horizontally, proof of the connection between effectiveness and the type of relationship can be found. Assessment of effectiveness needs the customers and groups originating the SC. The larger the organisation or industry being assessed the greater will be the number of DAS chains experienced. They will eventually all line up in what is called a DAS chain stack. These stacks can represent a whole industry or supply chain, or just a company level group. An example is shown in Figure 33.1.

DAS chain stack – Multiple layers of DAS chains – this stack displays a de-linked DAS chain stack

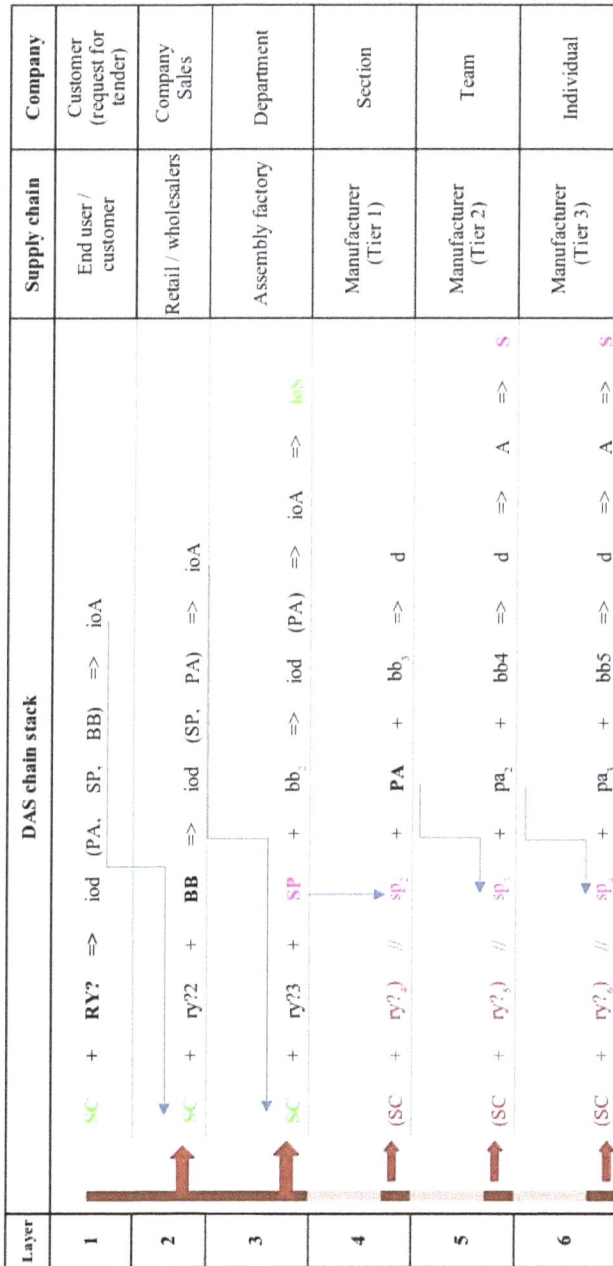

Layer	DAS chain stack	Supply chain	Company
1	SC + **RY?** => iod (PA, SP, BB) => ioA	End user / customer	Customer (request for tender)
2	SC + ry?2 + **BB** => iod (SP, PA) => ioA	Retail / wholesalers	Company Sales
3	SC + ry?3 + **SP** + bb2 => iod (PA) => ioA => ioA	Assembly factory	Department
4	(SC + ry?4 // sp2 + **PA** + bb3 => d	Manufacturer (Tier 1)	Section
5	(SC + ry?5 // sp3 + pa2 + bb4 => d => A =>	Manufacturer (Tier 2)	Team
6	(SC + ry?6 // sp4 + pa3 + bb5 => d => A =>	Manufacturer (Tier 3)	Individual

The solution provided is de-linked from the specific challenge of the end user customer and therefore is in danger of being not fit to resolve the specific challenge defined by the end user customer. In a highly competitive industry the Tier 1 manufacturer risks being not selected to supply the assembly factory because they are de-linked from the specific challenge as defined and passed to them by the assembler.

Figure 33.1 The DAS chain stack, showing vertical and horizontal de-linking

A DAS chain stack not only links between components within the individual DAS chain at each level but also links vertically up and down the stack between DAS chains. How these horizontal DAS chains fit together with the ones above and below will determine the effectiveness of the groups within the multi-layered stack: this is termed the vertical effectiveness of the group. This delinking from the end user customer becomes more obvious in a vertical effectiveness assessment. It can happen in a large multi-company stack or inside a company with multiple layers of subgroups.

The solution provided is de-linked from the SC of the end user customer and is therefore in danger of being not fit to resolve the SC as defined by the end user customer and supplier. In a highly competitive industry the Tier 1 manufacturer risks not being selected to supply the assembly factory because they are de-linked from the SC as defined and passed to them by the assembler.

This is where procurement teams and Request For Tender (RFT) documents come under scrutiny. Are they written in order to provide a solution that is exactly the same between all suppliers and therefore should in theory only differ in price at the minimum quality standards required? This makes it easier for the procurement team to selecting a supplier based on price. Conversely, is the RFT written to ensure that the SC is fully understood, thereby giving potential for the standard to be exceeded and a new, better, solution to the challenge to be provided?

Figure 33.1 shows the DAS stack, where the red arrows display the path that conveys the end users' SC between the DAS chains at each level. The red diagonal marks (//) demonstrate where the delinking occurs with the solution being just a normal solution rather than an initiative-owned solution (ios). The use of lower case letters and numbers displays the different subgroup support and proposed actions done at each different level, which fit into the higher level DAS chain solution. The upper case components indicate where the component has been defined. The subgroup levels' lower case components are redefined within the upper case component definitions so that they can be understood and kept specific and relevant to that subgroup level.

In terms of effectiveness each level should be working to produce a solution that makes the higher level more effective at their solution not just more efficient. Those where the red arrow leaves the upper DAS chain and enters the next DAS chain at any component other than SC (level 3 to 6) demonstrate a de-linked vertical chain. At this stage the lower level becomes just an efficiency measure in the upper DAS chain. The lower chain should be striving to add value to the upper DAS chain's SC and effectiveness.

Suppliers, marketers and sales personnel will focus on what makes them better than others. Often it is just price, which makes them a cost efficiency in the higher level DAS chain. Some marketing teams quote a unique selling point (USP), but a USP that does not relate to making the higher level more effective at providing a fit for challenge solution becomes an efficiency for the DAS chain of the higher level and can be compared with another supplier, being labelled as a cost. USPs that do not add to higher level effectiveness are just differences with no consequences.

The vertical effectiveness in groups will be affected by the type of relationships used within the groups. For groups that seek an initiative-owned solution to add value to the higher level it is an initiative-owned leadership relationship that is most likely to produce this. The connection between 'success' and leadership has substance provided the definition of success means effectiveness in resolving the group's SC.

Chapter 34: Leadership resolved

'The mind is not a vessel that needs filling but wood that needs igniting'

Plutarch

The paradox of leadership is one that has been in need of a solution in order to help improve the effectiveness of identifying, measuring and developing leaders. In particular there is a need to distinguish between the general leader–follower hierarchical or positional understanding, and the co-constituently authored, positive initiative-owned leadership relationship. There has been a tacit knowing that there is a difference between leadership and management, and now with accurate definition it can be considered more explicit knowledge: the difference is initiative ownership.

Much of the confusion has been caused by poor definition of terms, which leads to a blurring of what the factors are that apply to leaders and the relationships they are in. Analysing individuals without looking at the other factors that make up the compound solution, such as the followers and the group as an entity, has greatly blinkered the development of the theory of leadership. Stripping readers of their blinkers and engaging in the broader picture of the group and all of its co-constituents has allowed the leader to be viewed in the context of the whole group as an entity, with its followers and the leader as a bridge in the relationship.

The interaction between the co-constituents, and in particular the messages used to transfer the concepts, ideas and intentions between the co-constituents in order to get the group to act, is where the relationship is built, rather than the external situation or challenge being faced. The relationship acts as an internal structure or framework on which the situation external to the group acts as an initiator or catalyst, influencing but not constituting the relationship.

The relationship is like a sphere with an outer shell floating in a liquid environment. The situation and pressure of the liquid will affect the sphere. All the occupants, or co-constituents, of the sphere are affected equally by the pressure and external situation; it is how the occupants chose to bind and structure themselves within the sphere that will determine whether they will withstand the pressure or collapse. Creating processes for and making decisions to form relationships in the group could be considered one of the oldest languages known, the language of decision making.

As a language it needs interpreting and confirming against current behaviours and terms in groups. The language used in leadership consists of 'bits' or packages of information. Maslow, and others after him, identified the motivators that relate to the individual and help give clarity to the terms and priority in the decision-making process. These motivators provide the factors which make up the components in the language of the group relationship. Comparison with current established practices shows how these components are assembled and communicated to establish and maintain these relationships.

With these foundation components as building blocks the patterns of the message can be analysed and compared. The different patterns match descriptors and terms in common use, which help to identify and define the types of relationships.

Through Michael Polanyi's definition of tacit knowing and tacit knowledge it is possible to understand and unlock the seeming paradox that we can know more than we can tell. Terms such as *initiative* and *leadership* present these situations, where it seems possible to know what it is when seen or experienced, although it is difficult to define what or how it happens. Tacit knowledge demonstrates how a leader inspires followers into positive group-focused actions without telling the group members what to do. It is this tacit knowledge that helps distinguish the difference between leadership and management. Tacit knowledge allows for the focused positive, logical actions of initiative ownership and proves willingness in the action expressed.

The clues are now available to see how the solution 'leadership' is arrived at in the blank crossword puzzle. The decision equation has acted as a key or Rosetta stone to decipher the language of the group and act as a teaching, planning and assessment tool. The equation can be used to increase the effectiveness of the positional leader and the group's relationships. The decision equation provides the clues to demonstrate why and how initiative-owned leadership is different from management. Environments can now be made to engage with and inspire individuals to use their knowledge, ideas and actions to show the path and enable greater group effectiveness rather than just produce what they are told.

Knowing the path from components to effective initiative-owned leadership relationships will allow resources to be focused on developing aspects of the group that make it more effective. The groups that make better use of technology, communications and logistics to make themselves more effective as well as more efficient will thrive. The connection between effectiveness and initiative-owned leadership relationship is proven and the better the theory of leadership is understood, the better relationships can be developed to engage and inspire others to be more effective and exceed expectations and resolve the challenges rather than just beat the competition.

Leadership, as an adjective, describes a relationship between a group, leader and followers where the group purpose is co-authored and produces initiative-owned actions by the group.

Leadership as a verb is the action of initiating and facilitating the co-authorship and communicating of a group purpose in order to create and maintain initiative ownership in that group purpose by the group.

Leadership as a noun describes the act or ability to initiate and facilitate the co-authorship and communicating of a group purpose in order to create and maintain initiative ownership in that group purpose by the group.

The presence of positive initiative-owned actions is the defining indicator of the presence of an initiative-owned leadership relationship. All leadership relationships are defined by the presence of positive initiative ownership. Therefore the term *initiative-owned leadership* can be abbreviated to *leadership relationships.* This can further be abbreviated to apply to the verb describing an individual's actions in creating and maintaining that relationship or as a noun describing the act itself as the ability to perform this action. Positive initiative-owned actions define leadership.

Example 34.1 The leadership equation as derived from a DAS chain

$$SC + RY? + BB => iod\ (SP,PA) => ioA => ioS$$

$$+ioA <=> ioLR <=> LR <=> L$$

$$+ioA <=> L$$

Bibliography

[1] Xenophon, *Cyrus the Great, The Arts of Leadership and War* (New York, Truman Talley Books, 2006), edited with an introduction by Larry Hedrick.

[2] B. Bass and R. M. Stogdill, *Handbook of Leadership* (New York, Free Press, revised and expanded version, 1981).

[3] John Adair, Effective Leadership – How to be an Effective Leader, (Basingstoke and London, Pan Books, revised edition, 2009).

[4] Paul Hersey, Ken Blanchard, and Dewey Johnson, Management of Organisational Behaviour – Leading Human Resources (Prentice Hall, 9th edition, 2007).

[5] James MacGregor Burns, Leadership (New York, Harper & Row, 1978).

[6] Noel Tichy, The Leadership Engine (New York, Harper Business Essentials, 2002).

[7] Jim Collins, Built to Last: Successful Habits of Visionary Companies (New York, HarperCollins, 1994).

[8] Warren Bennis, On Becoming a Leader (New York, Addison-Wesley, 1989).

[9] Richard Holmes, The Age of Wonder: How the Romantic Generation Discovered the Beauty and Terror of Science (London, Harper Press, 2009).

[10] Thomas Kuhn, The Structure of Scientific Revolutions (Chicago, University of Chicago Press, 1962).

[11] Arthur O. Lovejoy, The Great Chain of Being: A Study of the History of an Idea (Cambridge, MA, Harvard University Press 1936).

[12] BBC videos – Interview by the BBC with Michael Ventris in 1952 shortly after he cracked the Linear B script. This quote is taken from the BBC website at http://www.bbc.co.uk/news/magazine-22782620, as they do not play the whole interview but write a number of extracts in the article; this quote is one of the written extracts.

[13] Robert K. Greenleaf, *The Servant-Leader within* (New York, Paulist Press, 2003).

[14] MOD UK Army, Article: *The History of RMA Sandhurst* (London, MOD, 2009).

[15] M. T. Clanchy, *A History of England: Early Medieval England* (London, Folio Society with permissions from HarperCollins, 1997).

[16] Victor Gourevitch, *The Social Contract and Other Later Political Writings*, (Cambridge, Cambridge University Press, 1997).

[17] Geert Hofstede, *Cultures and Organisations: Software of the Mind*, (Maidenhead UK, McGraw Hill,1991).

[18] British Army Field Manual Volume 1 – Combined Arms Operations and AATAMs All Arms Tactical Aide Mémoires.

[19] Joseph Maciariello, *Lasting Value – Lessons from a Century of Agility at Lincoln Electric* (John Wiley & Sons, 1999).

[20] Chris Argryis and Donald Schön, *Organisational Learning II: Theory, Method and Practice*, (Reading Mass., Addison-Wesley, 1996).

[21] Abraham Maslow, *Motivation and Personality*, 3rd edition (Pearson, 1997).

[22] Frederick Herzberg, *The Motivation to Work* (New York, John Wiley, 1959).

[23] Frederick Herzberg, One more time: how do you motivate employees? *Harvard Business Review*, **46**(1), 1968, pp. 53–62.

[24] Clayton Alderfer, *Existence, Relatedness and Growth: Human Needs in Organisational Settings* (New York, Free Press, 1972).

[25] Iain McGilchrist, *The Master and his Emissary – The Divided Brain and the Making of the Western World* (New Haven and London, Yale University Press, 2009).

[26] Bob Lutz, *Car Guys vs Bean Counters: The Battle for the Soul of American Business* (Penguin Books, 2011).

[27] Amy Wilson, Ford overhauls way forward plan (*Autoweek* magazine article, Automotive News, 9/15/2006). http://www.autoweek.com/apps/pbcs.dll/article?AID=/20060915/FREE/60915001/1024/LATESTNEWS

[28] *Concise Oxford Dictionary of Current English* (London, BCA with permission from Oxford University Press, 1991).

[29] Michael Polanyi, *The Tacit Dimension* (London, Random House, University of Chicago Press edition, 2009).

[30] Henry Ford, *My Life and Work* (BN Publishing, 2009).

[31] Dominic Scott, *Plato's Meno* (Cambridge University Press, 1992).

[32] Field Marshall Viscount Slim, *Defeat into Victory* (New York, First Cooper Press, edition 2000).

[33] Douglas McGregor, *The Human Side of Enterprise,* (McGraw Hill, 1960).

[34] Kathleen Broome Williams, *Grace Hopper: Admiral of the Cyber Sea* (Annapolis Maryland, Naval Institute Press, 2004).

[35] Simon Sinek, *Start with Why* (London, Penguin, 2009).

[36] Website of the National Archives, http://www.legislation.gov.uk/.

[37] Aneurin Bevan, *In Place of Fear* (Kessinger Publishing, 2010).

[38] Jim Collins, *Good to Great: Why Some Companies Make the Leap… and Others Don't* (New York, Harper Collins, 2001).

[39] Christopher Browne, *Getting the Message – The Story of the British Post Office* (Sutton Pub Ltd, 1993).

Index

Endnotes

1   Xenophon, *Cyrus the Great, The Arts of Leadership and War* (New York, Truman Talley Books, 2006) edited with an introduction by Larry Hedrick

2   Reproduced here with kind permission from Universal Uclick the distributors of the official Dilbert comic strips archive © 2013 Scott Adams

3   Reference taken from B. Bass and R. M. Stogdill, revised and expanded version, *Handbook of Leadership* (New York, Free Press, 1981) p. 26–27.

4   John Adair, *Effective Leadership – How to Be an Successful Leader* (Basingstoke and London, Pan Books, revised edition, 2009).

5   Paul Hersey, Ken Blanchard and Dewey Johnson, *Management of Organisational Behaviour – Leading Human Resources* (Prentice Hall, 9th edition, 2007).

6   *Ibid.*, p. 62

7   J. M. Burns, *Leadership* (New York, Harper & Row, 1978).

8   Stogdill's *Handbook*, Preface, p. xvii.

9   Taken from Richard Homes, The Age of Wonder – How the Romantic Generation *Discovered the Beauty and Terror of Science* (London, HarperPress, 2009) p. 122.

10 Stogdill's *Handbook*, Preface, p. xvii

11 Thomas Kuhn, *The Structure of Scientific Revolutions,* (Chicago, University of Chicago Press, 1962)

12 Arthur O Lovejoy, *The Great Chain of Being: A Study of the History of an Idea* (Cambridge Mass., Harvard University Press 1936)

13 Taken from an interview by the BBC with Michael Ventris in 1952 shortly after he cracked the Linear B script. This quote is taken from the BBC website at http://www.bbc.co.uk/news/magazine-22782620. As they do not play the whole interview but write a number of extracts in the article, this quote is one of the written extracts.

14 Referenced from a later book by Robert K. Greenleaf, *The Servant-Leader within* (New York, Paulist Press, 2003)

15 It is interesting to note that the British army officer training academy known as the Royal Military Academy Sandhurst adopted the motto 'Serve to Lead' in 1947 on its reorganisation.

16 *Ibid.* Stogdill's *Handbook of Leadership*, Preface extract, p. xvii

17 The Decision → Action → Solution chain is referred to as the DAS chain throughout the rest of the book unless the full form is written to focus on a specific aspect of the chain.

18 M.T. Clanchy, *A History of England: Early Medieval England* (London, Folio Society with permissions from Harper Collins, 1997), p. 142.

19 Geert Hofstede, *Cultures and Organisations: Software of the Mind*

(Maidenhead UK, McGraw Hill, 1991). Identifiers are mentioned throughout the book.

20 To be found in British Army Field Manual Volume 1 – Combined Arms Operations and AATAMs All Arms Tactical Aide Memoires, Restricted issue

21 Information extracted from Joseph Maciariello, *Lasting Value – Lessons from a Century of Agility at Lincoln Electric* (John Wiley & Sons, 1999)

22 Hersey, Blanchard, Johnson, p. 53

23 *Ibid.* 22, p. 52

24 In accordance with standard symbolic logic practices used in mathematics.

25 John Adair, *Effective Leadership*, p. 38

26 John Adair, *Effective Leadership* p. 77

27 Joseph Maciariello, *Lasting Value – Lessons from a Century of Agility at Lincoln Electric* (John Wiley & Sons, 1999), pp. 4–6.

28 These abbreviations will continue throughout the book.

29 Reproduced here with kind permission from Universal Uclick the distributors of the official Dilbert comic strips archive © Scott Adams 2013.

30 Iain McGilchrist, *The Master and his Emissary: The Divided Brain and the Making of the Western World* (New Haven and London, Yale University Press, 2009) pp. 33–54.

31 The Ford company recovery plan was called the 'Way Forward Plan' and was written about and published in many local and national papers, as it spelled out the closures and future plans for production.

32 *Concise Oxford Dictionary of Current English* (London, BCA with permission from Oxford University Press, 1991), p. 609.

33 Michael Polanyi, *The Tacit Dimension* (London, Random House, University of Chicago Press edition 2009), p. 4.

34 *Ibid.*, pp. 19–20

35 The quote could not be directly attributed to Henry Ford. Information on Henry Ford is taken from Henry Ford, *My Life and Work* (BN Publishing, 2009).

36 Examples of the situational leadership curve are on pp. 188, 192, 199 and 209 of Hersey, Blanchard and Johnson.

37 Field Marshall Viscount Slim, *Defeat into Victory* (New York, First Cooper Press, 2000), pp. 210–211.

38 Warren Bennis, *On Becoming a Leader*, pp. 47–48

39 *Ibid.*

40 Clips of this speech are available on YouTube and a transcript is available at this link: http://er.jsc.nasa.gov/seh/ricetalk.htm.

41 Warren Bennis, *On Becoming a Leader*, pp. 47–48

42 Kathleen Broome Williams, *Grace Hopper: Admiral of the Cyber Sea* (Annapolis Maryland, Naval Institute Press, 2004)
43 Remarks at the Annual Conference of the Society for Personnel Administration, 12/5/54
44 Simon Sinek, *Start with Why* (London, Penguin, 2009), pp. 36, 37, 156
45 As issued on the government publication and can be seen on the website of the National Archives:
http://www.legislation.gov.uk/ukpga/2006/41/contents
46 Called in full the 'Report of the inter-department committee of social insurance and allied services'
47 Aneurin Bevan, *In Place of Fear* (Kessinger Publishing, 2010) p. 100
48 *Ibid.*, p. 100
49 Jim Collins and Jerry Porras, *Built to Last: Successful Habits of Visionary Companies* (New York, HarperBusiness, 1994) Chapter 5, pp. 91–114

www.ingramcontent.com/pod-product-compliance
Lightning Source LLC
Chambersburg PA
CBHW052009030426
42334CB00029BA/3152